LIFE APPLICATION® BIBLE COMMENTARY

1 PETER 2 PETER JUDE

Bruce B. Barton, D. Min.
Mark Fackler, Ph.D.
Linda K. Taylor
Dave Veerman, M. Div.

Series Editor: Grant Osborne, Ph.D.
Editor: Philip Comfort, Ph.D.

Tyndale House Publishers, Inc.
Wheaton, Illinois

Contributing Editors: James C. Galvin, Ed.D. and Ronald A. Beers

Life Application is a registered trademark of Tyndale House Publishers, Inc.

Scripture quotations marked NIV are taken from the *Holy Bible,* New International Version®. Copyright © 1973, 1978, 1984 by International Bible Society. Used by permission of Zondervan Publishing House. All rights reserved. The "NIV" and "New International Version" trademarks are registered in the United States Patent and Trademark Office by International Bible Society. Use of either trademark requires permission of International Bible Society.

Scripture quotations marked NKJV are taken from The New King James Version. Copyright © 1979, 1980, 1982, Thomas Nelson, Inc., Publishers.

Scripture quotations marked NRSV are taken from the New Revised Standard Version of the Bible, copyrighted, 1989 by the Division of Christian Education of the National Council of the Churches of Christ in the United States of America, and are used by permission. All rights reserved.

(No citation is given for Scripture text that is exactly the same wording in all three versions—NIV, NKJV, and NRSV.)

Scripture quotations marked NASB are taken from the *New American Standard Bible,* © 1960, 1962, 1963, 1968, 1971, 1972, 1973, 1975, 1977 by The Lockman Foundation. Used by permission.

Scripture verses marked NEB are taken from *The New English Bible,* copyright © 1970, Oxford University Press, Cambridge University Press.

Scripture quotations marked RSV are taken from the *Holy Bible,* Revised Standard Version, copyright © 1946, 1952, 1971 by the Division of Christian Education of the National Council of the Churches of Christ in the United States of America, and are used by permission. All rights reserved.

Scripture verses marked TJB are taken from *The Jerusalem Bible,* copyright © 1966, 1967 and 1968 by Darton, Longman, & Todd, Ltd., and Doubleday & Company, Inc.

Scripture verses marked TLB are taken from *The Living Bible,* copyright © 1971 owned by assignment by KNT Charitable Trust. All rights reserved.

Library of Congress Cataloging-in-Publication Data

1 Peter, 2 Peter, and Jude / Bruce B. Barton ... [et al.].

   p.   cm. — (Life application Bible commentary)

   Includes bibliographical references and index.

   ISBN 0-8423-3031-3 (SC : alk. paper)

   1. Bible. N.T. Peter—Commentaries.   2. Bible. N.T. Jude—

Commentaries.   I. Barton, Bruce B.   II. Series.

BS2795.3.A18   1996

227'.9207—dc20   95-37612

Printed in the United States of America

05   04

12 11 10 9   8

CONTENTS

Gospels

MATTHEW:

MARK: between

LUKE:

ACTS:

Paul's Epistles

ROMANS: about 57

1 CORINTHIANS: about 55

2 CORINTHIANS: about 56–57

GALATIANS: about 49

EPHESIANS:

PHILIPPIANS:

COLOSSIANS:

1 THESSALONIANS: about 51

2 THESSALONIANS: about 51–52

1 TIMOTHY:

2 TIMOTHY:

TITUS:

PHILEMON:

General Epistles

JAMES: about 49

1 PETER:

2 PETER:

JUDE:

NEW TESTAMENT

AD 30	40	50	60

The church begins (Acts 1)

35 *Paul's conversion* (Acts 9)

46 *Paul's first missionary journey* (Acts 13)

Jerusalem Council and Paul's second journey (Acts 15)

54 *Paul's third journey* (Acts 18) *Nero becomes emperor*

58 *Paul arrested* (Acts 21)

64 *Rome burns*

61–63 *Paul's Roman imprisonment* (Acts 28)

between 60–65
55–65
about 60

JOHN: probably 80–85

about 63–65

about 61
about 62
about 61

about 64
about 66–67
about 64
about 61

HEBREWS: probably before 70

about 62–64
about 67

1 JOHN: between 85–90
2 JOHN: about 90
3 JOHN: about 90

about 65

REVELATION: about 95

TIMELINE

| 70 | 80 | 90 | 100 |

67–68
Paul and
Peter
executed

Jerusalem
destroyed

79 Mt. Vesuvius
erupts in Italy

About 75
John begins
ministry in
Ephesus

About 98
John's
death
at Ephesus

68
Essenes hide
their library
of Bible
manuscripts
in a cave
in Qumran
by the
Dead Sea

75
Rome begins
construction
of Colosseum

FOREWORD

The *Life Application Bible* Commentary series provides verse-by-verse explanation, background, and application for every verse in the New Testament. In addition, it gives personal help, teaching notes, and sermon ideas that will address needs, answer questions, and provide insight for applying God's Word to life today. The content is highlighted so that particular verses and phrases are easy to find.

Each volume contains three sections: introduction, commentary, and reference. The introduction includes an overview of the book, the book's historical context, a time line, cultural background information, major themes, an overview map, and an explanation about the author and audience.

The commentary section includes running commentary on the Bible text with reference to several modern versions, especially the New International Version and the New Revised Standard Version, accompanied by life applications interspersed throughout. Additional elements include charts, diagrams, maps, and illustrations. There are also insightful quotes from church leaders and theologians such as John Calvin, Martin Luther, John Wesley, A. W. Tozer, and C. S. Lewis. These features are designed to help you quickly grasp the biblical information and be prepared to communicate it to others. The reference section includes an index and a bibliography.

INTRODUCTION TO 1 PETER

Remember when the attacks began? At first, they were subtle—junior high friends decided that going to church was "stupid." In the later teen years, you found that your Christian lifestyle contrasted sharply with that of most of your peers, and often they would make fun of your purity and stand for Christ. As you grew in age and experience, you discovered that the attacks increased, especially when you spoke up against wrongdoing, took time to help those in need, and shared your faith. Your strong witness by life and word cost you friends and threatened your job.

Regardless of your personal persecution, you probably have not come close to what first-century believers experienced. A quick perusal of Acts will reveal stonings, beatings, imprisonments, murderous plots, and executions—all for spreading the truth about Christ. Some of the most severe of the persecutions came at the hands of Nero. This Roman emperor became obsessed with eliminating Christians and their faith. The Roman historian Tacitus said, "Besides being put to death, [Christians] were made to serve as objects of amusement; they were clad in the hides of beasts and torn to death by dogs; others were crucified, others set on fire to serve to illuminate the night when daylight failed" (*Annales* 15.44). The price for following Christ was high.

First Peter was written to persecuted Christians, to those living in Rome and throughout the Roman province of Asia. This letter encourages believers to remain strong; it explains how to live during difficult times; it offers hope to all who suffer for the faith. First Peter speaks to believers in all ages—those in the first century and in our century. God tells us how to respond to our tough times, especially when we are persecuted for what we believe. Read 1 Peter and discover courage, strength, and hope.

AUTHOR

Peter: apostle of Christ, one of the original twelve disciples, outspoken leader, and courageous preacher.

1 PETER

INTRODUCTION TO
1 PETER, 2 PETER, AND JUDE

Watch out! Beware! On guard!

Warnings alert us and urge us to prepare. Potential danger lurks nearby, so we need to be ready by bolstering our courage, building our defenses, and designing our response.

First Peter, Second Peter, and Jude—three small books tucked near the end of the Bible—convey crucial warnings to believers:

- *Watch out for persecution. Let your suffering build your faith, not crush it. Be strong! (1 Peter)*

- *Beware of false teachers, those who would draw you away. Keep focused on Christ. Be alert! (2 Peter)*

- *Guard against heresy, twisted truth, and outright lies. Stay close to God's Word. Be faithful! (Jude)*

Besieged on all sides, the early church faced external and internal threats. Followers of Christ could easily have been defeated or diverted. A distinct minority in a pagan society, they could have capitulated to their culture. But challenged by God through these holy writers and strengthened by the Holy Spirit, they stood fast, even to death.

We, too, live in a hostile environment, a God-denying culture where many would enjoy eliminating all traces of Christian faith. Crossing the centuries, these short and profound letters have been written for us. Watch out! Beware! On guard! Be prepared!

We first meet Peter when his brother, Andrew, brings him to Jesus (John 1:40-42). The sons of John (John 1:42; 21:15-17) and probably from Bethsaida in Galilee (John 1:44), Peter and his brother were fishermen on the Sea of Galilee (Matthew 4:18; Mark 1:16) and partners of James and John (Luke 5:10). Peter and Andrew first followed John the Baptist. When John pointed out Jesus as the "Lamb of God" (John 1:29), Andrew accepted his teacher's testimony and immediately left to get his brother, Simon, to introduce him to the Messiah. Jesus addressed Andrew's brother as "Simon son of John" and then changed his name to "Peter," meaning "rock" or "stone" (John 1:42).

This initial encounter seems to have had little effect on Peter because he returned to Capernaum to continue his vocation as a fisherman, perhaps awaiting further instructions. Subsequently, Jesus twice called Peter to follow him. The call first occurred on the Sea of Galilee, where the four business partners were fishing together. They left their nets to become "fishers of men" (Matthew 4:18-22). The second, confirming call occurred when Jesus selected the Twelve (Mark 3:13-19).

Almost immediately, Peter assumed the unofficial role of leader of the disciples. He regularly served as their spokesman and is named first in all the lists (see, for example, Matthew 14:28; 15:15; 18:21; 26:35, 40; Mark 8:29; 9:5; 10:28; John 6:68). More than likely, Peter's leadership arose from his character and personality. Totally devoted to his Lord, Peter enthusiastically spoke out and took the lead.

Belonging to the inner circle of disciples and being a powerful force in the early church, Peter is mentioned in the New Testament more often than all of the other eleven put together. Peter was present when Jesus raised Jairus's daughter from the dead. He also was privileged to be one of just four to hear Jesus' discourse on the fall of Jerusalem and the end of the world (Mark 13:3ff). He and only two others (James and John) were at the Transfiguration (Matthew 17:1) and were very close to Jesus in Gethsemane (Mark 14:33). Peter and one other disciple (John) were sent to prepare for the Last Supper (Luke 22:8). Peter also was present when Christ gave the great commission (Matthew 28:16-20) and when he ascended into heaven (Luke 24:44-53).

Although Jesus had renamed him "rock," at first Peter was anything but rock solid. Impulsive and impetuous, he often spoke without thinking (see, for example, his rebuke of Christ in Matthew 16:22 and his comments after the Transfiguration in Matthew 17:4), and he jumped to defend Jesus with a sword (John 18:10). Despite his best intentions, Peter tended to respond quite

poorly under pressure, falling asleep in the garden during Jesus'
most difficult hour (Matthew 26:40-41) and vehemently denying
the Lord when accused of being his follower (Matthew 26:69-74).

A Changed Life. Peter's life provides strong testimony to the
reality of the Resurrection and the power of the Holy Spirit. Consider the great contrast between his earlier pattern as leader of the
disciples and his later actions as leader of the early church. Peter
preached boldly and powerfully, at Pentecost (Acts 2) and
beyond. Jailed and then warned by the Jewish religious leaders
not to speak or preach in the "name of Jesus," instead of capitulat-
ing to their demands, Peter and John answered, "Judge for yourselves whether it is right in God's sight to obey you rather than
God. For we cannot help speaking about what we have seen and
heard" (Acts 4:13-20). Later, Peter was jailed again, this time by
civil authorities. Herod already had executed James, and Peter
would be next. But God miraculously released Peter, who continued to minister in Jesus' name (Acts 12:1-19). He would never
deny Christ again! The reason for this miraculous turnaround?
Peter saw the risen Christ (Acts 2:31-32). Peter knew that the gospel was true and that "Salvation is found in no one else, for there
is no other name under heaven given to men by which we must
be saved" (Acts 4:12).

Other significant events in the life and ministry of Peter
include: leading the disciples through the process of choosing a
successor to Judas Iscariot (Acts 1:15-26), condemning Ananias
and Sapphira for lying to the Holy Spirit (Acts 5:1-11), denouncing Simon the Sorcerer (Acts 8:18-23), healing Aeneas and restor-
ing Tabitha to life (Acts 9:34-40), baptizing the first Gentile
Christians (Cornelius and his household, Acts 10), and participating significantly in the Council at Jerusalem (Acts 15:1-11).

At first, Peter ministered exclusively among the Jews (Acts 1:1–
5:41). But that began to change when persecution against Christians
intensified in Jerusalem. At this time, many Christians scattered
throughout Judea and Samaria, but they preached the gospel as they
went, and many Samaritans responded (Acts 8:4-8). Soon thereafter,
Peter and John were sent to verify that, in fact, the conversions were
real (Acts 8:14-25), and Peter's ministry began to expand. Not long
afterward, on a journey throughout the country, teaching believers,
healing the sick, and telling the Good News about God's salvation,
Peter received a vision from God (Acts 9:32–10:16). Through this
vision, Peter realized that Gentiles were no longer to be considered
"unclean" and should be told about Christ. Thus, when invited by
Roman servants to come to the home of Cornelius, the centurion, Peter
agreed and traveled to Caesarea. There, in the home of this Roman

soldier, Peter preached and then witnessed the power of God transform these uncircumcised Gentiles (Acts 10:22-48). Later, when Peter explained his actions, the apostles and others praised God and declared, "So then, God has granted even the Gentiles repentance unto life" (Acts 11:18). Peter had learned from personal experience that God's message was for all the world. Later, Peter seems to have become an intermediary between the two main factions of the early church: Jewish Christianity, centered in Jerusalem, and the ministry to the Gentiles, championed by Paul (see Acts 15:6-11).

As described above, after the Ascension, Peter's early ministry was focused in Jerusalem. But then he seems to have traveled beyond, perhaps even to "Pontus, Galatia, Cappadocia, Asia and Bithynia" (1:1), the areas mentioned as destinations for this epistle. Eventually, Peter traveled to Rome, where he ministered among the beleaguered believers. This must have occurred after Paul's first imprisonment (A.D. 59–62), for Paul's prison epistles make no mention of Peter. This letter probably was written around A.D. 64, just before the terrible persecution of Christians by Emperor Nero (A.D. 65–67). Strong tradition holds that Peter was executed in Rome by Nero in A.D. 67, crucified upside down, feeling that he was unworthy to die as Jesus had. Jesus' words to Peter in John 21:18-19 seem to imply a death by crucifixion, but no historical proof has been found to confirm this tradition.

By God's mercy Peter became a fearless and outspoken servant of his risen Lord, eventually dying for his faith. God changed this man, and he can change you, too, into a rock-solid witness for Christ!

Questions of Authorship. That Peter wrote this book bearing his name is attested to by its content. Reminiscences of personal acquaintance with Christ fill this letter (for example, compare 5:5 with John 13:3-5). The writer claims to be an eyewitness of the sufferings of Jesus (5:1) and speaks with deep affection for Jesus, as though having known him personally. In addition, the admonition to "be shepherds of God's flock" (5:2) recalls Christ's charge to Peter by the Sea of Tiberias (John 21:15-17). The content of this epistle also seems to parallel Peter's speeches recorded in Acts. Compare, for example, 1:17 with Acts 10:34; 1:21 with Acts 2:32-36 and Acts 10:40; and 2:7-8 with Acts 4:10-11.

Peter's authorship also has been affirmed by the early church. Polycarp, who lived about A.D. 70–155, quoted several references (1:8; 2:11; 3:9) in his *Epistle to the Philippians.* Irenaeus, who lived about A.D. 104–203, quoted 1 Peter in *Against Heresies* (4.9; 4.16; 5.7). Tertullian, Clement of Alexandria, and Origen also supported Peter as the author.

Despite this evidence, a few scholars have disputed Peter's authorship. The main objection stems from the high quality of the Greek used in this letter. At times the Greek appears to be almost classical, and the style, extensive vocabulary, and syntax seem to be more consistent with a writer fluent in Greek rather than a simple Galilean fisherman (see Acts 4:13). In addition, the quotations of the Old Testament come from the Septuagint (the Greek translation of the Hebrew Old Testament), probably not the translation of choice for Peter, who would have been raised on either a Hebrew version or an Aramaic translation.

In answering this objection, note first that it underestimates Peter. When Peter and John appeared before the Sanhedrin, Caiaphas and the others "saw the courage of Peter and John and realized that they were unschooled, ordinary men [and] they were astonished and they took note that these men had been with Jesus" (Acts 4:13). Far from disparaging Peter and John's intellect or ability to think and write, this reference simply refers to the fact that these followers of Jesus were not rabbinical students; instead, they "had been with Jesus." Remember, John also was an "unschooled, ordinary" man, a fisherman; yet he wrote the Gospel that bears his name, three epistles, and Revelation. That Peter was not a professionally trained scribe does not mean that he was unacquainted with Greek. He lived in a Greek-dominated world (the language of commerce), and the Jerusalem church had experienced an influx of Greek-speaking Jews. Also, it is now realized that the Septuagint was widely used in Israel at this time. In fact, both James and Hebrews quote extensively from it. So Peter as a Jew from Galilee would have been well acquainted with it. In addition, Peter had several decades to polish his Greek from the time of the Ascension until 1 Peter was written. It also seems clear that Peter had the help of Silvanus (Silas) in writing this letter (5:12). This may account for the classical style of Greek used.

It is important to note here that the traditional author of nearly every book in the Bible has been disputed, especially in the last century with the rise of liberal theology and higher criticism. If certain scholars reject the notion that the Scriptures are the divinely inspired Word of God, inerrant and totally reliable, then they have no reason to worry about the integrity and accuracy of specific Bible books. In fact, they can propose (and often have) a wide variety of speculative theories of authorship based on a curious twist of text, the latest theological fad, or the push to be politically correct. As *evangelical* scholars, however, we take the Bible seriously and believe in verbal, plenary inspiration. In fact, the compelling motivation for researching and writing this commentary series rests in the fact that we believe the Bible truly is *God's Word*. We don't study it because it reads well, contains interesting stories and teachings, and has been revered for centuries. We take seriously Paul's admonition in 2 Timothy 2:15 to "correctly handle the word of truth." Thus, when 1 Peter claims to be written by Peter (1:1, "Peter, an apostle of Jesus Christ"), we assume that Peter was, in fact, the writer. God's Word speaks accurately. Thus, to believe or seek to prove otherwise would be a foolish waste of time.

SETTING

Written from Rome in about A.D. 64.

Peter gives a hint of his location with the phrase, "She who is in Babylon, chosen together with you, sends you her greetings" (5:13). Scholars have identified three possible geographical locations that may be identified with "Babylon":

1. One proposed location is what was an insignificant Egyptian military depot near the site of modern Cairo. Although the Egyptian site bore the name "Babylon" and the North African church has traditionally accepted this place as Peter's location, it seems very unlikely that Peter, Silvanus, and Mark would be together at such a remote outpost. In addition, no evidence has been found that Peter was ever in Egypt.

2. Another possibility is the village named "Babylon" located on the Euphrates River. Peter's readers would have understood this reference, and there had been a small colony of Christians there. However, again there is no evidence for Peter's presence in this location.

3. It is much more likely that "Babylon" is a figurative reference to Rome. According to the unanimous testimony of the early church, Peter ministered in Rome until his martyrdom. Choosing Rome as the location makes it easier to explain the presence of Silvanus (Silas) and Mark (5:12-13) because both had traveled with Paul. In fact, Paul had asked Timothy to send Mark to Rome to be with him (2 Timothy 4:11).

Paul had been taken to Rome as a prisoner in A.D. 59. There he had remained under house arrest, enjoying freedom to entertain guests and to teach, preach, and write (Acts 28:17-31). Likely Paul was released after two years. Then he probably left Rome for another missionary journey, traveling to Ephesus, where he left Timothy (1 Timothy 1:3), then to Colosse (Philemon 22) and on to Macedonia. He may also have traveled to Spain (Romans

15:24, 28) and Crete (Titus 1:5). It is during this time (A.D. 62–67) that Peter likely came to Rome and during which he wrote 1 Peter. Eventually, during Nero's crackdown, Paul was arrested again and returned to Rome. In this prison experience, he was isolated and lonely, awaiting execution (2 Timothy 4:9-18). Paul was martyred in the spring of A.D. 68.

Date. The only problem with identifying Rome with "Babylon" concerns determining when this letter was written. Some scholars hold to a late date (for example, A.D. 67, 70, or even after 100) by an unknown author. They reason that Christians did not call Rome "Babylon" until after Nero—for example, in Revelation, which was written in about A.D. 95. But this line of reasoning ignores the Old Testament passages that use Babylon as a symbol of godless prosperity (for example, Isaiah 14). Certainly Peter would have been familiar with this symbolism and could have used it to identify his location to those who also knew the meaning and significance of the name. Rome, far more than any other city of that day, would qualify as "Babylon" to Peter's readers.

Thus Peter wrote this letter from Rome, around A.D. 64, just before the intense persecution of the church under Nero.

Rome. Rome was the capital city of the vast and mighty Roman Empire, which stretched from Britain to Arabia. With a population of approximately one million, Rome was the diplomatic and trade center of the world and the largest city.

At first, Christianity was tolerated in Rome as a sect of Judaism. But in the last few years of Emperor Nero's reign (he ruled from A.D. 54 until his death in 68), he authorized capturing, torturing, and killing Christians. In A.D. 64, a large part of Rome was destroyed by fire, probably started at Nero's order. The emperor publicly accused the Christians in the city, giving him an excuse for terrible atrocities, including throwing believers to wild dogs in the Colosseum, as a spectator sport. During these terrible persecutions, believers were forced to choose between the emperor and Christ; those who chose Christ often died for their faith. Both Paul and Peter are believed to have been victims of Nero's reign of terror.

Certainly Peter would have seen the mounting persecution, leading him, under the inspiration of the Holy Spirit, to warn believers of "all kinds of trials" (1:6), beatings "for doing good" (2:20), suffering "for what is right" (3:14, 17), participating "in the sufferings of Christ" (4:13), and suffering "according to God's will" (4:19). With all these warnings, Peter includes words of encouragement and hope (1:7-9; 4:12-19; 5:10-11) and instructions for how to live (1:13-21; 2:1-3, 11-25; 3:1-17; 4:1-11; 5:1-9).

AUDIENCE

Christians scattered throughout Asia Minor.

The opening sentence of 1 Peter, identifying the audience as "God's elect, strangers in the world, scattered throughout Pontus, Galatia, Cappadocia, Asia and Bythynia," has also been translated "to the exiles of the Dispersion in . . ." (RSV). "Dispersion" usually is associated with Jews living in foreign cities. This phrase and the numerous Old Testament quotes have led many to believe that Peter was writing to Jewish Christians. This probably is not the case, however, because none of the problems of the dispersed Jews are discussed. In fact, the letter also contains a number of phrases that identify it with Gentile Christians: for example, the name, "Lord Jesus Christ" (1:3); the description, "the word that was preached to you" (1:25); and the reference to the readers as those who once "were not a people, but now you are the people of God" (2:10). Remember also that in most locations outside of Judea, Jewish and Gentile Christians worshiped together at this time (A.D. 64) and most likely would not be addressed separately. Thus we can conclude that Peter was writing to Christians of all nationalities.

"Pontus, Galatia, Cappadocia, Asia and Bithynia" (1:1) refer to formerly independent territories in northern Asia Minor (modern Turkey). Since 130 B.C., all of these territories had been under Roman control. The population was a mix of many races and cultures, including the native peoples, cultured Greeks, Orientals, and Jews. At the end of the first century A.D., the total population of these five huge provinces was approximately 8.5 million, one million of whom were Jews and eighty thousand, Christians. Luke explains in Acts that Paul did not minister in these northern provinces on any of his missionary journeys. On one occasion he was forbidden by the Holy Spirit to travel there and directed, instead, to Troas and then to Macedonia (Acts 16:6-12). How this area was evangelized is unknown; perhaps it was through Peter, who may have traveled there with his wife (see 1 Corinthians 9:5) after the Council of Jerusalem (Acts 15:1-29), or perhaps through the "scattering" of the believers (1:1).

OCCASION AND PURPOSE FOR WRITING

To offer encouragement and hope to Christians scattered throughout northern Asia Minor.

Peter had suffered much for preaching the gospel of Christ (see Acts 5:17-42; 8:1; 12:1-19)—he was no stranger to persecution. Nor were the Jewish believers who had been ostracized by their unbelieving families and hounded by the Sanhedrin. But this was a new experience for the Gentile Christians. Christianity was beginning to be considered a separate religion and not simply a Jewish sect. Thus Christians were no longer protected and were being persecuted by the state. This letter implies that these persecutions were just beginning on the local level. As a small minority, believers certainly must have felt like "strangers in the world" (1:1). Writing from Rome, Peter could see the change in Nero. Surely he could sense the growing threat and would know that more severe persecutions by the state would follow shortly. Peter wrote to encourage and comfort his beloved brothers and sisters and to prepare them for the persecution that was sure to come.

Peter's letter overflows with feelings of triumph in adversity, looking forward to God's glorious future. Even as they were suffering, believers could have the confident assurance of God's work in their lives and of their ultimate salvation. They could have a "living hope" (1:3).

Peter provides a powerful example of an encourager. He was not writing from a secure location, removed from the hardships of Roman life. Peter lived at the center of the persecution; yet, as he had for decades, he continued to preach courageously about his risen Lord until he, too, became a victim of Nero's murderous schemes. Despite personal hardships, Peter, like Paul, wrote to encourage others, to build them up in their faith, and to give them direction and guidance. In your struggles, do you look inward or outward? Do you tend to feel sorry for yourself or to encourage others?

MESSAGE

Salvation, Persecution, Christian Living, God's Family, Family Life, Judgment.

Salvation (1:1-5, 10-12, 18-20; 2:4, 6, 21-25; 3:18-22; 5:4). Salvation is a gracious gift from God. We are God's "elect" (1:1); that is, he *chose* us out of his love for us, sending Jesus to die in our place, to pay the penalty for our sin. (Seven times in five chapters, 1 Peter refers to believers being "elect" or "chosen.") The Holy Spirit cleansed us from sin when we believed (1:2; 2:23-24; 3:18). Eternal life belongs to those who trust in Christ. God has promised it, so we can count on it (1:3-5; 5:4).

Peter reminded his readers of the reality of their relationship with Christ. He explained that their salvation was based, not on feelings or circumstances, but on the truth, goodness, and sovereignty of God. They were chosen by God and saved by grace. That truth is the basis of hope.

Importance for Today. No matter what we are going through—pain, persecution, loneliness—we can be confident in our relationship with God if we put our faith in Christ. Our safety, security, and identity rest in him. And think of it: If we experience joy in our relationship with Christ now, how much greater our joy will be when he returns and we see him face-to-face! God has a wonderful future for us; God has chosen us and we belong to him. Such a hope should motivate us to serve Christ with great commitment.

Persecution (1:6-9; 2:19-21; 3:14-17; 4:12-19; 5:10). The recipients of this letter were suffering because of their commitment to Christ. Peter realized this and knew that the persecutions would increase dramatically in the next few years, during Nero's reign. So Peter wrote to offer faithful believers comfort and hope.

Christians should expect to be ridiculed and rejected for their faith; after all, Christ's values and virtues contrast greatly with those of the world. Persecution should make believers stronger, however, because it can refine their faith. God's message through Peter is that followers of Christ can face suffering victoriously, as the Lord did, if they rely on him.

Importance for Today. Christians still suffer for what they believe. In some countries, Christians are punished or even killed for their faith. In other countries, they face ridicule and rejection at school, at work, in the neighborhood, and even at home. We should expect persecution, but we don't have to be terrified by it. We know that God is with us in our suffering, giving us courage, comfort, and peace and strengthening our faith. We also know that one day we will live eternally with Christ. These truths should give us the confidence, patience, and hope to stand firm, even when persecuted.

Christian Living (1:13-25; 2:1-5, 9-21; 3:8-16; 4:1-11, 19; 5:1-12). As a distinct minority in a non-Christian world, Peter urged believers to be holy, "But just as he who called you is holy, so be holy in all you do; for it is written: 'Be holy, because I am holy'" (1:15-16). This meant keeping their focus on Christ, obeying him, and living as citizens of God's "holy nation" (2:9). It would involve submitting to authorities (2:13), respecting others (2:17), doing good (3:9-13; 4:19), sharing the Good News (3:15), keeping a clear conscience (3:16), being disciplined (4:7; 5:8), and being humble (5:1-6).

Importance for Today. We also live in a non-Christian society, one that is filled with pressures and temptations that threaten to conform us to the world's values and lifestyles. Instead of giving in, we should be "holy," standing out from the crowd because of our love, humility, and discipline—all evidence of our strong commitment to Christ. And we should be ready "to give an answer . . . for the hope that [we] have" (3:15), pointing family, friends, coworkers, and neighbors to Christ.

God's Family (1:14, 22; 2:4-10; 3:8; 5:12-14). Believers are privileged to belong to God's family, a community with Christ as the founder and foundation. Everyone in this community is related—all brothers and sisters, loved equally by God. The recipients of this letter were far from Peter, but they were his brothers and sisters in Christ. Although Peter was an apostle and a revered teacher and leader in the church, he was also their brother, a fellow member of God's royal family.

Importance for Today. Because Christ is the foundation of our family, we must be devoted, loyal, and faithful to him. By obeying our Lord, we show that we are his children. We may be "strangers in the world" (1:1), but we are "a chosen people, a royal priesthood, a holy nation, a people belonging to God" (2:9). This means that regardless of the rejection we feel in society, we can feel accepted and loved by our spiritual family. It also means that we should live differently from those who don't know the Lord and make a difference for Christ in the world.

Family Life (3:1-7). Peter encouraged the wives of unbelievers to submit to their husbands' authority as a means of winning them to Christ. He also urged all family members to treat each other with respect, displaying sympathy, love, compassion, and humility.

Importance for Today. The family is under attack today, by Satan and by a society that values living for oneself and for the moment. So families are falling apart, with soaring divorce rates and mothers and fathers deserting their spouses and children. Christians should model what the family can and should be. We must treat our family members lovingly, especially those who don't know the Lord. Although it isn't easy, willing service is the best way to influence loved ones. To gain the strength we need for self-discipline and submission, we should pray for God's help.

Judgment (1:17; 3:18-22; 4:7, 17-18; 5:4). God will judge with perfect justice. Everyone who has ever lived will face God, who will punish evildoers and those who have persecuted God's people. Those who have placed their trust in Christ and who love God will be rewarded with life forever in God's presence.

Importance for Today Every person is accountable to God for what he or she has done with Christ and for how he or she has lived. Thus we must leave judgment of others to him. This means not hating or even resenting those who persecute us. Instead, we should pray for them, that they may come to know the Savior too. We also should realize that we will be held responsible for how we live each day. This truth should motivate us to obey God and do what is right.

VITAL STATISTICS

Purpose: To offer encouragement to suffering Christians

Author: Peter

To whom written: Jewish Christians driven out of Jerusalem and scattered throughout Asia Minor, and all believers everywhere

Date written: About A.D. 64

Setting: Peter was probably in Rome when the great persecution under Emperor Nero began. (Eventually Peter was executed during this persecution.) In various places throughout the Roman Empire, Christians were being persecuted and killed for their faith, and the church in Jerusalem was being scattered throughout the Mediterranean world.

Key verse: "These [trials] have come so that your faith . . . may be proved genuine and may result in praise, glory and honor when Jesus Christ is revealed" (1:7 NIV).

OUTLINE

1. God's great blessings to his people (1:1–2:10)
2. The conduct of God's people in the midst of suffering (2:11–4:19)
3. The shepherding of God's people in the midst of suffering (5:1-14)

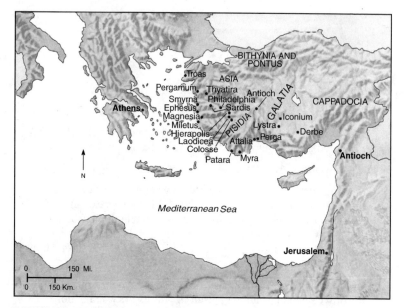

THE CHURCHES OF PETER'S LETTER
Peter addressed his letter to the churches located throughout Bithynia,
Pontus, Asia, Galatia, and Cappadocia. Paul had evangelized many of these
areas; other areas had churches that were begun by the Jews who were in
Jerusalem on the day of Pentecost and heard Peter's powerful sermon (see
Acts 2:9-11).

1 Peter 1

The apostle Peter wrote this letter to encourage believers who would likely face trials and persecution under Emperor Nero. During most of the first century, Christians were not hunted down and killed throughout the Roman Empire. They could, however, expect social and economic persecution from three main sources: the Romans, the Jews, and their own families. All Christians would very likely be misunderstood; some would be harassed; a few would be tortured and even put to death. Peter may have been writing especially for new Christians and those planning to be baptized. He wanted to warn them about what lay ahead—they needed his encouraging words to help them face opposition.

This letter continues to encourage Christians facing trials. Two-thirds of believers around the world live under governments more repressive than the Roman Empire of the first century. Christians everywhere face misunderstanding, ridicule, and even harassment by unbelieving friends, employers, teachers, and family members. In some countries, converting to Christianity is punishable by death. No one is exempt from catastrophe, pain, illness, and death—trials that, like persecution, make us lean heavily on God. The first verses of the first chapter show the perspective we should have in trials. We are chosen, but we must live as resident aliens. We know that we belong to the triune God rather than to this world. For today's readers, as well as for Peter's original audience, the themes of this letter are *hope and assurance* in Jesus Christ.

1:1 Peter, an apostle of Jesus Christ. In the style of ancient letters, *Peter* began by identifying himself. Peter was one of the twelve disciples chosen by Jesus (Mark 1:16-18) and, with James and John, was part of the inner group that Jesus had singled out for special training and fellowship. Peter's given name was Simon, but upon meeting Jesus, Jesus had said, "'You are Simon son of John. You will be called Cephas' (which, when translated, is Peter)" (John 1:42 NIV). Cephas is an Aramaic word that is *petros* in Greek. The word means "stone" or "rock." Jesus called him Peter because he knew that Peter would become a pillar and a foundation stone in the building of the first-century church (see Matthew 16:16-18; Galatians 2:9; Ephesians 2:20; 1 Peter 2:4-5). Peter was one of the first to recognize Jesus as the Messiah, God's Son, and Jesus gave him a special leadership role (Matthew 16:16-19; Luke 22:31-32; John 21:15-19). In fact, the first twelve chapters of the book of Acts focus on Peter's ministry in the establishment and expansion of the early church.

Peter was an *apostle,* the title Jesus had given to the twelve disciples (Luke 6:13). The title "apostle" designated one who had authority to set up and supervise churches and discipline them if necessary. Even more than a title of authority, "apostle" means one sent on a mission, like an envoy or ambassador. Peter had been sent by the Master himself—*Jesus Christ.* As an apostle of Jesus Christ, Peter wrote with authority because, like the Old Testament prophets, he wrote God's very words. The recipients of this letter (including us) should remember Peter's connection with Jesus, his powerful ministry, and his authority to speak.

Peter had denied even knowing Jesus, but Christ had forgiven and transformed him. Peter had disowned Jesus three times. Later, Jesus asked Peter three times if Peter loved him. When Peter answered yes, Jesus told him to feed his sheep (John 21). While it was one thing to say he loved Jesus, it would be another to actually do it. From that point, Peter's life changed dramatically—from fisherman to evangelist; from impetuousness to being rock solid; from one who had disowned to one who had been totally and completely forgiven. Peter willingly took on the job of "feeding the sheep." The book of Acts records how Peter ministered to, cared for, and shepherded the growing "flock" of believers in Jerusalem and was the first to take the gospel message beyond the bounds of Judaism to the Gentiles (Acts 10).

GOD'S TEAM
Peter reveals the tremendous depth and scope of God's plan. God chooses, destines, cleanses, and covers those who believe. All three members of the Trinity—God the Father, Son, and Holy Spirit—work together to take us to our final destination. What amazing teamwork and strategy. What a privilege to be on God's team!

With God's strength, we can try harder to do more at greater risk without fear. We can face trials knowing that the final victory belongs to God.

Next time you're faced with a tough decision—money, career, medical treatment—remember who's with you; ask God to give you strength.

**To God's elect, strangers in the world, scattered throughout
Pontus, Galatia, Cappadocia, Asia and Bithynia.**[NIV] The recipients of this letter were *God's elect,* that is, both Jewish and Gentile Christians. In the Bible, "God's elect" refers to those chosen
or "called out" who have responded to the gospel. Although we
can't totally understand the doctrine of election, it gives us tremendous insight into God's love and wisdom. (For more on the
elect, see notes on "chosen" in 1:2.) God chooses us, not based
on our character or actions, but on his own merciful purposes.
Although he initiated our calling, based totally on his wisdom,
we who are called still must respond and choose to follow him.
All believers have been called and chosen by God. We are God's
special chosen ones. God gave us new status.

THIS WORLD IS NOT MY HOME
Peter used two terms for how we are to live in this present
society:

  1. We are resident aliens (1:1; 2:11).
  2. We are tourists (1:17; 2:11).

  Both terms emphasize separation of our goals and desires
from those of our contemporaries in our culture (see also
Philippians 3:20). We should regard the pursuits of this world
as foreign, belonging to someone else. We should be polite to
those intrigued by possessions, achievements, and sinful
pleasure, but say, "No thanks, I'm just passing through." We
must not be so attached to this world that we are unprepared
for Christ's return. We should not be so preoccupied with
worldly gain that we neglect service for Christ.

When people accept Jesus Christ as Savior and Lord, God
transfers their citizenship from the world to heaven (Philippians
3:20). Thus, while they live on this earth, they are like *strangers
in the world.* So we should feel estranged from our society and
uncomfortable with its directions and values. The Greek word
translated "strangers" is *parepidemois* and refers to those living
temporarily in a foreign land. It does not refer to people
unrecognizable to their neighbors, nor does it mean that the
people live in these locations against their will (as the word
"exiles" in NRSV might suggest; it means "resident aliens"). The
world becomes a "foreign land" to believers because their real
home is heaven and they are only on earth temporarily. Christ's
followers in the first century also had a spiritual calling that made
them strangers on the earth as they awaited their real home with
Christ (see also 1:17 and Hebrews 11:13).

The church began in Jerusalem, but before long it had spread across the Roman Empire and beyond. Some of this had resulted from travelers hearing the gospel in Jerusalem, believing it, and then taking the message back to their homelands. However, persecution also had a role in the spread of the gospel. In Acts we read that, after Stephen was martyred, "a great persecution broke out against the church at Jerusalem, and all except the apostles were scattered throughout Judea and Samaria. . . . Those who had been scattered preached the word wherever they went" (Acts 8:1, 4 NIV), resulting in Jews and Gentiles all over the world hearing and believing the message. Thus Peter wrote this letter to both Jewish and Gentile believers in churches *scattered throughout Pontus, Galatia, Cappadocia, Asia and Bithynia,* Roman provinces in Asia Minor (see the introductory map). Some of the churches in these areas were begun by those who had heard Peter preach at Pentecost (see Acts 2:9-10). The Greek word for "scattered" is *diasporas,* originally referring to Jews who were separated from their homeland in Israel. Peter adopted the word to refer to the early believers who were separated from their homeland in heaven and to build up their identity as members of the church (see chapter 2).

But how does one address a letter to "scattered" people? Most likely, Peter planned for the letter to be circulated from one church to the next throughout each area. Paul had employed this method when he had requested the Colossian church to send his letter to the church in Laodicea, and for the Colossians to, in turn, read the letter he had written to the Laodiceans (Colossians 4:16). Galatia, Cappadocia, and Asia were Roman provinces, while Pontus and Bithynia were considered as one province (with both names). Peter may have separated the names of that province to indicate the circular route that the bearer of this letter would travel.

Although these believers were scattered, many of them would suffer persecution for their faith. Peter often referred to persecution in this letter as he comforted the believers who prepared to face harassment and harm because of their faith. Believers could expect persecution from at least one of the following sources:

- *The Jews.* The first believers and leaders of the early church were Jews. When they became Christians, they didn't give up their Jewish heritage, just as we didn't give up our nationality when we became followers of Christ. Many Jews did not appreciate being lumped together with Christians into the same religious category by the Romans and therefore given the same legal status. As the book of Acts frequently records, Jews occasionally harmed Christians physically, drove them out of town, or attempted to turn Roman officials against them. Saul, later the great apostle Paul, was an early Jewish persecutor of Christians.

■ *The Romans.* The legal status of Christians in the Roman Empire was unclear. Many Romans considered Christianity to be a Jewish sect; because the Jewish religion was legal, they considered Christianity legal also, as long as Christians obeyed the law. However, if Christians refused to worship the emperor or join the army, or if they were involved in civil disturbances (such as the one in Ephesus recorded in Acts 19:23ff.), they could be punished by the civil authorities.

■ *The family.* Another source of persecution was the Christian's own family. Under Roman law, the head of the household had absolute authority over all its members. Unless the ruling male became a Christian, the wife, children, and servants who were believers could face extreme hardship. If they were sent away, they would have no place to turn but the church; if they were beaten, no court of law would uphold their interests.

Peter began his letter with words of comfort. Despite the growing threat of organized persecution, he reminded the Christians that they were and would remain God's selected and loved people who, although strangers in this world and often persecuted by it, would eventually find their eternal rest and home with Christ.

1:2 Who have been chosen according to the foreknowledge of God the Father.[NIV] This verse mentions all three members of the Trinity—God the Father, God the Son (Jesus Christ), and God the Holy Spirit. All members of the Trinity work to bring about our salvation and provide a threefold assurance to believers. Because of his grace and love, the Father chose us before we chose him (Ephesians 1:4). Jesus Christ the Son died for us while we were still sinners, gaining our salvation by shedding his blood (Romans 5:6-10). The Holy Spirit applies Christ's sacrifice to our lives, bringing us the benefits of salvation, cleansing us, and setting us apart (sanctifying us) for God's service (2 Thessalonians 2:13).

Although Christians are "strangers in the world" (1:1), they take comfort in the fact that they are "God's elect," God's *chosen.* At one time, only the nation of Israel could claim to be God's; but through Christ, all believers—Jews and Gentiles—are his chosen people.

But how are God's people "chosen"? Don't people make their own choices? While doctrines of election, predestination, and

God's choice of believers have generated fierce doctrinal differences among Christians, most of these differences come from theological and philosophical points of view about what the Bible means. God alone originates and accomplishes our salvation because of his grace. We do nothing to earn it. God's choice of each believer is based on

- *his gracious mercy,* so there is no room for our pride. Sinners deserve nothing but wrath; God's mercy alone offers salvation.

- *his decision in eternity past,* so there is no room for us to doubt our salvation or our future in heaven. Nothing that happens in time can change God's promises to us.

- *his sovereign control,* so there is no room for fatalism. Some are saved, some are not, yet this does not make God unjust, for God owes mercy to no one. We should marvel not that he withholds mercy from some, but that he gives grace to any.

- *his love for us as provided in Christ,* so there is no room for apathy. God's incredible love for us should make us change our way of life and be willing to serve, honor, and glorify God alone.

Being "chosen" according to God's *foreknowledge* in no way removes the necessity for people to choose to follow him. The fact that God knows all events and decisions beforehand, even ordains them beforehand, does not mean that he forces the actions of his creatures, leaving them no choice.

The word translated "foreknowledge" means more than simply that God knew ahead of time who would respond to his call. It goes much deeper, into God's grace, sovereignty, and authorship of salvation (see Numbers 16:5; Deuteronomy 7:6-8; Amos 3:2). God's choice has more to do with his love and generosity. First, God's foreknowledge means that he took the initiative and chose people before they had done anything to deserve it. Second, God had intimate knowledge of these future believers; he knew who would believe, and he knew them personally. These chosen ones were known by God the Father as a father knows his children, except that God knew about them from eternity past. God is not trapped in time—what he knows is from eternity past into eternity future. Third, God makes his choice effective by the presence of the Holy Spirit in those who believe, resulting in obedience.

They were chosen, but not against their own will. When the time came, they would accept the gospel message. In 1:20, Peter described Christ as being "chosen before the creation of the world." God chose Christ, knew Christ intimately, and did not force Christ to pay the penalty for sin. Christ freely accepted the task assigned to him by the Father.

The Greek wording leaves open the possibility that the phrase "according to the foreknowledge of God" modifies "God's elect, strangers in the world, scattered . . ." If Peter meant this, he was telling these scattered and persecuted believers that God knew their situations and he had known this from the beginning of time. Everything was happening in accordance with God's fore-knowledge—he was not surprised.

Salvation and assurance rest in the free and merciful choice of almighty God; no trials or persecutions can take away the eternal life he gives to those who believe in him.

Through the sanctifying work of the Spirit.NIV These people are God's chosen only because of his grace and mercy and *through the sanctifying work of the Spirit.* (Paul used the same phrase in 2 Thessalonians 2:13.) Only the Spirit can draw people to a saving relationship with God. "The man without the Spirit does not accept the things that come from the Spirit of God, for they are foolishness to him, and he cannot understand them, because they are spiritually discerned" (1 Corinthians 2:14 NIV). The Spirit comes to the chosen people to sanctify them. Sanctification refers to the process of Christian growth through which the Holy Spirit makes us like Christ. We are set apart by God for his special use. We experience the inner trans-formation whereby the Spirit changes us. The Spirit draws us from sin toward obedience. He does that by reminding us of our new status in Christ (Romans 8:15-17; John 14:20) and by using Scripture to strengthen and guide us (John 17:17). Only the Holy Spirit can help us reach that goal; we cannot, in our own power, become like Christ. Sanctification is a gradual, life-long process that will be completed when we see Christ face-to-face (1 John 3:2).

For obedience to Jesus Christ and sprinkling by his blood.NIV The result of the chosen status of God's people and their sanctifi-cation is *obedience* to the gospel, which proclaims the saving act of Jesus Christ. *Sprinkling by his blood* refers to the initial cleans-ing of each believer because of Christ's blood shed on the cross (Hebrews 10:22) and to the day-to-day cleansing from sin through Christ's blood (1 John 1:7). The constant cleansing from sin available to us because of Christ's sacrifice enables us to obey God faithfully.

In these first two verses of his letter, Peter has already used decidedly Jewish, Old Testament terminology and applied it to New Testament believers. Many in Peter's audience were Jewish Christians, familiar with his references:

- The Old Testament Jews had been scattered from their homeland; Christians are scattered and awaiting return to their homeland in heaven (1:1).

- The Old Testament Jews had been called God's chosen and elect people (Isaiah 43:20); Christians are God's chosen and elect people, sanctified and willing to obey.

- In the Old Testament, three ceremonies involved the sprinkling of blood on the people. First, through Moses, God had sealed his first covenant with the Old Testament Jews by the sprinkling of blood, both on the altar and on the people (Exodus 24:3-8); Christians are metaphorically sprinkled with the spilled blood of the Savior, sealing God's new covenant with them (Luke 22:20). Second, the ordination of priests (Exodus 29:21); Peter called the Christians a royal priesthood (2:9), indicating each individual believer's access to God. Third, the purification ceremony of a leper who had been healed of the dread disease (Leviticus 14:6-7); Christians also have been cleansed from a deadly disease, the defilement of sin, by Christ's shed blood (Hebrews 9:14).

May grace and peace be yours in abundance.NRSV *Grace* means God's unmerited favor; *peace* refers to the peace that Christ made between sinners and God through his Son's death on the cross. Only God can grant such wonderful gifts; only he can give them *in abundance.* Peter wanted these believers, scattered as they were across the empire's provinces, to be united in their experience of grace and peace in their daily lives. Peter wrote to both Jewish and Gentile believers, and in this greeting he combined expressions from Jewish and Gentile customs. Jews wished each other "peace" *(eirene* or the Hebrew *shalom);* Gentiles wished each other "grace" *(charis).* The world offers a temporary and counterfeit version of each of God's wonderful gifts (for grace, good luck; for peace, a lack of conflict). For believers, life's great blessings are not good luck, but God's grace; and even hardships have a gracious purpose behind them. For believers, Christ's peace does not mean prevention of problems or turmoil, but it does mean an inner calm that permeates life itself. To these persecuted believers, these words held deep meaning and great comfort.

A GREAT START
When Peter says "Grace and peace," he's saying much more than "Have a nice day!" Grace describes God's character. It's a theological statement of immense importance. The heart behind the universe is a gracious heart of love. Although he is the center of all power, God cares for you as a person.

The meaning of peace goes far beyond merely the cessation of hostilities. Peace between you and God settles your biggest problem—sin. When God saves you, he removes all your rebellion and indifference to him. Peace with God gives you the base for solving your second tier of problems—relationships with everyone else in the world. With your relationship with God made right, you have the energy and insight to work on your human relationships. All this comes at a price you could not pay yourself; it was prepaid by Jesus on the cross.

Thank God for who he is and what he has done. Let the realization of God's grace and peace get your day off to a great start.

THE HOPE OF ETERNAL LIFE / 1:3-12

Peter opened his letter by thanking God for the salvation he gives, because of his mercy, to believers. Peter looked to their future reward, reminded them that God saw their present suffering and was protecting them, and spoke of the believers of the past (the prophets) who longed to see and understand the new birth that these believers experienced in their daily lives. Even as these believers faced persecution, they could remember God's grace and continue to live as God desired. Not all believers are persecuted for their faith, but everyone faces times of stress, discouragement, or despair. This section introduces the blessings of salvation (1:3-12) and the ethical responsibilities they produce (1:13–2:3). Peter's words echo through the centuries, reminding us of God's grace and sovereignty over all of life, encouraging us to glorify and live for him.

1:3 Praise be to the God and Father of our Lord Jesus Christ![NIV]
Peter launched into praise of God the Father, who had chosen and cleansed the believers (1:2). *Praise be* to God (or blessed be God) was an Old Testament format that Peter gave New Testament implications. (For examples of Old Testament praises to God, read Genesis 9:26; 14:20; 24:27; Ruth 4:14; 1 Samuel 25:32; 1 Kings 1:48; Psalms 66:20; 72:18.) The Old Testament believers praised God, but the New Testament believers praised him with an entirely new name, one never used in the Old Testament: *Father of our Lord*

Jesus Christ. (See Romans 15:6; 2 Corinthians 1:3; 11:31; Ephesians 1:3 for Paul's use of the same phrase.) God is "Father," the first person of the Trinity. He did not exist before the Son, for the Son has always existed (John 1:1-3; 17:5, 24). God the Father sent the Son, and the Son responded in full obedience.

By his great mercy he has given us a new birth into a living hope through the resurrection of Jesus Christ from the dead.^{NRSV} We find God's mercy always at the center of any discussion of salvation. Only God's mercy would allow him to have compassion for sinful and rebellious people. Salvation is all completely from God; we can do nothing to earn it. Salvation is *given* to us because of God's *great mercy* alone. Peter's words offer joy and hope in times of trouble. He finds confidence in what God has done for us in Christ Jesus, who has given us hope of eternal life. Our hope is not only for the future; it is "living." Eternal life begins when we trust Christ and join God's family. Regardless of our pain and trials, we know that this life is not all there is. Eventually we will live with Christ forever.

The term *new birth* refers to spiritual birth (regeneration)—the Holy Spirit's act of bringing believers into God's family. The words "has given . . . new birth" translate *anagennesas,* meaning "beget again," "regenerate," or "cause to be born again" (the same word is used in 1:23). Jesus used this concept of new birth when he told Nicodemus that he had to be "born again" in order to see God's kingdom (see John 3). In the new birth, we become dead to sin and alive to God with a fresh beginning. People can do no more to accomplish their "new birth" than they could do to accomplish their own natural birth. In his introductory comments, Peter thanked God for the new spiritual lives of the believers to whom he was writing.

Believers are reborn into a *living hope.* The "hope" refers to our confident expectation of life to come. "Living" means that it grows and gains strength the more we learn about our Lord. It is not dependent on outward circumstances; it is dynamic and vital. Hope looks forward in eager anticipation to what God will do. We have hope based on our conviction that God will keep his promises. We base our hope in a future resurrection on *the resurrection of Jesus Christ.* It is living because Christ is alive (see 1:13, 21; 3:5, 15). By rising from the dead, Christ made the necessary power available for our resurrection (1 Corinthians 15:22). Christ's resurrection makes us certain that we too will be raised from the dead. Believers are "born again" from their sinful state into the life of grace, which, in the end, will become a life of glory. We shouldn't be discouraged by earthly trials, for we have the Resurrection to be our backup.

BORN AGAIN!
Is "born again" politically correct? ("New birth" means the same as "born again"; see 1:23.) Ever since Jimmy Carter's presidency, news commentators have struggled to understand what Christians mean by "born again." Currently the phrase is used to label Christians on the political right wing. Almost always in the news media, "born again" is a term of derision.
  So let's unravel the facts:

- All Christians are born-again. The term is a wonderful metaphor of new life from God. You cannot be a Christian without a fresh beginning based on the salvation Christ brings.
- Born-again people have a new set of priorities and values, but not a prescribed political agenda. God calls us to pursue justice and love, but how we do so varies. No political party is born-again.
- To be born-again is a magnificent gift from God. It is also a dividing line. Cross it, and you enter God's kingdom. Not everyone will understand. But that's no cause for arrogance or defensiveness. Just demonstrate God's love and justice. That's your new job that accompanies your new birth.

1:4 And into an inheritance that can never perish, spoil or fade— kept in heaven for you.[NIV] There are two results of the new birth: the living hope (1:3), and our inheritance, as shown here by the use of *eis,* meaning "into." The word translated *inheritance (kleronomia)* is also used in the Old Testament to describe the inheritance to which the Jews had looked forward in the Promised Land of Canaan (Numbers 32:19; Deuteronomy 2:12; 19:8-10). God gave the land of Canaan to his people as an inheritance (Exodus 15:17; Joshua 22:19; Psalm 79:1). God first promised this to Abraham and then to his children. The word occurs frequently in the books of Numbers and Deuteronomy, which describe the future allotment of the Promised Land to the tribes, and in the book of Joshua, where this allotment was carried out. God divided the land among his people, each tribe receiving an "inheritance."

Although the nation had received that right of inheritance, eventually they defiled their faith through the influence of foreign nations. The people's sins had caused the promise to become only a fading memory. Christians can look forward to another "inheritance"—eternal life with God, described in various ways in Scripture (see the chart below). Jesus Christ is God's only Son; thus he is sole heir (Mark 12:7). As children of God, believers become heirs with Christ. "Now if we are children, then we are heirs—heirs of God and co-heirs with Christ, if indeed we share in his sufferings in order that we may also share in his glory" (Romans 8:17 NIV). Believers

THE INHERITANCE

Our promised inheritance comes from our loving Father. We cannot earn an inheritance; it is a gift. The word *inheritance* is described in various ways in Scripture.

The Promised Land	Numbers 32:19; Deuteronomy 12:9; 15:4; 19:10; Joshua 11:23; Psalm 105:11
God Himself	Psalm 16:5
Eternal Life	Daniel 12:13; Matthew 19:29; Mark 10:17; Titus 3:7
The Earth	Matthew 5:5
The Kingdom of God	Matthew 25:34; 1 Corinthians 15:50; Ephesians 5:5
Glory with Christ	Romans 8:17
Sealed by the Holy Spirit	Ephesians 1:13-14
A Reward	Colossians 3:24
Salvation	Hebrews 1:14
Eternal	Hebrews 9:15
A Blessing	1 Peter 3:9
Holy City, New Jerusalem	Revelation 21:2-7

inherit Christ's blessing. An inheritance comes freely to the heirs; they cannot obtain it by their own efforts. Thus, the word fittingly describes what God gives to believers.

Peter used three words, each beginning with the same letter and ending with the same syllable in Greek, to describe this inheritance. It can never *perish (aphthartos),* meaning it will never pass away, disappear, or come to ruin as the result of hostile forces. Neither can it *spoil (amiantos),* meaning it will never become unfit for us or polluted by sin. And it won't *fade (amarantos)*; it won't lose its glory or freshness, nor will it die away. These words contrast this inheritance with all earthly, human possessions. Nothing in the natural order—catastrophe, sin, age, evil—can affect it. God has made it indestructible, existing for all eternity.

Believers have uncancelable and untransferable reservations in heaven. The inheritance is *kept in heaven* for us. The word "kept" is in the perfect tense in Greek, expressing a past activity with results that continue in the present; God has been keeping and still keeps the inheritance there—prepared, reserved, certain, and waiting. No matter what harm might come to believers on earth, the inheritance awaits, for it is kept safe with God. "Heaven" is where God dwells—

untouched by the evil and corruption of the natural world. An inheritance in heaven is in the safest possible place. As Jesus advised, "Do not store up for yourselves treasures on earth, where moth and rust destroy, and where thieves break in and steal. But store up for yourselves treasures in heaven, where moth and rust do not destroy, and where thieves do not break in and steal. For where your treasure is, there your heart will be also" (Matthew 6:19-21 NIV).

INFLATIONPROOF INVESTMENT
If people have too much money, prices go up and dollars buy less. Then the Federal Reserve Board raises prime interest rates, people have less money, and prices stabilize. So the theory goes. Fortunately, none of the laws of economics apply to salvation: Everyone can have it; money cannot buy it; and the value never depreciates.

This investment tops anything your retirement plan can offer. God makes all the payments, gives you daily interest, and keeps a huge escrow account for you in heaven.

That's why we must take the Bible as our only real Prospectus. It reads: Don't worry; serve God heartily; the future looks really good with God in control.

Do you suppose this financial tip might interest your neighbor? You be the first to tell him.

1:5 Who are being protected by the power of God through faith for a salvation ready to be revealed in the last time.[NRSV] In these words, Peter answered concerns that might have arisen in the minds of persecuted believers: Will we be able to endure and remain faithful to Christ if persecution becomes more intense? What good is an inheritance in heaven, kept safe and sound, if we are not kept safe and sound on earth?

Peter explained that, in spite of persecution and even violent death, believers *are being protected.* The word translated "protected" (guarded, shielded) is *phrouroumenous,* a military term used to refer to a garrison within a city (see also 2 Thessalonians 3:3; Jude 24). It's an inner area of protection; though the city wall is taken, the garrison is not. No matter how the world persecuted or killed believers' bodies, God was guarding their souls. Peter gave a double-locked security for believers. First, our inheritance is protected (1:4); second, we are protected. Like a safe within a safe, nothing could be more secure. We have this continuous protection *by the power of God* working *through* the *faith* of those protected. Believers reading Peter's letter could rest in the fact that God would constantly protect their faith, thus enabling them to receive their promised inheritance. We may have to endure trials, persecution, or violent death, but our souls cannot be harmed if we have accepted Christ's gift of salvation. We know we will receive God's promised rewards.

The goal of that protection is *salvation*. Believers have already received salvation through their acceptance of Jesus Christ as Savior, but the fullness of that salvation, its complete rewards and blessings, will be *revealed in the last time*. Salvation refers not just to regeneration; it is a summary term for all the blessings of the Christian life. These blessings are ready, but will not be revealed until the "last time"—that is, the judgment day of Christ (see Romans 14:10; Revelation 20:11-15). Peter said these were *ready* to be revealed, indicating that he knew he was living in the "last time" (see also 1:20). Peter lived in the last time (or last days), and so have all believers since. The "last time" comprises the period (however long it will be) between Christ's first and second comings. The last act of history has begun. What has started will be fully disclosed when he returns.

1:6 **In this you greatly rejoice, though now for a little while you may have had to suffer grief in all kinds of trials.**[NIV] *In this* (referring to the entire future hope of believers discussed in 1:3-5) the believers *greatly rejoice*. The Greek word *agalliasthai* (also translated "to exult") is not used by secular Greek writers; in the New Testament it refers to deep, spiritual joy (see Luke 1:46-47; Acts 16:34; 1 Peter 4:13). This type of rejoicing remains, unhindered and unchanged by what happens in this present life.

Believers, at that time and even today, *may have had to suffer grief in all kinds of trials*. Peter mentioned suffering several times in this letter (1:6-7; 3:13-17; 4:12-19; 5:9). In 1:11, he mentioned that the Spirit of Christ predicted the suffering and glory of Christ. When Peter wrote of trials, he was not referring to natural disasters or God's punishments; instead, he meant the response of an unbelieving world to people of faith. Christians became the target of persecution for four main reasons: (1) They refused to worship the emperor as a god and thus were viewed as atheists and traitors. (2) They refused to worship at pagan temples, so business for these moneymaking enterprises dropped wherever Christianity took hold. (3) They didn't support the Roman ideals of self, power, and conquest, and the Romans scorned the Christian ideal of self-sacrificing service. (4) They exposed and rejected the horrible immorality of pagan culture. (See the introduction to 1 Peter for more about the persecution of believers.)

> No pain, no palm; no thorns, no throne; no gall, no glory; no cross, no crown. *William Penn*

The words "may have had [to suffer]" are literally translated "if (or since) it is necessary." Peter made the point that no individual's suffering escapes God's notice and control. God uses that person's experience according to his infinitely wise plans for that person. Grief and suffering do not happen without cause or reason. While it may never be clear to us, God must be trusted to carry out his purposes, even in times of trial. All believers face such trials when they let their lights shine into the darkness. We must accept trials as part of the refining process that burns away impurities and prepares us to meet Christ. Trials teach us patience (Romans 5:3-4; James 1:2-3) and help us grow to be the people God wants.

Peter made it clear to these suffering believers that even as they grieved *now* (in their present existence), it was only *for a little while* compared to the glorious eternity awaiting them. Because of this they could rejoice, even as they suffered grief. Peter pointed out that grief and joy can be simultaneous in the Christian life. Grief is the natural response to the difficulties in this fallen world, but faith looks forward to an eternity with God and rejoices.

WHY ME?
The problem has vexed philosophers since they first asked questions: Why does an all-powerful, good God permit suffering? To which most people add: "And if someone has to suffer, why me?" Instead of answering these questions on the philosophical level, Christians face suffering by adopting a new set of responses:

- *Confidence* that God knows, plans, and directs our lives for the good. It's hard to calculate sometimes, but God always provides his love and strength for us. God leads us toward a better future.
- *Perseverance* when facing grief, anger, sorrow, and pain. Christians believe in expressing grief, but we should never give in to bitterness and despair.
- *Courage* because with Jesus as Brother and Savior, we need not be afraid. He who suffered for us will not abandon us. Jesus carries us through everything.

Instead of asking, "Why me?" respond to your trials with confidence, perseverance, and courage.

1:7 So that the genuineness of your faith—being more precious than gold that, though perishable, is tested by fire—may be found to result in praise and glory and honor when Jesus Christ is revealed.NRSV While God may have different purposes in the trials that face his people, one overriding result of all trials is clear: Suffering refines people's faith. Peter described the *genuineness* of believers' *faith* as being *more precious than gold,* the most valuable and durable substance of the time. As gold is heated, impurities float to the top and can be skimmed off, leaving extremely valuable "pure

REASONS TO REJOICE IN TRIALS

Reason	Verses	Application
1. Trials strengthen our faith.	"Not only so, but we also rejoice in our sufferings, because we know that suffering produces perseverance" (Romans 5:3 NIV) *(See also 1 Peter 4:19.)*	Trials and suffering burn away self-reliance and promote reliance on God.
2. Trials help us look forward to the glory we will experience when Christ comes to restore us.	"And after you have suffered for a little while, the God of all grace, who has called you to his eternal glory in Christ, will himself restore, support, strengthen, and establish you" (1 Peter 5:10 NRSV).	Trials and suffering teach us not to be so comfortable or dependent upon this life.
3. Trials expose a deep vein of patience in us.	"But the fruit of the Spirit is love, joy, peace, patience, kindness, goodness, faithfulness" (Galatians 5:22 NIV).	Trials and suffering are the only way for us to develop patience.
4. Trials help us resist worldly desires.	"Since therefore Christ suffered in the flesh, arm yourselves also with the same intention (for whoever has suffered in the flesh has finished with sin)" (1 Peter 4:1 NRSV).	Trials and suffering help us see the futility of worldly desires so we can devote ourselves to God.
5. Trials can bring rewards from Jesus.	"Blessed is anyone who endures temptation. Such a one has stood the test and will receive the crown of life that the Lord has promised to those who love him" (James 1:12 NRSV). *(See also Romans 8:18; 2 Corinthians 4:17; 1 Peter 5:4.)*	Trials and suffering are slight compared to the eternity of joy that we have been promised.

gold." Yet gold is not eternal; like everything else on earth, it too will eventually perish. Genuine faith, on the other hand, is indestructible for all eternity. However, it may take the "fire" of trials, struggles, and persecutions to remove impurities and defects. God values a fire-tested (or "stress-tested") faith. All of us have faith that may be mixed with improper attitudes or sinful motivations (sometimes even the good we do is for selfish reasons). In the crucible of life, God our Goldsmith skims off our impurities. Through trials, God burns away our self-reliance and self-serving attitudes, so that our genuineness reflects his glory and brings praise to him.

How do trials prove the genuineness of one's faith? A person living a comfortable life may find it very easy to be a believer. But to keep one's faith in the face of ridicule, slander, persecution, or even death proves the true value of that faith. The fire of difficulty and suffering tests the genuineness of faith. If believers can trust God and rejoice when surrounded by persecution and when they cannot see the outcome or understand the reason, then their faith has been proved genuine and will not be forgotten by God.

Such faith results in *praise and glory and honor.* Although it is unclear whether these will be directed to the believers or to Jesus Christ, most likely Peter was encouraging these scattered believers. Their genuine faith would be rewarded by praise, glory, and honor bestowed upon them by God himself when Jesus Christ returns *(is revealed)* to judge the world and take believers home.

WHILE WE WAIT
Christians look toward the return of Jesus, when pain will end and perfect justice begin. Faith will be rewarded and evil will be punished. But what should we do until then?

The Bible's answer is simple but not easy: Because we know the future, we must faithfully serve God here and now. If today that means resolving a conflict, mending a hurt, working a dull job, confronting a belligerent child, rebuilding a marriage, or just waiting for guidance—do it all with the joy of God, who will return with his reward!

1:8 Although you have not seen him, you love him; and even though you do not see him now, you believe in him and rejoice with an indescribable and glorious joy.NRSV Peter had known Jesus Christ personally—talked with him, walked with him, questioned him, professed faith in him. Yet Peter understood that most of the believers to whom he wrote had not known Jesus in the flesh. He commended their faith because they believed and loved without having seen the object of their faith. Certainly Peter remembered Jesus' words to another disciple: "Thomas, because you have seen Me, you have believed. Blessed are those who have not seen and yet have believed" (John 20:29 NKJV). The Holy Spirit enables believers to have a personal relationship with Jesus Christ. The word *love* is in the present tense, indicating a regular and continual activity. They were continually loving Christ, even though they had never seen him in the flesh. The word *believe* means "to trust," "to put one's confidence in," "to depend upon."

Christian faith does not focus on some abstract idea or some fallible person. It focuses on one person—Jesus Christ—who was sent by God to live in a fallen world and then to die for that world in order to save it. We, like Peter's audience, *do not see him now* (in this present life, see also 1:6), but one day our faith will be rewarded when Christ returns to take us home. On that day and for eternity, we shall see him face-to-face (Revelation 22:3-5). Until then, we live by faith, with hope and joy. Peter says believers can, in this present life, *rejoice with an indescribable and glorious joy.* As in 1:6 above, rejoicing can be a present reality no matter what occurs in the world. The realization of the joy we will have in the future permeates and enlivens the present.

This makes no sense to the unbelieving world. Christians rejoice despite trials and suffering, have faith in someone they have never seen, and stake their lives on promises. Why? Because they know the Lord. Before his death, Paul wrote in his last letter: "I know whom I have believed and am persuaded that He is able to keep what I have committed to Him until that Day" (2 Timothy 1:12 NKJV). Paul, Peter, and all believers know that they have put their confidence in the right Person and that they have given their lives for the right cause.

The word "indescribable" (or "unutterable," used only here in the New Testament) describes joy so deep and profound that words cannot express it. Our joy is also described as "glorious," infused with a heavenly glory. While we await Christ's return, we are already experiencing a touch of heaven through the joy of our relationship with God.

Grief, suffering, and persecution drive us to think of our pain and what we are going through. Because we can easily be absorbed in our own difficulties, we need the three active responses of faith, hope, and love. They will keep us from being neutralized, inactive, and inert.

JOY
"Why don't I have joy?" a wife asks her husband. She believes in God, she believes in Jesus, but is there something more?

It's a common question. All of life's checkpoints add up—family, job, paycheck, health—but something's missing.

Peter had it—a sure, steady, and satisfying focus on Christ as the source. For Peter, joy was the presence of the living Christ in his heart and mind.

As you trust Christ each day and live in his company, you're on the road to the joy you seek. Rise today expectantly; God has something more for you today.

1:9 For you are receiving the outcome of your faith, the salvation of your souls.[NRSV] Believers express joy (1:8) because of their belief in and love for Jesus Christ. Peter explained that his readers *are receiving the outcome* of their faith as they believe and rejoice in

their Savior. The final outcome of their faith refers to full and
complete *salvation.* The present tense, "are receiving," indicates
the tension between what we received when we accepted Jesus
Christ, what we already possess as believers, and what we will
yet receive when Christ returns. We received salvation when we
accepted Jesus Christ as Savior, yet our salvation will not be complete until Jesus Christ returns and makes everything new. In the
meantime, we continue growing in the Christian life and experiencing more and more of the blessings of salvation. As we continue to
believe and rejoice, we also continue to grow toward maturity in
Christ and to our promised salvation.

Some have suggested that Peter used the phrase *of your souls* to
indicate that salvation included the soul only, not the body (according to Greek thought). However, Peter's use of "salvation of your
souls" means "salvation of yourselves" (see also 2:11; 4:19).

1:10-11 **Concerning this salvation, the prophets, who spoke of the
grace that was to come to you.**NIV *This salvation* refers to believers' progressive obtaining of more and more blessings of salvation (as explained in 1:9). *The grace that was to come* refers to
the suffering Messiah, who has made salvation by grace available
to all who believe. Both had been foretold by God's prophets in
the Old Testament. The prophets were so amazed by the prophecies God gave them that they **searched intently and with the
greatest care, trying to find out the time and circumstances to
which the Spirit of Christ in them was pointing when he predicted the sufferings of Christ and the glories that would follow.**NIV Peter was saying, "How can you be discouraged? Don't
you realize that you are the fulfillment of all the prophets' yearn-
ing?" The prophets wanted to know more about what they had
been told. They wondered when the Messiah would come, what
circumstances would surround his coming, why he would have to
suffer and die, and what glories would come after his death. They
not only wondered, but they also actively *searched* (through earlier written Scriptures and their own prophecies) to learn more, to
find answers to their questions, to understand the far-reaching
implications of God's words through them. Jesus once said to his
listeners, "For I tell you the truth, many prophets and righteous
men longed to see what you see but did not see it, and to hear
what you hear but did not hear it" (Matthew 13:17 NIV; see also
Luke 10:23-24). The believers of Peter's day (as well as believers
today) had the privilege of understanding the prophets' writings
better than the prophets themselves had understood them. All of
those prophets' predictions regarding the life, death, and resurrec-

tion of Jesus Christ had been completely fulfilled. Other prophecies concerning the end times are being or are yet to be fulfilled.

Throughout the rest of 1 Peter, the apostle shows that sufferings are the path to glory. In chapters 2, 3, and 4, we see Jesus as the model for us to follow. *Spirit of Christ* is another name for the Holy Spirit. The Old Testament prophets wrote under the Holy Spirit's inspiration; the Spirit of Christ was within them as they spoke and wrote God's words (see 2 Peter 1:20-21). The Spirit did the predicting ("the Spirit of Christ in them . . . when *he* predicted"). The prophecies describing various aspects of the Messiah's birth, life, death, and resurrection revealed that everything that would happen to the Messiah had been ordained by God. God gave the Holy Spirit to many who lived before Jesus' coming, and the Spirit would empower certain people for specific tasks. As Jesus prepared to leave his ministry on earth to return to heaven, he promised to send the Holy Spirit, the Counselor, to teach, help, and guide his followers (John 14:15-17, 26; 16:7). The Holy Spirit would explain the prophecies that told about Jesus (John 15:26; 16:14). The New Testament apostles, through the inspiration of the same Holy Spirit, then went out to preach the crucified and risen Lord. The Holy Spirit now resides in all believers—giving strength, help, and guidance as they continue to grow spiritually.

1:12 It was revealed to them that they were serving not themselves but you, in regard to the things that have now been announced to you through those who brought you good news by the Holy Spirit sent from heaven.^{NRSV} The Spirit *revealed* to the prophets that the prophecies would not be fulfilled in their lifetimes. Therefore, as the prophets continued to speak and write God's words, and as they labored and faced persecution, they *were serving not themselves*; instead, the words were for another era, to be understood by the believers in Peter's day, as well as believers today. The prophets had the great honor of having Christ's Spirit speak through them, but the privileges of our understanding are even greater and should move us to an even deeper commitment to Christ.

All the experiences regarding the coming salvation that the prophets had so wanted to see and hear *have now been announced* by those who brought the *good news,* the gospel of Jesus Christ. As the Spirit inspired the prophets, so he inspired the apostles and missionaries in the first century. The persecuted believers scattered across Asia could take comfort in the "big picture":

■ The believers to whom Peter wrote were living what the Old Testament prophets had only desired to experience.

■ The prophets had written and spoken God's messages; sometimes these messages were fulfilled in their lifetimes, and other messages would be fulfilled much later.

■ The prophets had continued to write and speak in spite of persecution; even though they did not fully understand what God was saying through them about a coming Savior, they knew that someday some people would understand.

■ The Good News that the believers had received—whether from apostles, missionaries, or new converts—was that this Savior had come.

■ The Good News had been given to God's apostles and other faithful believers by the same Holy Spirit who had inspired the prophets' writings.

■ The Holy Spirit is divine, came from heaven (as part of the Trinity), had been promised by Jesus, and lives in believers to help them continue to spread God's Good News of salvation.

Even angels long to look into these things.^NIV Angels are spiritual beings created by God who help carry out his work on earth. Peter explained that even the angels *long* (strongly desire) to understand the mysteries of salvation. The angels want to watch the mystery unfold in the lives of believers and in the church. It is unclear whether the word "long" refers to a longing fulfilled or unfulfilled. If the angels have "inside knowledge" and their longing is being fulfilled as they watch events unfold on earth, the word could refer to their intense interest in those events. If their longing is unfulfilled, the word could mean that, just as the prophets could not understand or experience the coming salvation and grace because it would occur after their lifetimes, neither can the angels understand or experience it because they are spiritual beings who do not need the blood of Christ to save them.

The word *parakupto* (translated "to look") means to peek into a situation as an outsider. The angels watch (and often are sent to minister to) believers as they struggle and face ridicule or persecution. The angels know that God's people are recipients of God's grace and blessings and that one day they will be highly honored in the coming kingdom.

The mention of angels parallels the function of the prophets. The two major figures whom Peter's readers looked up to were the prophets and the angels. Both were intensely interested in seeing the plan of salvation unfold. The angels were interested in Peter's readers! Peter could give no stronger encouragement of the blessings of salvation.

A CALL TO HOLY LIVING / 1:13-25

Peter gave a bold challenge. The next four paragraphs (1:13-16; 1:17-21; 1:22-25; and 2:1-3) detail the ethical responsibilities of those who have experienced the blessings of salvation described in 1:3-12. The promises God makes to believers and the hope we have based on what we know about God should motivate us to holy living. Christ is coming soon. His imminent return should motivate us to live for him. This means being mentally alert, morally disciplined, and spiritually focused. This is hard work. Are you ready to meet Christ?

1:13 Therefore prepare your minds for action.^NRSV The word *therefore* ties Peter's following challenge with the previous passage. Because the prophets had foretold the great privileges of the gospel and, with even the angels, long to understand them better, believers should show the same kind of earnest and alert concern regarding the way they live. The believers did not need to be holy in order to be saved, but they were called to holy living in order to portray God's nature and his grace to an unbelieving world. The price the Lord paid for our redemption ought to result in our faithful obedience to him.

Peter challenged these scattered believers to *prepare your minds for action* or "roll up your sleeves." Obedience does not always come naturally or easily. In Greek, the phrase is "gird up the loins of your minds," picturing a person "girding up his loins" by tucking his long robes into the belt around his waist in order to run (see, for example, 1 Kings 18:46; 2 Kings 4:29; 9:1). The word "minds" refers to spiritual and mental attitudes. To lead holy lives in an evil world, the believers would need a new mind-set. Like "robes" that are already "girded up," their minds should be set and prepared, ready for "action" at God's prompting. As the Israelites ate the Passover meal with their "loins girded" ("your cloak tucked into your belt, your sandals on your feet and your staff in your hand" Exodus 12:11 NIV), to be ready when God called, so believers must also be prepared for action—ready to obey, follow, speak, and go with Christ when he returns.

> The effective Christians of history have been men and women of great personal discipline— mental discipline, discipline of the body, discipline of the tongue, and discipline of the emotions. *Billy Graham*

Be self-controlled.^NIV The believers needed to monitor and restrain their sexual and material desires, anger, and words. "Be self-controlled" is also translated "discipline yourselves." Believers must avoid drunkenness, addictions, or attitudes that can overwhelm and take control of their minds and bodies. Even "good" things in life can take control if they are allowed to—such as one's career, education, or creative pursuits. Peter wanted the believers to remember that, as they lived in the world, they needed to keep full possession of their minds and bodies so as not to be enticed away from God and lose the "preparedness" they needed in order to stand for him (see above). Peter used the same word in two other verses, encouraging self-restraint to resist those temptations that would draw us away from God:

- "Be clear minded and self-controlled so that you can pray" (4:7 NIV).

- "Be self-controlled and alert. Your enemy the devil prowls around like a roaring lion looking for someone to devour" (5:8 NIV).

Set all your hope on the grace that Jesus Christ will bring you when he is revealed.^{NRSV} This sentence forms a bridge from the first section to the remainder of the letter. Peter has described true faith in 1:1-13, and in 1:14 he begins a series of moral commands that stretch throughout the rest of his letter. In these few words, Peter explained how believers can reflect God's character and priorities and follow God's commands. As they *set all* their *hope* fully on the grace to be given them, they will be encouraged to change their mind-sets to be in line with God's plans for them, to change their lifestyles to glorify God, and to persevere during difficulties and persecutions.

SHOULD CHRISTIANS GAMBLE?
Peter urges us to set all our hope on Jesus Christ. That means we should live under a different set of goals, looking for a different future, setting aside distractions and disturbances.

With the rapid spread of lotteries, floating casinos, and offtrack betting on horses, Christians have more opportunity to gamble money on luck and hunch. Should we?

TV ads for state lotteries say "Yes, it's OK." You could win. If you lose, a portion of your dollar may go to fund education or other worthy state enterprises.

Many Christians gamble—for entertainment, leisure, maybe for the chance to win big. What's worse, losing a couple of bucks on a ticket or spending it on a fat-filled restaurant meal?

Yet if we look at the culture and appeal of gambling, its ethos and its hope is a universe away from where the Bible points us. Next time you line up for a lottery ticket, ask which direction the line is facing, toward or away from 1 Peter 1:13.

Believers' "hope" is not a hazy desire that we wish would come true. Instead, it is a confident expectation of what God has promised; it is our sure destination. *The grace that Jesus Christ will bring* to

believers refers to salvation. We have already received salvation
through our acceptance of Jesus Christ as Savior. However, the fullness of salvation (the fullness of the grace given to us in Christ) with
its complete rewards and blessings will be revealed when *he* (Jesus
Christ) *is revealed,* that is, when he returns. Therefore, we can place
our hope fully, completely, and unreservedly on that grace to be given;
we know that we will receive our promised inheritance (1:4). That
knowledge should affect the way we live for Christ in the world.

**1:14 As obedient children, do not conform to the evil desires you
had when you lived in ignorance.**^NIV All believers are part of
God's family; we are his *children.* Children all have different
character traits; parents often marvel at how different each of
their own children are. Yet despite the many differences among
God's children, we ought to all have one characteristic in common: We are *obedient.* We have been chosen (1:2), and the result
of our chosen status is obedience to the Savior.

Peter first explained what obedient children do *not* do (he
then explains what they *should* do in this verse). Believers
ought not to live in the same manner that they lived before
they were saved. At that time, they had *lived in ignorance,*
giving in to their evil desires, insensitive to sin or to God's
desires. But when Christ saved them, they received a new
mind-set, new goals, a new sensitivity to sin, a new desire to
please God, and an altogether new way of living. The word for
conform (used elsewhere only in Romans 12:2) means "to pattern one's life or actions after." Unbelievers pattern their lives
after their desires, with no power to conquer or control them.
But believers' lives are to be radically different. Believers
must not be conformed to their evil desires because they have
been transformed by the renewing of their minds (Romans
12:2). The evil desires still exist, but believers have a new
goal for their lives. They must break with the past and depend
on the power of the Holy Spirit to help them overcome evil
desires and conform themselves to God's will.

**1:15 But as He who called you is holy, you also be holy in all your
conduct.**^NKJV After people commit their lives to Christ, they usually
still feel a pull to return to their old ways. Peter wrote to the first-
century believers that they were to not conform to their old ways
and desires (1:14), but were to be like their heavenly Father—*holy*
in everything they did. Why? Because God had *called* them; they
had been chosen (see also 1:2; 2:9, 21; 3:9; 5:10; 2 Peter 1:3). God
initiated their salvation; they were called not only to be saved, but
to live to please God.

God's holiness means that he is completely separated from sin and evil. Holiness pervades his character—he *is* holiness. He is the opposite of anything profane. Holiness for God's people means being totally devoted or dedicated to God, set aside for his special use and set apart from sin and its influence. The God of Israel and of the Christian church is holy—he sets the standard for morality and integrity. Unlike the Roman gods, he is not warlike, adulterous, or spiteful. Unlike the gods of the pagan cults popular in the first century, he is not bloodthirsty or promiscuous. He is the God of mercy and justice who cares personally for each of his followers. Our holy God expects us to imitate him by following his high moral standards.

WHO WANTS TO BE HOLY?
Holiness is a tough sale for pastors, teachers, and youth leaders to make today! Who really wants to be holy? In most people's minds, holiness stands for moral superiority, a judgmental spirit, and nonparticipation in the world's pleasures. How can we persuade reticent readers of 1 Peter that they should be holy?

Most churches don't teach "separation from sin." If we did so, we'd have to eliminate TV and most movies. We'd have to stay away from professional sporting events where many are drunk and foul language prevails. We'd have to purge our desires for this world's goods and pleasures. Where do we draw the line? Wouldn't we then become hypocrites?

Yes, it's a tough sale to make . . . if it were merely Peter or Pastor Smith who was doing the promoting. But Christ himself told us to be holy. He said, "In the same way, let your light shine before others, so that they may see your good works and give glory to your Father in heaven" (Matthew 5:16 NRSV). So we should be holy because we love our holy Lord. If that doesn't motivate us, we must remember that our lives will be judged. Live according to God's standards, not the world's.

Believers should be set apart and different because of God's qualities in our lives. Our focus and priorities must be his. We have already been declared holy because of our faith in Christ, but we must work out that divine family likeness in our day-by-day walk, behavior, and conduct. We cannot become holy on our own, but God gives us his Holy Spirit to help us. We will not achieve perfect holiness in this life; Peter's words mean that all parts of our lives and character should be in the process of becoming conformed, both inwardly and outwardly, to God's holy standards.

1:16 Because it is written, "Be holy, for I am holy."NKJV Peter quoted the Old Testament Scriptures, which would be familiar to the Jewish Christians in his audience, to confirm his words in

1:15. These words are from Leviticus 11:44-45; 19:2; 20:7. Originally this command applied to the Jews, God's chosen nation, but Peter applied it to the Christians, God's chosen people from all nations.

TOUGH TASK
We are called to be holy. Like the Israelites who received the commandment from Moses to be holy as God is holy, Christians should remain spiritually separate from the world's wickedness. Even though we are different from unbelievers, we rub shoulders with them every day. It isn't easy to be holy in an unholy world, but God doesn't ask you to accomplish this on your own. The Holy Spirit will help you make good decisions and right choices. Pray for help in setting a holy course for your life that steers away from both moral compromise and acting "holier than thou."

1:17 If you invoke as Father the one who judges all people impartially according to their deeds.^{NRSV} The word *if* could also be translated "since." Peter assumed that these believers already did constantly *invoke* God, meaning that they prayed regularly to him and habitually called upon him for help. God was their loving *Father,* yet he was also a strong disciplinarian and the impartial Judge of the entire universe. This judging could refer to God's future judgment of believers when they will be rewarded for how they have lived, but the present tense of the verb *judges* makes more sense if it is applied to God's present judgment and discipline on believers during their lives on earth ("as strangers here," see below).

God judges and disciplines *all people impartially according to their deeds.* The phrase "all people" referred to the believers, whose judgment and discipline are personal and certain. God hears all prayers and sees all sin. Peter explained that just as these believers constantly called on God for help because they knew he loved them, they should also be careful how they lived: **Live your lives as strangers here in reverent fear.**^{NIV} *Reverent fear* is not the fear of a slave for a ruthless master, but the healthy and fervent respect of a believer for the all-powerful God. Because God is the Judge of all the earth, believers dare not ignore him or treat him casually. We ought to truly fear God's discipline and live so as to

> There is no fear like that which love begets. We do not fear God with the fear of the slave or felon, but with the fear of the love that cannot endure the thought of giving pain to the one loving and loved. *F. B. Meyer*

avoid it. We should live as tourists who are passing through, with no thought of permanent stay or becoming assimilated into the culture. Such fear is not inconsistent with our love for God or our understanding of his love for us. Rather, it is fear of offending him, of taking him for granted and becoming sloppy in our Christian lives. We should not assume that our privileged status as God's children gives us freedom to do whatever we want. A good parent administers discipline without favoritism. Many Christians may take Peter to mean, "God will judge others harshly but look favorably on me." But God does not overlook sin. God judges impartially, so we must remain morally alert. We should not be spoiled children, but grateful children who love to show respect for our heavenly Father.

1:18-19 **For you know that it was not with perishable things such as silver or gold that you were redeemed from the empty way of life handed down to you from your forefathers.**NIV Peter again reminded us of the blessings of salvation from 1:3-12. Another reason that we should fear displeasing God is that he paid the enormous price to buy us back from sin. The word *redeemed* was used when someone paid money to buy back a slave's freedom. In Old Testament times, a person's debts could result in that person's being sold as a slave. The next of kin could redeem the slave (buy his or her freedom), a transaction involving money or valuables of some kind. Yet all valuables are perishable—even silver and gold are susceptible to corruption. The transaction God made to buy us back from sin is not refundable; it is a permanent transaction.

However, silver and gold can do nothing to change anyone's spiritual condition. No amount of money can buy our salvation. It had to be done God's way, not with money, **but with the precious blood of Christ, like that of a lamb without defect or blemish.**NRSV That Christ "redeemed" us means that he paid the price to set sinners free from slavery to sin. Christ paid the debt we owed for violating the righteous demands of the law. Christ purchased our freedom, and it cost him his own life. The word "precious" means flawless, unblemished. Jesus had moral integrity and perfection. He did not have to die for his own sin; thus, he could take ours. Christ has provided all that we need to stand in God's presence as though we had never done wrong.

Why blood? From the very beginning God said, "For the life of a creature is in the blood, and I have given it to you to make atonement for yourselves on the altar; it is the blood that makes atonement for one's life" (Leviticus 17:11 NIV). But the blood Peter mentioned here is *the precious blood of Christ.* Only the sacrificial death of Christ on the cross was effective atonement

for our sins. Christ stands in our place, having paid the penalty of
death for our sin, having completely satisfied God's demands.
The Old Testament saints sacrificed lambs *without defect or blemish* in order to atone for their sins, but New Testament believers
have had their sins covered by the blood of the sinless Savior. We
have been redeemed from sin in order to live for God. (See also
Romans 6:6-7; 1 Corinthians 6:20; Colossians 2:13-14; Hebrews
9:12.) We could not escape from sin on our own; only the sacrifice of God's Son on our behalf could buy us back and set us free.

BREAKING FAMILY TRADITIONS
It may be very difficult for a new Christian to go against the
wishes of an unbelieving family. In Peter's day, it would be like
Jews going against their ancestors. Yet the Good News is so
radically different from normal, everyday religion that every
Christian family, at some point, must break from the past and
start anew with God. We trade in all the world's precious goods
(and all of religion's perks and privileges) for allegiance to
Christ, who died to win our salvation.

    If your family resents your allegiance to Christ, that's normal.
If your mother cries over your stubborn refusal to "stay with the
family," comfort her. If your father cuts off your allowance, gives
his business to loyal siblings, or grows silent in your presence,
be generous to him with talk, good cheer, and respect.

    You stand at the beginning of a new family tradition. Your
family may not follow Christ if you badger and preach. Instead,
simply show them what a difference God makes.

1:20 **He was chosen before the creation of the world, but was
revealed in these last times for your sake.**^{NIV} Christ's sacrifice
for the world's sins was not an afterthought, not something God
decided to do when the world spun out of control. This plan was
set in motion by the all-knowing, eternal God *before the creation
of the world.* In eternity past, God chose his people (1:2) and
planned that Christ would redeem them. Christ has always
existed with God (John 1:1), but *was revealed in these last times*
to the world in his incarnation. The "last times" refers to the time
between Christ's first and second comings. The redemption God
accomplished for believers through Christ—not understood even
by the prophets who wrote about them (1:10-11)—should cause
us to be even more concerned to live according to his high moral
standards. Peter's words, *for your sake,* provided an intensely personal note, encouraging his readers that Christ's coming and the
entire plan of salvation are for individual believers, loved and
chosen by God.

MIXED SIGNALS
Christ was revealed for our sake, to reassure us and to
stabilize our faith. In our daily life, we constantly "check out"
other people to see where we stand. We worry about how
others regard us.

A wife wonders whether or not her husband still loves her, or
if he loves his work or something else more. A child wonders if
she is loved when her father is too busy to spend time with her.
A young man wonders about his date, and the wonder
escalates as dating grows serious.

Do you ever wonder about God? What does he think of you?

If so, look at the evidence: God sent his Son for you and
raised his Son as sure evidence that you are loved. "Checking
out" this relationship gives you every reason for hope and faith.

1:21 Through him you believe in God, who raised him from the dead and glorified him, and so your faith and hope are in God.NIV Only through the death of Christ on the cross could sinful humanity approach the holy God. Jesus had told his disciples, "I am the way, the truth, and the life. No one comes to the Father except through Me" (John 14:6 NKJV). It is through Christ that we can know and believe in God. The fact that God *raised him from the dead and glorified him* is the foundation for our faith for two reasons: (1) Through Christ's resurrection and glorification, God openly declared that he has accepted Christ as our righteous substitute, thereby giving us access to God. (2) Through Christ's resurrection and glorification, believers can receive power from the Holy Spirit (John 16:5-15). The power that resurrected and glorified Christ is the same power that enables us to believe. Because Christ ransomed us, we must no longer fear God and face his judgment; instead, we set our *faith and hope* in him, trusting in the one who planned our salvation from eternity past. As God raised Christ from the dead, we believe and expect that he will also raise us.

> Our Lord has written the promise of the resurrection not in books alone, but in every leaf in springtime.
> *Martin Luther*

1:22 Now that you have purified your souls by your obedience to the truth so that you have genuine mutual love, love one another deeply from the heart.NRSV Peter continued his call to holy living (1:15-16). Believers ought to be holy because of who God is and what he has done on our behalf. However, human beings cannot, on their own, be holy in all their conduct, because the struggle between the new nature and the old, sinful nature continues throughout our lifetimes (Paul described this in Romans 7:14-25). But, with the Holy Spirit's help, believers can grow toward holiness because their souls have been purified by their obedience and love. Peter did not mean that they were completely pure, but that they would move in the direction of purity as they matured in the Christian life. Their *obedience to the truth* could refer to the time of their conversion, when they believed the gospel message, or it could refer to daily obedience to God's commands. In either case, Peter was pointing out that their conversion had changed their lives. The transformation that Christ had made in their lives was toward purity and holiness.

This change was not meant to be internal only; it must be acted out in their daily behavior, attitudes, and conduct. This is one of the strongest statements of brotherly love in the New Testament, for it virtually makes brotherly love the goal of our conversion. Peter expected that growth in purity and holiness would result in deeper love among Christians. Not merely outward appearance or profession, *genuine mutual love* for our Christian brothers and sisters comes from the heart. In order to do this, we must willingly let go of evil thoughts and feelings toward fellow believers. Peter used the word *philadelphia* (love of the brothers) in the phrase "genuine mutual love," and then changed to the more intense form of the word love, *agapao,* to describe strong and deep love in the next phrase, *love one another deeply.* The Greek word for "deeply" is an athletic term meaning "with every muscle straining." Despite our differences and disagreements, we can have genuine affection for one another, and as we grow in holiness, we can learn to love one another deeply because of the Holy Spirit within us.

Such love is not possible in the world at large, for it doesn't understand the love that results when people's sins are forgiven and their souls are purified. This experience brings together even very different believers on the common ground of forgiveness in Christ and requires them to love one another as Christ loved them. Peter no doubt remembered Jesus' words to him and the other disciples at their last supper together: "A new commandment I give to you, that you love one another; as I have loved you, that you also love one another. By this all will know that you are My disciples, if you have love for one another" (John 13:34-35 NKJV).

1:23 **For you have been born again, not of perishable seed, but of imperishable, through the living and enduring word of God.**^{NIV} Peter gave the second reason to love others: Believers have a common ground in Christ. We have all *been born again;* we are sinners saved by grace. Because we have all received new life in Christ, we should be motivated to live to please God, obey the truth, keep ourselves pure, and love our Christian brothers and sisters. The change that took place in our lives is eternal. As we move toward purity and holiness, we will eventually reach the end goal. Our new birth was *not of perishable seed,* meaning of human origin, so that we will one day wither and die; rather our new birth originated from *imperishable* seed, described as *the living and enduring word of God.* The contrast between "perishable" and "imperishable" is key to verses 23-25. Our lives and earthly pursuits are transitory (1:24); only the word is eternal (1:23, 25). God's word lives and endures forever, because God who gave it lives and endures from eternity past to eternity future. The powerful, "living" word of God himself, recorded in Scripture, brings new life to believers; the "enduring" word of God himself assures the permanence of that new life. It is only through hearing and/or reading these words that people can find eternal life, for the Scriptures tell the gospel message and make the way of salvation clear to those who seek it.

> This was the real mountaintop experience. Above and around me the world was filled with joy and love and beauty. For the first time I felt truly free, even as the fortunes of my life seemed at their lowest ebb. *Charles Colson*

1:24-25 **For "All flesh is like grass and all its glory like the flower of grass. The grass withers, and the flower falls, but the word of the Lord endures forever."**[NRSV] Quoting Isaiah 40:6-8, Peter reminded believers that everything in this life—possessions, accomplishments, people—will eventually fade away and disappear. *All flesh* refers to every person, all human existence. As the grasses and flowers bloom for a season then wither and fall, so all of this life is transitory in nature; it will pass away. *Glory* refers to all earthly attainments. Only God's will, word, and work are permanent. We are mortal, but God's word is eternal and unfailing. Peter's readers would face suffering and persecution, but that would be only temporary. As the word of the Lord endures forever, so their salvation and subsequent eternal glory would endure forever.

That word is the good news that was announced to you.[NRSV] What gives reason for life? What gives peace and patience in the middle of suffering and persecution? Why have hope? Peter answered the questions in this phrase: They believed in the eternal word of God. Believers have been born again "through the living and enduring word of God" (1:23) because they believed the *good news* that had been *announced* (or proclaimed) to them through the apostles or other believers.

1 Peter 2

In describing the church as God's spiritual house, Peter drew on
Old Testament texts that would be familiar to his Jewish Christian readers: Psalm 118:22; Isaiah 8:14; 28:16. They would have
understood the living stones to be Israel; then Peter used the
image of the "cornerstone" for Christ. Again Peter was demon-
strating that Christ did not cancel the Jewish heritage but had fulfilled it. Peter encouraged his readers by emphasizing their true
identity and unity in Christ. We too should strive to be usable,
obedient elements in God's work.

**2:1 Therefore, rid yourselves of all malice and all deceit, hypoc-
risy, envy, and slander of every kind.**NIV The word *therefore* ties
Peter's following words with the end of chapter 1, specifically
1:22, where Peter had explained that believers' new lives in
Christ should result in genuine mutual love so that they would
love one another deeply. Such love binds believers together as
they face struggles and persecution. Believers need to get rid of
any attitude or hindrance that could threaten this love for brothers
and sisters in Christ.

Rid yourselves is also translated "put away" or "put off." The
same phrase is used in other New Testament passages, always
indicating removing one's former life of
sin as one would take off a garment (see
also Romans 13:12; Ephesians 4:22, 25;
Colossians 3:8; James 1:21). The Greek
tense indicates that this is a decisive act.

> Whoever gossips to you
> will gossip of you.
> *Spanish proverb*

Peter addressed this command to rid oneself of sin only to born-
again Christians (1:23) who, having a new God-given nature
within them, have the ability to break with their past life of sin.
While we cannot become completely sin-free in this life, no matter how hard we try to put aside sin, we are commanded to get rid
of sin in order to become more like Christ.

Peter listed several types of sin to remove from our lives. The
sins Peter listed here fight against love and cause dissension

among believers. The first two sins mentioned refer to general categories. The last three sins refer to the specific acts that flow out of them.

■ *Malice* means doing evil despite the good that has been received; the desire to harm other people. Malice may be hidden behind good actions. Christians should have no part in evil actions toward others (see Colossians 3:8; James 1:21).

■ *Deceit* means deliberately tricking or misleading by lying (see also 3:10).

■ *Hypocrisy* means that people say one thing but do another; playacting; presenting good motives that mask selfish desire.

■ *Envy* means desiring something possessed by someone else. This causes discontent and resentment as believers make unhealthy comparisons to one another. It also makes them unable to be thankful for the good that comes to others.

■ *Slander* means destroying another's good reputation by lies, gossip, rumor-spreading, etc. Malice often manifests itself through slander. We should not treat fellow Christians the way the world treats us (3:16).

SO MUCH FUN TO TALK
Most of us wince to admit it, but having "the goods" on someone and commanding a group's attention by reporting our news is just plain fun. We like to share intimate details of someone else's weakness.

Peter warns that our conversation should not slip into slander. You're getting close to the border when you are glad that the subject is out of earshot. You've crossed the border when your report begins: "It doesn't leave this room, but . . ."

If you cannot avoid gossip or spreading rumors, tell your story to a tape recorder, and don't bother using a tape.

Real friends don't broadcast each other's weaknesses. Real Christians strive to build each other up in love. When it comes to gossip, *don't* pass it on.

2:2 Like newborn babies, crave pure spiritual milk, so that by it you may grow up in your salvation.NIV In the Greek text, this verse is part of one long command beginning at verse 1: "Rid yourselves . . . crave pure spiritual milk." As newborn babies crave milk, so born-again believers should *crave* (long for) *pure spiritual milk* that will nourish them and help them grow to maturity. The Greek word translated "spiritual" is *logikos*; it means "logical, reasonable, and spiritual." As such, it probably points to the Word of God, which provides spiritual life to those who partake of it. The Word of God, as described by Peter in 1:23-25, is living and enduring. Thus, like milk, the essential nourishment for babies, it sustains life and gives growth. The psalmist described God's words as pure: "The words of the Lord are pure words, like silver tried in a furnace of earth, purified seven times. . . . The commandment of the Lord is pure" (Psalm 12:6; 19:8 NKJV). The purity of God's Word means that there is no imperfection, no flaws, no dilutions, and that it will not deceive or lead people astray.

By using the term *newborn babies,* Peter was not implying that his readers were young believers; indeed, some of them had been Christians for as many as thirty years. Instead, he may have been picking up the reference to being "born again" in 1:23. Peter was saying that believers should always crave more and more of God's Word in the same way that a baby eagerly desires milk. (Note that "milk" is used in a positive context. This verse should not be compared to 1 Corinthians 3:2 and Hebrews 5:12-13, where the writers employed a similar metaphor but used milk— in contrast to meat—as depicting the diet of immature believers.)

While believers receive *salvation* when they accept Christ as Savior, salvation is an ongoing experience from the time of the new birth until the time Christ returns. At that time, salvation will be completed (1:5). In the meantime, as we live on this earth, we must constantly partake of God's Word so that we can *grow up* in our salvation. We must not remain spiritual babies, but become mature in Christ (2 Peter 3:18).

GROW UP
One characteristic all children share is that they eagerly want to grow up—to be like big brother or sister or like their parents. When we are born again, we become spiritual newborn babies. If we are healthy, we will yearn to grow. How sad it is that some people never grow up. The need for milk is a natural instinct for a baby, and it signals the desire for nourishment that will lead to growth. Once we see our need for God's Word and begin to find nourishment in Christ, our spiritual appetite will increase, and we will start to mature. How eagerly do you desire God's Word?

2:3 Now that you have tasted that the Lord is good.^{NIV} Peter picked up the beautiful invitation in Psalm 34:8 and placed it in the past tense for these believers: "Taste and see that the Lord is good" (see

also Jeremiah 15:16). The believers had already taken that first step
in following God by accepting his salvation. At that time, they had
tasted, that is, they personally had experienced God's goodness and
kindness. As they lived out their Christian lives, growing to maturity
in the faith, they were tasting more and more of the Lord's goodness.
That should only serve to whet their appetites. *Now that* they had
tasted God's goodness, they should continue to crave the spiritual
milk of God's words. Most likely, Peter had all of Psalm 34 in mind
as he wrote these words; he would refer to it again in 2:12-16. The
theme of Psalm 34 is that God's people can call upon him during
their distress and troubles, knowing that he will deliver them; this is
also the theme of Peter's letter to God's scattered people as they
faced problems and persecutions.

The more we taste God's goodness, the more tasteless other
worldly options will become. We must not fill our lives with
cheap substitutes so that we lose our craving for the truth con-
tained in God's Word.

BIG HELPINGS
"Try this," Mom urges. But Junior resists. What if it's bitter, sour,
or salty?

"It's good," Mom assures. *Whoa,* thinks Junior. *If Mom really
wants me to eat this green stuff, it's gotta be bad!*

"You'll like it," Mom says, speaking from experience. "Yeah,"
Junior counters, "like I crave broccoli for breakfast and cauli-
flower for dessert."

When Junior finally tries it, he agrees that Mom was right.
"Delicious, great, seconds please!"

So God wants us to enjoy the satisfaction of knowing him.
Don't pass the plate without taking a big helping. Dig into his
Word for nourishing and delicious food and drink.

**2:4 Come to him, a living stone, though rejected by mortals yet
chosen and precious in God's sight.**[NRSV] Using a new metaphor
here, Peter employed Old Testament imagery to describe believers' relationship with God. Believers can constantly *come to* (or
approach) Christ. The words "come to" do not refer to initial salvation, but to constantly drawing near and coming into Christ's
presence. In the Old Testament, only the priests had that privilege; under the new covenant, all believers can enter into God's
presence at any time, with any need.

Peter described the one to whom believers come, Christ, as *a living stone*; the "stone" imagery is taken from Psalm 118:22 and other
Old Testament passages quoted in the following verses. Jesus had
applied these words to himself when he spoke of being rejected by

his own people (Matthew 21:42; Mark 12:10-11; Luke 20:17). In fact, rejection by the world signaled spiritual victory to believers in the early church. Also, Peter had quoted Psalm 118:22 in his speech on the day of Pentecost, "Jesus is 'the stone that was rejected by you, the builders; it has become the cornerstone.' There is salvation in no one else, for there is no other name under heaven given among mortals by which we must be saved" (Acts 4:11-12 NRSV). Peter carried on the imagery of Christ as the "stone" by adding the adjective "living." Christ lives and imparts life to those who believe in him. He is the starting point for all our faith.

The phrase *though rejected by mortals* continues the thought from Psalm 118:22, "The stone that the builders rejected has become the chief cornerstone" (NRSV). When Jesus quoted this verse, he was speaking to unbelieving Jews; Peter used a more general term when he referred to Jews and Gentiles who rejected Jesus. Although rejected by many, Christ is now the "cornerstone" of the church, the most important part. Paul had written to the Ephesian believers:

■ *You are . . . members of the household of God, built upon the foundation of the apostles and prophets, with Christ Jesus himself as the cornerstone. In him the whole structure is joined together and grows into a holy temple in the Lord; in whom you also are built together spiritually into a dwelling place for God. (Ephesians 2:19-22 NRSV)*

Although rejected by many people, Christ is *chosen and precious in God's sight.* The word "chosen" echoes back to 1:2, where Peter called God's people "chosen," meaning "selected in love." The word "precious" means highly valued or esteemed. Although chosen and precious to God, Christ had to suffer greatly in order to accomplish God's will—it was his "precious blood" (1:19) that redeemed us. Therefore, believers are also very precious to God. To side with Christ often means to be rejected by people. It sometimes even means persecution and suffering for the faith. Jesus had warned his disciples at the Last Supper, "Remember the words I spoke to you: 'No servant is greater than his master.' If they persecuted me, they will persecute you also. . . . They will treat you this way because of my name, for they do not know the One who sent me. . . . But this is to fulfill what is written in their Law: 'They hated me without reason'" (John 15:20-21, 25 NIV). Peter encouraged these persecuted believers by telling them that they, like Christ, had been chosen by God.

2:5 Like living stones, let yourselves be built into a spiritual house, to be a holy priesthood, to offer spiritual sacrifices acceptable

to God through Jesus Christ.^{NRSV} Peter carried the imagery further, describing believers also as *living stones* because they are made alive by Christ, the Living Stone. (It is interesting to note that many of Christ's names in the singular are also assigned to Christians in the plural: Son/sons, High Priest/priests, King/kings, Lamb/lambs, Living Stone/living stones.) These are stones cut into shape for building materials, not just boulders or fieldstone randomly gathered. We must each ask, "Am I willing to be shaped and used as a living stone for God's purposes?" Too many Christians seem to want to be the whole temple or to take Christ's place as the cornerstone.

If these "stones" are "living," then what activities should they be doing? First of all, they should welcome being *built into a spiritual house.* The Greek word for house, *oikos,* is often used to refer to the temple in Jerusalem. Peter was using words that normally described the activities in the temple to describe God's new house on earth, the "spiritual house" made up of all believers. Because God is spirit (John 4:24), he lives in a spiritual house among his people, no longer in any particular physical building. It is a high privilege to be a part of the spiritual building that God is constructing—a "house" made up of "living stones." No doubt Peter remembered Jesus' words to him, "You are Peter, and on this rock I will build My church" (Matthew 16:18 NKJV). The believers "are being built," meaning that God is doing the building. The "house" that God builds is the church, and so Peter was seeing Jesus' words fulfilled in the churches to whom he was writing. Believers are not left alone in the world; God lives among them in the spiritual home that he is building, only to be completed when Christ Jesus returns. (See also 1 Corinthians 3:9-17; 2 Corinthians 6:16; Ephesians 2:19-22 [quoted above]; 1 Timothy 3:15; Hebrews 3:2-6.)

Believers not only are the stones that make up God's spiritual house, but they also serve there as *a holy priesthood [offering] spiritual sacrifices.* This is a twofold metaphor. We are both the temple (see 1 Corinthians 6:19) and the priests who serve in it. Just as priests served in the temple, so believers are to be priests. Peter used words from Exodus 19:6, where God promised Israel that they would be "a kingdom of priests and a holy nation" (NKJV) if they remained obedient to God. God's people, all who believe in Jesus Christ, have become this holy priesthood. The Old Testament priests entered God's presence at specific times and only after carefully following ritual cleansing instructions; God's people can enter God's presence at any time, for they have been cleansed by the Holy Spirit (Hebrews 4:16). The Old Testament priests offered animal sacrifices in the temple; God's people offer sacrifices too, but these are "spiritual sacrifices."

What comprises these spiritual sacrifices? The answer is found in other New Testament letters (quoted from the NIV):

- "I urge you, brothers, in view of God's mercy, to offer your bodies as living sacrifices, holy and pleasing to God—this is your spiritual act of worship" (Romans 12:1). We offer ourselves and our wills to God's control.

- "Live a life of love, just as Christ loved us and gave himself up for us as a fragrant offering and sacrifice to God" (Ephesians 5:2). We offer love, to God and to others.

- "[The gifts the believers had sent to Paul] are a fragrant offering, an acceptable sacrifice, pleasing to God" (Philippians 4:18). We offer our money and possessions freely to help spread the gospel.

- "Through Jesus, therefore, let us continually offer to God a sacrifice of praise—the fruit of lips that confess his name" (Hebrews 13:15). We center our lives around continual praise to God.

- "And do not forget to do good and to share with others, for with such sacrifices God is pleased" (Hebrews 13:16). We do good and share freely with others.

We see from Scripture that every part of our lives—our jobs, activities, recreation, attitudes, giving, outlook, goals—should be given as a spiritual sacrifice to God. When we learn to please God and follow his directions and guidance, all we do delights him. These sacrifices are "spiritual" because we can only give ourselves to God with the Holy Spirit's help. Just as the aroma of the Old Testament sacrifices pleased God, so our service can be a sweet aroma to God, continually giving him delight.

OFFERING OURSELVES
When sacrificing an animal according to God's law, a priest would kill the animal, cut it in pieces, and place it on the altar. Sacrifice was important, but even in the Old Testament God made it clear that obedience from the heart was much more important (see 1 Samuel 15:22; Psalm 40:6; Amos 5:21-24). God wants us, his "holy priesthood," to offer ourselves, not animals, as living and spiritual sacrifices—daily laying aside our own desires and following him, putting all our energy and resources at his disposal and trusting him to guide us.

The sacrifice of ourselves is *acceptable to God through Jesus Christ*. We are imperfect and sinful, yet we are made acceptable to God because of Jesus Christ's sacrifice of himself on our behalf. Only because of Christ have believers received this high and holy calling to be living stones and a holy priesthood in the spiritual house of God.

HOUSE BEAUTIFUL
Peter portrays the church as a living, spiritual house, with Christ as the foundation and cornerstone and each believer as a valuable element. Paul portrays the church as a body, with Christ as the head and each believer as a contributing member (see, for example, Ephesians 4:15-16). Both pictures emphasize community. One stone is not a temple or even a wall; one body part is useless without the others. In our individualistic society, we can easily forget our interdependence with other Christians. When God calls you to a task, remember that he is also calling others to work with you. Together your individual efforts will be multiplied. Look for those people and join with them to build a beautiful house for God.

2:6 For it stands in scripture: "See, I am laying in Zion a stone, a cornerstone chosen and precious; and whoever believes in him will not be put to shame."^NRSV To support his words in 2:4-5, Peter quoted from what *stands in scripture* by citing several Old Testament passages. Words from Scripture stand forever and can be trusted completely. First, Peter quoted from the prophet Isaiah (Isaiah 28:16). In these words, God promised to establish a *cornerstone*. (For an explanation of the words "chosen and precious," see 2:4 above.) A cornerstone, the first stone laid in a building, starts a new work. Therefore, it holds a place of honor. The cornerstone makes the foundation stable and the walls plumb and square. Christ, our cornerstone, is our solid foundation for living and our guideline for morality and truth.

That this stone would be laid in Zion meant not only that Christ had lived in and around Jerusalem, but also that this new building (the Christian church and the new covenant) with Christ as the cornerstone would actually replace the old building (the Jerusalem temple and the old covenant).

Peter, like Paul, described this cornerstone as a person: *whoever believes in him* (see also Romans 9:33; 10:11). Peter promised those who believe that they *will not be put to shame*. Christians will sometimes be put to shame or face disappointment in this life, but their trust in God is never misplaced. God

will not let them down. These words greatly comforted believers
facing persecution. As a building rests on its cornerstone, so
believers rest on Christ. We can safely put our confidence in
Christ because he will certainly give to us the eternal life he
promises.

2:7 Therefore, to you who believe, He is precious.^{NKJV} The word
therefore refers back to the "Living Stone" in 2:4 and the "chosen
and precious cornerstone" in 2:6—both referring to Jesus Christ.
To you who believe addressed the Christians to whom Peter wrote
as well as Christians today. Jesus Christ is indeed *precious.* The
word "precious" means highly valued or esteemed. Not only is
Christ precious to the Father (2:4), he is also precious to those
who follow him.

While this is true, most scholars take issue with this translation
of the Greek text (as translated above, and basically the same in
NIV and NRSV), saying that this is an unlikely rendering of the
Greek. They prefer that this phrase be translated, "Therefore the
honor [or preciousness] is to you, the believers" or "This honor
belongs to you who believe." This would follow from Peter's
words in 2:6 that believers will not be put to shame and will
instead receive honor from God. It also contrasts the preciousness
of believers, and the honor they will receive, with the dishonor
and shame facing those who reject Christ (see the next sentence).

THE ROCK AND CORNERSTONE
No doubt Peter often thought of Jesus' words to him right after
he confessed that Jesus was "the Christ, the Son of the living
God": "You are Peter, and on this rock I will build my church,
and the gates of Hades will not overcome it" (Matthew 16:16-18
NIV). What is the stone that really counts in the building of the
church? Peter answers: Christ himself. What are the characteristics of Christ, the cornerstone?

- He is completely trustworthy.
- He is precious to believers.
- Though rejected by some, he is the most important part of
  the church.

Because Christ is supreme, we must constantly trust him and
exalt him in our lives.

**But for those who do not believe, "The stone that the builders
rejected has become the very head of the corner."**^{NRSV} While
believers receive preciousness and honor from God, unbelievers
face a different result. They do not regard the Stone as precious

and chosen; instead, they reject him. Jesus referred to these words when he spoke of being rejected by his own people (Matthew 21:42; Mark 12:10-11; Luke 20:17). In Matthew 21:42 and Acts 4:11, the *builders* who rejected Christ were the Jewish religious leaders. Peter used "builders" to refer to all people across the ages who toss Christ aside like an unwanted stone, choosing to build the foundations of their lives on something else. However, they were mistaken to reject him because God took the rejected stone and made it *the very head of the corner,* the cornerstone. These words are quoted from Psalm 118:22. Although he was rejected by people, God glorified Jesus and made him the "head of the corner," the foundation of the church.

2:8 And, "A stone that makes them stumble, and a rock that makes them fall." They stumble because they disobey the word, as they were destined to do.[NRSV] Quoting once again from the prophet Isaiah (see Isaiah 8:14), Peter further explained that not only were the builders who rejected the stone humiliated that it later became the cornerstone, they also had stumbled and fallen over this stone. The word "stumbled" can mean tripping and falling, or it can mean taking offense at or rejecting something or someone. Peter explained that they stumble because they *disobey the word*—this disobedience refers not to slipups by one who tries to obey; rather it means outright rejection of the Word and the Messiah that the Word promised, and a rebellious stance toward God. Some stumble over Christ because they reject him or refuse to believe that he is who he claims to be. Those who refuse to believe in Christ have made the greatest mistake of their lives. They have stumbled over the one person who could save them and give meaning to their lives, and they have fallen into God's hands for judgment.

Their stumbling and disobedience *were destined* by God. Peter used the word here in contrast to 2:6. In that verse, God laid (or established) the Stone in Zion; here, God destined (or established) rebellious people to their stumbling and disobedience.

What does it mean to be "destined"? How can some be destined to disobey? Isn't that unfair of God? Some scholars take 1 Thessalonians 5:9 and Romans 9:22-23 to prove double predestination. This means that some are predestined to belief unto salvation, and others are predestined to disbelief unto damnation. It would be more natural here to take Peter's point to be that God has predestined punishment for those who disbelieve, so that only the consequence of disbelief is ordained. "He is patient with you, not wanting anyone to perish, but everyone to come to repentance" (2 Peter 3:9 NIV). The fact of predestination does not imply that all our choices are predetermined. Because God is not limited by time as we are, he "sees" past, present, and future at the same time. Parents sometimes "know" how their children will behave before the fact. We don't conclude from these parents' foreknowledge that they made their children act that way. God's foreknowledge, insofar as we can understand it, means that God knows who will accept the offer of salvation and who will reject it.

To explain foreknowledge and predestination in any way that implies that every action and choice we make has been not only preknown, but even predetermined, seems to contradict those Scriptures that declare that our choices are real, that they matter, and that there are consequences to the choices we make. Those who choose to disobey will stumble and fall.

2:9 But you are a chosen generation, a royal priesthood, a holy nation, His own special people, that you may proclaim the praises of Him who called you out of darkness into His marvelous light.^{NKJV} This verse contrasts the privilege and destiny of believers with that of unbelievers (described in 2:8).

Believers are *a chosen generation,* a distinct group from the rest of the world, unified by the Holy Spirit. Isaiah prophesied God's blessings on those God called "my people, my chosen" (Isaiah 43:20 NIV; see also Deuteronomy 10:15). Just as the nation of Israel had been God's chosen people, Christians have become God's people, not by physical birth into a certain race but by spiritual rebirth into God's family through Jesus Christ.

Believers also are *a royal priesthood, a holy nation* (1:1; Ephesians 2:19). At Mount Sinai when the nation received God's laws, Moses had told all Israel: "And you shall be to Me a kingdom of priests and a holy nation" (Exodus 19:6 NKJV). In 2:5, Peter referred to believers as "a holy priesthood, offering spiritual sacrifices acceptable to God through Jesus Christ" (NIV). Being part of a "priesthood" is a high honor for believers. Christians speak of "the priesthood of all believers." In Old Testament times, people did not approach God directly. Instead, a priest would act as intermediary between God and sinful human beings. With Christ's victory on the cross, that pattern changed. Now believers can come directly into God's presence without fear (Hebrews 4:16). Also, they have been given the responsibility of bringing others to him (2 Corinthians 5:18-21). United with Christ as members of his body, believers join in his priestly work of reconciling God and people. This priesthood is called "royal" because believers have become members of God's family, brothers and sisters of Christ, the King of kings. As members of the King's family, we are royalty! "Holy nation" refers to Christians as a people who are distinct from all the others because of their devotion to God.

Believers are God's *own special people.* This phrase is more literally translated "a people for his possession." Similar language is found in Exodus 19:5 ("Now therefore, if you will indeed obey My voice and keep My covenant, then you shall be a special treasure to Me above all people" NKJV) and in Malachi 3:17 ("'They will be mine,' says the Lord Almighty, 'in the day when I make up my treasured possession'" NIV). God's "special people," his "special treasure," and his "treasured possession" are those who are faithful to him; thus this refers to Christians.

ON HIS KNEE
When a father puts a youngster on his knee, gives a hug, and tells how much he loves that child, neither one of them doubts the message: "Of all the children in the world—some of them brighter, healthier, less troublesome—*you* are special, you are mine!" Later, that child crawls into bed at peace with the world.

God gives us the same tender treatment. If not a bounce and a squeeze, surely the equivalent in peace and affirmation: We are God's special people.

Face tomorrow's troubles assured that your heavenly Father goes with you each step. Don't worry. Rest well tonight.

The remainder of the Isaiah 43:21 verse quoted in the preceding paragraph reads, "that they may proclaim my praise" (NIV). This ties in with Peter's explanation of what God's special people are to do: *proclaim the praises of Him who called you out of darkness into His marvelous light.* Christians were not redeemed just so they could enjoy their redemption and proclaim their own praises; they were redeemed with a special purpose—to glorify and praise the one who has called them out of the darkness of sin and of their hostile surroundings into the light of eternal life. The word "praises" is also translated "wonderful deeds" or "excellencies" (referring to moral excellence and virtue). We are called to "proclaim" who God is and what he has done, specifically the act of salvation. We proclaim him by

- *conducting* our lives so that they manifest his character, and

- *telling* others of the salvation he accomplished for us and of his work in our individual lives.

2:10 **Once you were not a people, but now you are God's people; once you had not received mercy, but now you have received mercy.**NRSV This verse is an adaptation of Hosea 1:9-10 and 2:23. Hosea, God's prophet, was describing God's rejection of Israel, followed by future restoration. Paul used these same verses from Hosea and applied them to the Gentile believers (Romans 9:25-26). Peter applied these verses to the New Testament church as a whole.

CREATIVE WITNESSING
How do we proclaim God's praises in a hostile world? A bank manager wants his staff to hear God's Good News. He considers inviting them all to church, giving each a devotional book, or hosting a dinner party with a gospel magician entertaining. Will these plans reach the goal?

In many settings, no. Surely not as the first approach. People are often offended by pushy evangelists, and some people consider a Bible on your desk overly aggressive.

A Christian's first approach to skeptics, cynics, and burned-out saints must be to serve them in love, with justice as the keynote. A consistent servant-leader appears so odd, by today's standards, that soon the difference God makes becomes apparent, and then words start to take root. Try communicating Christ through love and service.

Just as Israel had been, at one time, rejected by God without any hope of forgiveness for their sins, so Christians had been, at one time, rejected by God without any hope of mercy. But believers are now *God's people* because they have been chosen by him (2:9) and *have received mercy.* "Mercy" means God's compassionate treatment of us even though we deserve the full measure of his justice. God had no obligation to gather a people together to whom he would show mercy; not one of us deserves his slightest concern. God drawing a people unto himself and lavishing mercy on them gives overwhelming evidence of his great love. This mercy ought to affect the way every believer lives, as Peter will point out in the following verses.

> There's a wideness in God's mercy, like the wideness of the sea.
> *Frederick William Faber*

CHOSEN BY GOD
People often base their self-concept on their accomplishments. But our relationship with Christ is far more important than our jobs, successes, wealth, or knowledge. We have been chosen by God as his very own, and we have been called to represent him to others. Remember that your value comes from being one of God's children, not from what you can achieve. You have worth because of what *God* does, not because of what you do.

OBEY THOSE IN AUTHORITY / 2:11-25

At this point in Peter's letter, the focus changes from theological to practical. Up to this point, Peter had explained that the believers were to live holy lives, revealing their status as God's chosen people. In this section, Peter offered practical advice for holy living in an unholy and often hostile world. As believers who have received God's mercy (2:10), we ought to live worthy of our calling. This begins the next major section of 1 Peter (2:11–3:12). It centers on the Christians' relationship to non-Christians. Because we are the community of God (2:4-10), we must live like it.

2:11 **Dear friends, I urge you, as aliens and strangers in the world, to abstain from sinful desires, which war against your soul.**^{NIV} Peter

called these scattered believers *dear friends* (other versions say "beloved") describing the love he had for these brothers and sisters in the faith. He did not know each reader personally, but he loved them all "deeply, from the heart" (1:22) because of their mutual bond in Christ.

NOT HOME YET
We believers are "aliens and strangers" in this world because our real home is with God. Heaven is not the pink-cloud-and-harp existence popular in cartoons. Heaven is where God lives. Life in heaven operates according to God's principles and values, and it is eternal and unshakable. Heaven came to earth in the symbolism of the Jewish sanctuary (the tabernacle and temple), where God's presence dwelt. It came in a fuller way in the person of Jesus Christ, "God with us." It permeated the entire world as the Holy Spirit came to live in every believer.
Someday, after God judges and destroys all sin, the kingdom of heaven will rule every corner of this earth. John saw this day in a vision, and he cried out, "Now the dwelling of God is with men, and he will live with them. They will be his people, and God himself will be with them and be their God" (Revelation 21:3 NIV). Our true loyalty should be to our citizenship in heaven, not to our citizenship here, because the earth will be destroyed. Our loyalty should be to God's truth, his way of life, and his dedicated people. Because we are loyal to God, we often will feel like strangers in a world that would prefer to ignore God. When that happens, remember that you're not home yet.

Peter "urged" (more forceful in the Greek: Peter "strongly urged") the believers to remember their status as *aliens and strangers in the world.* The word "aliens" *(paroikos)* refers to people living in a place that is not their true home. The word *strangers (parepidemois,* see 1:1) is slightly different from "aliens," describing a visitor staying briefly in a foreign land. These words are also used together in Genesis 23:4 and Psalm 39:12. The world is not the Christian's true home; our real home is with Christ. We are here temporarily, awaiting the return of Christ when he will take us to our true home in heaven.

We are passing through this world on the way to our home in heaven's glory; therefore, we ought to remain as untouched as possible by this world's rampant sin. Peter explained that the best way to do that is *to abstain from sinful desires.* Because we will not escape our sinful surroundings until Christ returns, and because we still have a sinful nature that wants us to act on its desires, we will not be able to remain completely free of sin and its effects. But we can "abstain"; that is, we can put away our sinful desires by controlling them right from the start. The verb tense literally means to "continually keep away from." It takes alertness and self-control to continually abstain from sinful desires (5:8).

Why must we abstain? Why does it matter that we keep away from sinful desires? Because those desires *war against your soul.* Once we become believers, a battle has begun, for Satan is the enemy of Christ and his followers. The verb tense literally means "continually waging war." Believers must "continually abstain" because the evil desires are "continually waging war." This battle will continue throughout our lives on this earth. The word "soul" refers to the inner, spiritual part of a person (see also 1:22). Desires come from deep within us; often our sinful desires never actually become sinful actions. Some believers may take pride in their clean lives, yet have hearts filled with all kinds of evil thoughts and desires. Peter wrote that while believers know that their lives and actions must be changed by Christ, they also must have their inner lives transformed. Sinful desires may seem much less evil than sinful actions, but Peter explained that they too can hurt us as they war against our souls.

How do they wage war? Jesus had told his followers, "You have heard that it was said, 'Do not commit adultery.' But I tell you that anyone who looks at a woman lustfully has already committed adultery with her in his heart" (Matthew 5:27-28 NIV). Entertaining evil desires, even if those desires are never acted upon, takes our focus off of Christ and turns our hearts from heavenly to earthly desires. All evil actions begin with a single thought; therefore, Peter advised believers to kill sin right at its root.

2:12 **Live such good lives among the pagans that, though they accuse you of doing wrong, they may see your good deeds and glorify God on the day he visits us.**[NIV] This thought follows from 2:11 without a break in the Greek text—the believers were to have their inner selves under control so that their outer lives would be honoring to God. *Live . . . good lives* refers to daily living and day-by-

day interactions; a "good life" is filled with *good deeds*. (For more
on good deeds, see Ephesians 2:8-10; Titus 3:1, 8, 14; James 1:22;
2:14-26; 3:13.) Believers are called to honor God by living honorably and morally upright in and in spite of an unholy world. We
must live "good lives" so that *pagans* (unbelievers) will glorify
God. Peter's progression of thought has four steps:

1. The pagans slander us as evildoers.

2. Our good deeds prove their slander a lie.

3. Our good lives convict them of their sin and slander
   (implied).

4. The pagans become converted (they "glorify God").

Peter's advice sounds like Jesus' advice recorded in Matthew
5:16, "Let your light so shine before men, that they may see your
good works and glorify your Father in heaven" (Matthew 5:16
NKJV). If believers' actions are above reproach, even hostile people
might end up praising God. Peter's readers were scattered among
unbelieving Gentiles who were inclined to believe and spread
vicious lies about Christians, accusing them of wrongdoing, blaming
them without cause. Attractive, gracious, and upright behavior on
the part of Christians could show these rumors to be false and could
even win some of the unsaved critics to the Lord's side.

But why would people *accuse* Christians *of doing wrong?* During the last part of the first century, Christianity became suspect
as seditious.

- The founder of this Christian sect, Jesus Christ, had been cruci-
  fied under Roman law for leading a movement that challenged
  Caesar as ruler and god—the inscription on Jesus' cross read,
  "The King of the Jews" (Mark 15:26).

- Christians had been accused of defying Caesar. When the apostle Paul had visited Thessalonica, his enemies stirred up trouble
  by going to the city officials and exclaiming, "These men who
  have caused trouble all over the world have now come
  here. . . . They are all defying Caesar's decrees, saying that
  there is another king, one called Jesus" (Acts 17:6-7 NIV).

- Wherever the gospel was taken, it usually caused a spiritual
  upheaval because both pagan and Jewish systems were threatened by this new religion based on faith (see Acts 16:16-22;
  19:23-41).

- Christians often were blamed for social disturbances. Business
  people, like silversmiths, who made a living off of religion,

were threatened by Christianity. Riots often ensued when the gospel was preached, not because the speakers stirred up the people, but because someone's power or livelihood was affected when people began following Christ and rejecting pagan idols. Leaders in other cities found that mere accusations against Christians could be used effectively against them.

Peter urged the believers not to be surprised when persecution and false accusations arose, and to live above reproach so that the accusations would have to be dropped.

The phrase *on the day he visits us* (or "on the day of visitation") has caused much discussion among scholars. At first reading, it sounds like Peter was referring to the final Day of Judgment, when unbelievers will be forced to glorify God. However, arguments against this understanding are:

■ There is no definite article in the Greek, so most likely no definite "day" is meant. Some scholars point to Isaiah 10:3, where Isaiah wrote of "the day of punishment," but again the same problem arises because there are two definite articles in Isaiah's phrase and none in Peter's. In fact, Peter's exact phrase occurs nowhere else in the Old or New Testament, so he probably was not quoting a reference to the last judgment.

■ The "visitation" could refer to a decisive intervention when God comes to judge, or when he comes to bring blessing or deliverance. Most likely, Peter was referring to the times when God brings mercy to unbelievers, offering them salvation.

■ At that time, unbelievers will "glorify" God. The Greek word *doxazo* is used over sixty times in the New Testament, but never to refer to unbelievers being forced to glorify God. Therefore Peter most likely referred to the voluntary praise of believers.

Thus, in 2:11-12, Peter gave four reasons for self-discipline:

1. Our citizenship is in heaven; we are aliens in this world, so we must live by the rules of God's country.

2. Sinful desires war against our souls. Our bodies are good servants, but tyrannical masters.

3. Our lives will influence others.

4. Christ will return, and we will want to glorify him with our lives when he comes.

What are some of the "good deeds" (2:12) that Christians can live out? Peter offered some of these in the following verses.

GOODY TWO-SHOES
Peter's call to live virtuously may strike you as self-defeating, since nobody admires a goody-goody. Perfect people are no fun, and often they are so obsessed with not trespassing some rule that their goodness becomes its own prison.

But remember, the good that Peter urges includes humility, forgiveness (self-forgiveness too), and a dose of laughter and frolic. This life is no stiff-collared Puritanism; it is vibrant, loving, curious, engaging, active, prayerful, and devoted to others in God's service.

Don't neglect doing good deeds and being good neighbors. Live honorably and discreetly. The energy comes from God, who promises that the energy will never run out.

2:13 **For the Lord's sake accept the authority of every human institution, whether of the emperor as supreme.**^{NRSV} Peter commanded believers to accept *authority*. The expression "accept the authority" means "submit to" (see 2:18–3:1). The phrase *of every human institution* broadens the scope to refer to more than just governmental authority (2:13-17), to other institutions of authority established for orderly relations among people, such as household slaves to masters (2:18-20) and the mutual cooperation between husband and wife (3:1-7). The word "every" leads us to conclude that not in these situations alone, but in every area where authorities have been placed (parents/children, employer/employee, church leaders/church members) God is honored when we accept and respect those in authority over us. We do this *for the Lord's sake,* so that he is glorified by our orderly submission. We glorify God when we accept others' authority over us

- because the authority is divinely ordained; thus, we are doing God's will;

- because Christ accepted the Father's authority—we must follow in his steps;

- because our actions commend Christ to others.

Peter's meaning goes even deeper. The word *authority (ktisei)* literally means "creature" or "that which is created." Thus Peter explained that believers should, in a sense, accept every other person as an authority because God was their Creator. In other words, believers ought to defer to others, willingly putting them first, showing respect for everyone, friends and enemies alike.

In telling his readers to accept the authority of *the emperor,* Peter was speaking of Emperor Nero, a notoriously cruel tyrant who ruled from A.D. 54–68. The emperor was the supreme ruler over all Roman provinces—including the areas to which Peter addressed this letter. The emperor Nero was considered the *supreme* authority by his subjects, even worshiped by them. The Christians should never worship the emperor, but they should obey his laws because he was an authority put in place by God. Paul had written, "Let every person be subject to the governing authorities; for there is no authority except from God, and those authorities that exist have been instituted by God. Therefore whoever resists authority resists what God has appointed, and those who resist will incur judgment" (Romans 13:1-2 NRSV).

But here is a word of warning: Peter was not telling believers to compromise their Holy Spirit–directed consciences. Remember, Peter had told the high priest years before, "We must obey God rather than any human authority" (Acts 5:29 NRSV). At other times, God had approved disobedience to human authorities (see, for example, Exodus 1:17; Daniel 3:13-18; 6:10-24; Acts 4:18-20; Hebrews 11:23). In those cases, the government had called upon God's people to sin against God and God's people had to submit to the higher power—God himself. But in most aspects of daily life, it was desirable for Christians to live according to the law of their land, whether or not they agreed with the policies. Christians were not to rebel against Rome—Roman law was the only restraint against lawlessness. In addition, it wouldn't take much for an imperial edict to fall on a group who had become known for causing unrest within the empire. The Christians' quiet submission might allow them to continue to spread the gospel freely. If they were to be persecuted, it should be for obeying God, and not for breaking moral or civil laws. Peter himself would later be put to death for his faith during Emperor Nero's intense persecution of Christians.

2:14 Or of governors, as sent by him to punish those who do wrong and to praise those who do right.NRSV The king (or emperor), with supreme authority, would delegate responsibility to representatives in the territories under the empire's control. These *governors* would carry out the emperor's commands, enforce the laws, and keep the peace in the provinces. Both Pontius Pilate and Felix had the title of "governor" (see Matthew 27:2; Acts 23:24).

The words *by him* could mean that these governors were sent out by the emperor. While that may be true, another underlying meaning is also possible. The phrase could be translated "through him," meaning that God sent out these governors "through" the edicts of the emperor.

Peter outlined the God-ordained functions of those in authority.

They had been given authority in order *to punish those who do wrong and to praise those who do right.* While no government carries out these functions perfectly, most attempt to do so in order to maintain peace and safety for their citizens.

IT'S JUST WAR

Christians differ on the question of how to respect the government when it comes to war. Many believe that these verses and others teach that Christians should support "just wars." That is, when the cause is right, we should take up arms and destroy enemy targets by government order.

Mennonites, Quakers, and others strongly disagree. They believe that submission to a government's ordered killing violates God's commands and is strictly wrong.

Let each believer pursue the Bible's guidelines with devotion and intelligence. All Christians must limit their allegiance to the state because the laws of God must come first, and they must draw lines where they feel the Word of God and the Spirit of God require. While disagreement can be heated on this issue, both sides should continue to listen to the other, perhaps to learn, and surely to share each other's struggle, for both pacifists and "just war" believers find pain in the violence they confront.

Today, one-third of all Christians live in freedom while the other two-thirds live under repressive governments. Scripture does not recommend one form of government over another. Rather, it simply asks Christians to accept the government under whose authority they find themselves and to cooperate with the rulers as far as the Holy Spirit–directed conscience will allow. Believers must do this "for the Lord's sake"—so that his Good News and his people will be respected.

2:15 **For it is God's will that by doing right you should silence the ignorance of the foolish.**NRSV *Doing right* refers to the submission that Peter just described in 2:13-14. The *foolish* are unbelievers who speak about and act in *ignorance* toward Christians. Peter exhorted the believers to live so righteously that even those foolish people's lies and slander would be silenced. The word *silence* is more literally "to muzzle"—in other words, to shut them up. This repeats the idea of 2:12. These unbelievers should finally have to admit that they could hold nothing against Christians except their faith.

> If Christ lives in us, controlling our personalities, we will leave glorious marks on the lives we touch. Not because of our lovely characters, but because of his. *Eugenia Price*

2:16 Live as free men, but do not use your freedom as a cover-up for evil; live as servants of God.^{NIV} Here Peter was outlining a paradox of the Christian life. Christians are *free* yet they are *servants.* They can live as free people but must use their freedom to glorify God. We glorify God when we serve him faithfully. Christian freedom does not mean that anything goes; believers are not free to do whatever they want or to use their freedom *as a cover-up for evil.* In other words, believers must not hide behind their freedom in Christ in order to sin. We cannot use freedom and forgiveness as a cloaking device for self-indulgence, adultery, or poor spending habits. Christ is our leader, and serving him provides our limits.

RESPONSIBLE FREEDOM
Christians have freedom in Christ, but the apostles defined freedom more narrowly than the normal use of the word in common language. Christians use freedom as a tool for a life of exuberant service. It's the foundation that God gives to us to reach our highest potential. Because God gives us freedom from religious rules and eternal guilt, we must not seek to indulge our own desires; instead, we should reach for the best God has for us.

Don't be fooled if someone tries to sell you other versions of freedom like:

- You're free, party on!
- Freedom! Let's get stoned!
- No more rules! Let's pick up some babes and . . .

Such "freedom" becomes a fast track to the prison of guilt and brokenness. Let your freedom sing of power, joy, and love—accountable to God, devoted to others.

Second Peter 2:19 states, "people are slaves to whatever masters them" (NRSV). Jesus said, "I tell you the truth, everyone who sins is a slave to sin" (John 8:34 NIV). If people follow their own sinful desires, they will be slaves to those desires. However, if people choose to follow God, they receive freedom from sin, from Satan's power and control, from guilt, and from having to be good enough in order to be saved. Christian freedom means that our salvation is not determined by good works or legalistic rules, but by the free gift of God. We are free from keeping the law as a way to earn salvation. We are still to obey God's laws (specifically his moral law, out-

> Stone walls do not a prison make, nor iron bars a cage; if I have freedom in my love, and in my soul am free, angels alone that soar above enjoy such liberty.
> *Richard Lovelace*

lined in the Ten Commandments), because they are expressions of God's will for us. Christian freedom ties inseparably to Christian responsibility. Christ frees us to serve him, a freedom that results in our ultimate good (see Romans 6:15; Galatians 5:13).

2:17 Show proper respect to everyone.^{NIV} These four short sentences summarize how believers can live peacefully in the world. First, *show proper respect to everyone.* The word "respect" means to honor, value, or esteem. Believers should be especially conscious that God made all people in his image, whether or not they believe in Christ. Therefore, we should show them proper respect.

Love the family of believers.^{NRSV} While all believers are called to "respect" everyone, they have an extra obligation to those in their *family,* the brothers and sisters in the family of God. They are called to *love* them. The word for "love" is *agapao,* referring to volitional, self-sacrificial love. The believers of Peter's day needed to stand together as a unified force against coming persecution. They needed to maintain the bond of love. When believers truly love one another, they maintain peace in the fellowship and can continue the work of the gospel.

Fear God. The word *fear* means to show deep respect, reverence, and awe. While believers are to respect and love God as well, they are also to fear him. Proper fear leads to obedience. They should *honor the king,* but they should "fear" God.

Honor the king.^{NIV} The word *honor* is from the verb *timao,* the same verb translated "respect" above. The respect due to "everyone" must also be given to those in authority, whether we agree with them or not. With a touch of irony, Peter deftly placed the emperor on the same level as "everyone else." While Rome's emperors claimed to be divine, God's people were only to respect the emperor as they would respect any other human being. They should "fear" God alone. When we honor the king, we should give the government its rights, what it owns, what it controls; but we may not give to the government those rights that belong to God alone.

2:18 Slaves, submit yourselves to your masters with all respect, not only to those who are good and considerate, but also to those who are harsh.^{NIV} Peter had already commanded believers to accept authority (2:13). Here he specifically addressed Christians who were servants in pagan homes. The Greek word is not *doulos,* the usual word translated "slave." Here it is *oiketes,* meaning a household slave or servant. These people were not permanent slaves, but neither were they merely servants. Their

positions were semipermanent. They did not have legal or economic freedom but often were paid for their services and could
eventually hope to purchase their freedom. For more on slaves,
see 1 Corinthians 7:21; Ephesians 6:5-8; 1 Timothy 6:1-2; Titus
2:9-10.

Peter called these servants to *submit . . . to [their] masters,*
meaning that they should cooperate, be loyal, and willingly obey.
Believers who were servants were not set free from serving their
masters, but they were set free from slavery to sin. While their
masters might not be Christians, that did not allow the servants to
be disrespectful or lazy. They needed to remember that their ultimate Master was God himself (Colossians 3:23-24).

Peter explained that God wanted Christian slaves to fulfill their
responsibilities with the right attitude—*with all respect.* The
Greek word for "respect" is not the same word used in 2:17. It is
phobos, which refers to healthy fear. The slave should do his or
her best not to incur the displeasure of the master.

Slaves played a significant part in this society, with several million in the Roman Empire at this time. Slavery was sanctioned by
law and part of the empire's social makeup. Because many slaves
and slave owners had become Christians, the early church had to
deal straightforwardly with the question of master/slave relations.
Colossians 3:22–4:1 and Ephesians 6:5-9 explain how Christian
masters and slaves should live together in Christian households.
In Paul's day, women, children, and slaves had few rights. In the
church, however, they had freedoms that society denied them.
Paul explained how masters and slaves should live out the dichot-
omy of being on different social levels yet equal in Christ.

Like Paul, Peter neither condemned nor condoned slavery. To
attempt to rebel against the system would only bring the wrath of
the powerful Roman Empire and would hurt the cause of the gospel. So the apostles suggested that the believers should live
within the system, hoping to transform it by first transforming
lives through salvation in Jesus Christ. Thus Peter commanded
that the believing slaves simply serve well and show respect, not
just to Christian masters or to those who were *good and considerate,* but also to masters who were *harsh.* (The Greek word is
skolios, meaning "crooked" or "perverse.")

A good and considerate master might have high expectations
but be willing to overlook small mistakes, care about the slave as
a person, and provide fair pay and good living conditions. However, a harsh master might use his power over a slave to inflict
severe punishments, withhold wages or not pay fairly, force his
slaves to live in squalor, and have unreasonable expectations. It

would take God's grace for Christian slaves to loyally and obedi-
ently serve such a master. Peter encouraged loyalty and perseverance even in the face of unjust treatment.

WHO'S IN CHARGE?
Peter was writing to slaves. Slavery hardly exists in our
twentieth-century society, but much in this section applies to
our work relationships.
   Because God is in control, we face each day with his power
and love. If you receive some hard knocks today, turn them
over to God. If you've been cheated, give the problem to God.
If employees do not fulfill their responsibilities, admit your loss
and trust God fully. Christians must never seek revenge, no
matter how bad the circumstances. The impulse for revenge
comes from people who think that systems or bosses or powerful people are in control. Christians believe that God has
ultimate power.
   Be careful. This verse does not advocate passivity or
weak-willed submission to cruel people. Rather, it frees victims
from screaming in pain to an empty sky.

**2:19 For it is commendable if a man bears up under the pain of
unjust suffering because he is conscious of God.**^{NIV} The
word *for* refers back to the topic of submission discussed in
2:18. Many slaves would have heard this letter read to them
because many of the early church members were slaves.
Roman law regulated the treatment of slaves, but ultimately
masters had power over their slaves. Many masters were
"good and considerate" (especially those who were Christians), but many were "harsh" (perhaps especially with slaves
who had become believers). As noted in 2:18 above, harsh
masters could inflict cruel punishments upon slaves, considered as property, usually by whipping or beating them with a
stick. Like thieves, runaway slaves were branded on the fore-
head. Others were imprisoned. Many slaves died from mis-
treatment or imprisonment, but it was illegal to take the life of
a slave without a court order. In some cases, a master might
take out his anger on his slaves, even though the slaves had
done nothing to incur any wrath.
   Many of the readers of this letter would have known all too
well what it meant to *[bear] up under the pain of unjust suffering*. Peter had learned about suffering from Jesus. He knew that
Jesus' suffering was part of God's plan (Matthew 16:21-23; Luke
24:25-27, 44-47) and was intended to save people (Matthew
20:28; 26:28). He also knew that all who follow Jesus must be

prepared to suffer (Mark 8:34-35). Thus it would be *commend-able* or praiseworthy if these believers trusted in God as they endured "pain" (referring to mental, not physical, anguish) caused by unjust suffering.

By being *conscious of God* when they suffered, they were remembering God's care and love for them even as they suffered. They focused on the fact that they were suffering injustice as Christ had suffered injustice, and they knew that one day God would right all wrongs. This gave them the proper attitude, enabled them to persevere, and kept their practice from being mere passive acceptance.

2:20 But how is it to your credit if you receive a beating for doing wrong and endure it?NIV While bearing the pain of unjust suffering is commendable before God, there is no special commendation for patiently bearing punishment that is deserved. The word for *beating* is *kolaphizein,* meaning to strike with one's fist (see also Mark 14:65).

But if you suffer for doing good and you endure it, this is commendable before God.NIV This repeats the thought of 2:19. Christian slaves who patiently endured suffering when they had done nothing to deserve it would be commended by God. If they *suffer* (because of someone's lies, the master's temper, or their faith) even though they have *done good* (by obeying God and their masters), and they *endure* the suffering (patiently taking it rather than lashing out in revenge or hatred), then God approves of this behavior, for it demonstrates his grace in a sinful world. It also shows that the believer has followed the example of Jesus Christ, as Peter will explain in the following verses.

THE FACE OF SUFFERING
We may suffer for many reasons. Some suffering comes as the direct result of our own sin; some happens because of our foolishness; and some is the result of living in a fallen world. Peter writes about suffering that comes as a result of doing good. Jesus never sinned, and yet he suffered so that we could be set free. When we follow Christ's example and live for others, we too may suffer. Our goal should be to face suffering as he did—with patience, calmness, and confidence, knowing that God controls the future.

2:21 For to this you have been called, because Christ also suffered for you, leaving you an example, so that you should follow in his steps.NRSV The phrase *for to this you have been called* refers back to suffering for doing good. Why have believers been "called" (see also 1:15; 2:9) to unjust suffering? Because such suffering was endured by Christ. Jesus had told Peter and the other disciples at the Last Supper: "No servant is greater than his master. If they persecuted me, they will persecute you also" (John 15:20 NIV). When we patiently suffer injustice, we are following our supreme example in Christ. He suffered great injustice in order to obtain our salvation:

- He endured the unbelief of his own people (John 1:11).

- He endured a trial by religious leaders already committed to his death (Mark 14:1; John 11:50).

- He endured the lies of false witnesses (Matthew 26:59-60).

- He endured beating and mockery from his people and from the Roman soldiers (Mark 14:64-65; 15:16-20).

- He endured merciless flogging (Mark 15:15).

- He endured an excruciatingly painful death by crucifixion (Mark 15:22-37).

- He endured the insults of bystanders as he suffered on the cross (Mark 15:29-32).

- He endured a time of separation from God (Mark 15:33-34).

That the believers were to *follow in his steps* does not mean that they would die for the sins of the world or die by crucifixion (although some first-century believers may have been crucified). Instead, the example to follow is Jesus' complete peace and trust in God. Peter had learned how to follow in Christ's steps; he had accepted the responsibility and had taught it to others. Jesus said, "If any want to become my followers, let them deny themselves and take up their cross and follow me" (Mark 8:34 NRSV). Christ has given believers an *example* of how they are to face injustice and persecution. The Greek word for "example" is *hupogrammaton,* which was a model of handwriting set up by masters for their pupils to copy. The word was used, as here, as a figure of speech for a model of conduct for imitation. Peter set up Christ as the model for the believers to follow; his example would have greatly comforted these believers, who soon would be persecuted for their faith. They should face injustice from harsh masters or from other authorities with supreme dignity, trusting God's control.

> You are never at any time nearer to God than when under tribulation, which he permits for the purification and beautifying of your soul.
> *Miguel de Molinos*

IN HIS STEPS
Topeka minister Charles Sheldon wanted to attract local college students to God, so he began preaching a series of practical, Sunday evening sermons on how to follow Jesus in business, in journalism, in other careers. From the popular series he wrote magazine articles, which in time became the best-selling book *In His Steps,* still available today.

Following Jesus' steps, for Sheldon, meant counting the value of his famous book not in dollars earned, but lives touched.

You, too, may have a chance to follow in Jesus' steps and so show a needy world that Christians run at a different pace, to a different tune, tracking a different leader.

2:22 "He committed no sin, and no deceit was found in his mouth."NRSV Verses 22-23 detail how Jesus was an example. Peter quoted from Isaiah 53:9, Isaiah's prophecy about the suffering of the coming Messiah. Christ's suffering was completely unjust because he never committed any sin or spoke any lies; there was no good reason for his being condemned to death (even Pilate saw that—see John 19:4). From personal experience Peter knew that Jesus was perfect. He had lived and traveled with Jesus for three years. Intimate relationships often reveal the worst in people, but Peter had seen the truth of the prophet's words. Christ was completely sinless in his life and in his words. (For other verses about Christ's sinlessness, see Matthew 27:4; John 8:29, 46; 18:38; 2 Corinthians 5:21; Hebrews 4:15; 1 John 3:5.)

2:23 When he was abused, he did not return abuse; when he suffered, he did not threaten.NRSV This is another allusion to Isaiah 53, this time verse 7: "He was oppressed and He was afflicted, yet He opened not His mouth; He was led as a lamb to the slaughter, and as a sheep before its shearers is silent, so He opened not His mouth" (NKJV). Christ faced horrible abuse and suffering (see the list in the notes for 2:21). The word *abused* is also translated "reviled" and refers to insulting and abusive speech (see, for example, Matthew 26:67-68; 27:27-30). Jesus did not *return abuse* nor did he *threaten.* How tempting it must have been to expose the liars at his trial, to come down from the cross in a great display of power (as the hecklers suggested—see Mark 15:30), or to blast his enemies with God's wrath. **Instead, he entrusted himself to him who judges justly.**NIV Jesus suffered patiently because he knew that God would have the final say. Jesus regarded God as sovereign, so he put the outcome of his life in God's hands. He was confident of God's righteous judgment. As Jesus *entrusted* (the verb is imperfect, he "kept entrust-

ing") *himself* and his sufferings to God, so all believers can
entrust themselves and their suffering into God's hands. Knowing
that God will ultimately right all wrongs is a great comfort to
believers who are suffering, and it helps them respond correctly
in their sufferings.

DEALING WITH ABUSE
Peter urged Christians not to retaliate with abusive speech;
instead, they were to endure government persecution as a
testimony to the Lord.

Some have taken this verse and verses like Matthew 5:38-42
to mean that people should be passive victims of violence, but
Peter did not have that in mind. When Christians are tortured
and martyred and have no recourse, they must call to God for
deliverance and strength. When we enounter people who have
a pattern of abusing others, however, we do not need to suffer
as victims.

If you grew up with or live with an abusive person, you should
not retaliate, but neither should you try to appease the person.
You should seek professional help and a safe location. Don't
minimize or deny the sick person's cruel behavior, for that will
only encourage the person to continue to be abusive and
discourage him or her from getting help. You may need to confront the problem in order to protect innocent family members
from danger.

Don't rationalize or excuse abuse. Seek help from the
professionals God has given us. Those who don't stop the
cycle of abuse may live to see those victims become abusers
themselves.

2:24 He himself bore our sins in his body on the cross.^{NRSV} This
phrase also comes from Isaiah 53: "He bore the sin of many"
(53:12); "by his wounds we are healed" (53:5 NIV). Only Christ
himself, the sinless Son of God, could bear our sins *on the cross.*
Christ took the death penalty for sin, dying in our place, so that
we would not have to suffer the punishment that we deserve. In a
transaction we cannot comprehend, God placed the sins of the
world on Jesus Christ.

Why did Jesus have to die? The problem began in the Garden of
Eden with the very first sin, and people have been sinning ever since
because they are born sinners. Because of sin, all people are separated from the holy God. The situation was hopeless, for sinful
people can never do enough or be good enough to make themselves
acceptable to God. God knew from eternity past that sin would enter
creation; he also knew the solution. In the Old Testament, people
would offer animals as sacrifices for their sins. Eventually Jesus,

God's only Son, entered this sinful world as a sinless human being. This sinless "Lamb of God" offered himself for the sins of all people. He suffered for our sakes, bearing our sins to make us acceptable to God. Only he could bridge the gap between the sinless God and sinful mankind. Jesus died on the cross in our place, taking all our wrongdoing upon himself, saving us from the ultimate consequences of our sin—eternal judgment.

Jesus took our past, present, and future sins upon himself **so that we might die to sins and live for righteousness; by his wounds you have been healed.**^{NIV} Because all our wrongdoing is forgiven, we are reconciled to God. All who believe in Jesus Christ as Savior can have this new life and live in union with him. Believers can *die to sins* by following Peter's advice in 2:11: "Abstain from sinful desires, which war against your soul" (NIV). Sin still exists, the sinful nature still rears its head, and temptations still come, but believers have the power of the Holy Spirit and the knowledge that their sins are already paid for and forgiven. Our evil desires, our bondage to sin, and our love of sin died with Christ on the cross. This is called substitutionary atonement. Jesus died as our substitute; his *wounds* have healed ours.

Now, united by faith with him in his resurrection life, we have unbroken fellowship with God and freedom from sin's hold on us. We should regard our old, sinful nature as dead and unresponsive to sin. Because of our union and identification with Christ, we are no longer obligated to carry out those old motives, desires, and goals. We are "dead to sin."

But to be simply dead to sin would leave a vacuum—if we are not to sin, then what are we to do? We are to *live for righteousness.* Because believers no longer need to live under sin's power, we are free to live for Christ. Paul wrote similar words to the Romans:

- *Count yourselves dead to sin but alive to God in Christ Jesus. Therefore do not let sin reign in your mortal body so that you obey its evil desires. Do not offer the parts of your body to sin . . . but rather offer yourselves to God, as those who have been brought from death to life. (Romans 6:11-13* NIV)

and to the Galatians:

- *For I through the law died to the law that I might live to God. I have been crucified with Christ; it is no longer I who live, but Christ lives in me; and the life which I now live in the flesh I live by faith in the Son of God, who loved me and gave Himself for me. (Galatians 2:19-20* NKJV)

SUBMISSION

Submission is voluntarily cooperating with someone, first out of love and respect for God, and second, out of love and respect for that person. Submitting to nonbelievers is a difficult but vital part of leading them to Jesus Christ. We are not called to submit to nonbelievers to the point that we compromise our relationship with God, but we must look for every opportunity to humbly serve in the power of God's Spirit.

Submission is:

Functional . . . . . distinguishing our roles and the work we are called to do

Relational . . . . . loving acknowledgment of another's value as a person

Reciprocal . . . . .mutual, humble cooperation with one another

Universal . . . . . .acknowledgment by the church of the all-encompassing lordship of Jesus Christ

---

Christ is the ultimate example for all believers (2:21-23), those scattered across the world in Peter's day as well as today. He deserves to be imitated because he is our Savior—having suffered the ultimate injustice and pain on our behalf. His suffering accomplished our salvation; his wounds healed ours. As we trust him for salvation, we can also trust him with every step of our lives, through joy and through suffering. He has shown us what to do and how to live.

2:25 **For you were like sheep going astray, but now you have returned to the Shepherd and Overseer of your souls.**[NIV] This verse also echoes Isaiah: "All we like sheep have gone astray" (53:6 NKJV). Sheep need the constant protection of a shepherd or they will wander away, following their noses and sometimes getting into great danger. People can be like that, wandering through life in whatever direction circumstances might take them. But that was in the past; *now you have returned to the Shepherd and Overseer of your souls.* At conversion, each believer returns from going his or her own way (the way of sin). Peter described God as a "Shepherd" who

> The King of love my shepherd is, whose goodness never faileth; I lack nothing if I am his, and he is mine forever.
> *Sir Henry Williams Baker*

tirelessly looks after the sheep, guiding and protecting them (see Psalm 23:1-4; Ezekiel 34:11-16; Luke 15:5-7; John 10:11-16). Whatever trials and difficulties they might face, the Shepherd would always be by their side, and the "Overseer of their souls" would protect and seal them for eternity.

1 Peter 3

In 2:11-25, Peter had explained that the believers needed to act in an exemplary manner before the unbelieving world. He tells them to be subject "to every authority instituted among men" (2:13); he then described three areas of that authority: citizens to the government (2:13-17), slaves to masters (2:18-20), and wives to husbands (3:1-7). Anarchy results if there is no authority. As Christians, we should not rebel against authority, but work within the system and serve God.

3:1-2 Wives, in the same way, accept the authority of your husbands.^{NRSV} The phrase *in the same way* (or "likewise," *homoios*) most likely referred to 2:13, "Accept the authority of every human institution" (NRSV). The word *homoios* has a slightly different slant than the word *kathos,* another word that is translated "in the same way." If Peter had used the word *kathos,* he would have meant that wives should serve their husbands in the same way that slaves serve their masters. However, the word *homoios* focuses the comparison in other areas. While wives are to serve their husbands "in the same way" as slaves serve their masters, Peter was not saying that wives were slaves. Instead, the wives' service should have positive motives ("for the Lord's sake," 2:13), should be consistent no matter what the attitude of the one in authority ("not only to those who are good and considerate, but also to those who are harsh," 2:18), and should have a positive attitude ("with all respect," 2:18). Christian wives were to accept the authority of their husbands in obedience to Christ to keep harmony in the family and to encourage unbelieving husbands to believe.

Submission of the wife to the husband is an often misunderstood concept, although it is taught in several places in the New Testament (see, for example, Galatians 3:28; Ephesians 5:24; Colossians 3:18; 1 Peter 3:5). It may be the least popular Christian teaching in society. These texts do not teach the general subjugation of all women under all men. The principle of submission does not require a woman to become a doormat. When a Chris-

tian wife interacted with an unbelieving husband, she needed to
be submissive according to cultural norms in order to save her
marriage and sometimes even her life. But she ought not participate in her husband's pagan religion or submit to actions that dis-
honored God. However, when both wife and husband were
Christians, the woman should respect the God-given authority of
her husband, while the husband exercised his authority in a loving and gentle manner. For marriage and family relationships to
run smoothly, there must be one appointed leader—and God has
appointed the husband and father. The wife should willingly follow her husband's leadership in Christ, acknowledging that this
is his responsibility. Submission does not mean blind obedience,
nor does it mean inferiority. A wife who accepts her husband's
authority is accepting the relationship that God has designed and
giving her husband leadership and responsibility.

SUBMITTING TO SUBMISSION
What should a wife do if her husband is an unbeliever or very
difficult to live with? Peter says she should accept the authority
of her husband. To accept authority means to cooperate
voluntarily with someone else out of love and respect for God
and for that person. For Christian couples, submission must be
mutual. Paul wrote, "Submit to one another out of reverence for
Christ" (Ephesians 5:21 NIV). When only one partner believes,
submission can be an effective Christian strategy to win
unbelievers. Jesus Christ submitted to God's will and died so
that we could be saved. A Christian wife may sometimes have
to submit in unpleasant circumstances so that her husband will
see that Christ is her Lord and come to believe. (Christian
submission never requires us to disobey God, submit to abuse,
or participate in what our Holy Spirit–directed conscience
forbids.) One-sided submission requires tremendous strength.
Ask for the power of the Holy Spirit to help you obey Christ in
your marriage.

**So that, if any of them do not believe the word, they may be
won over without words by the behavior of their wives, when
they see the purity and reverence of your lives.**NIV In the first
century, when a man became a Christian, he usually would bring
his whole family into the church with him (see, for example, the
story of the conversion of the Philippian jailer, Acts 16:29-34).
By contrast, a woman who became a Christian usually came into
the church alone. Under Roman law, the husband and father had
absolute authority over all members of his household, including
his wife. A wife who demanded her rights as a free woman in

Christ could endanger her marriage and her life if her husband
disapproved. Instead, she should live her new faith quietly and
respectfully. Peter reassured Christian women who were married
to unbelievers that they need not preach to their husbands; their
husbands could be *won over without words*. (Paul used the same
word describing the "winning" of unbelievers in 1 Corinthians
9:19-22.)

WITNESS WITHOUT WORDS
In an intimate relationship like marriage, actions often speak
louder than words. Words get preachy, but actions demonstrate
reality. Words create division, but loving action builds trust.
Words lay out propositional truth—the information about
salvation—but actions show the living Christ in the believer's
heart and life.
   Did Peter forbid a spouse to witness? Obviously not. Words
built on trust and love can transform a life. Does Peter down-
play street preaching, testimonies, sermons, and personal
witnessing? Truly not. He was advising married partners how
to treat unbelieving spouses. If your husband is a nonbeliever,
you can strengthen your marriage not by preaching, but by
living, loving, and letting God provide the opportunity for you to
witness.

Under the circumstances, the wives' best approach would be witnessing by their *behavior*. Their attitude should reflect loving service: They should show their husbands the kind of self-giving love
that Christ showed the church. Their lives should reflect both *purity*
and *reverence*. "Purity" refers to behavior that is free from moral
defilement. The wives should be pure for their husbands' sakes, yet
they would have to disobey should their husbands ask them to do
something morally wrong or to participate in pagan practices. "Reverence" is the same word translated as "respect" in 2:18 *(phobos)*,
referring to healthy fear. The wives had no protection from violence
(other than murder) under the law. So these wives should not do anything to incur the displeasure of their husbands. By being exemplary
wives, they would please their husbands. At the very least, the men
would then allow these wives to continue practicing their "strange"
religion. At best, their husbands would join them and become Christians too.

**3:3 Your beauty should not come from outward adornment, such
as braided hair and the wearing of gold jewelry and fine
clothes.**ᴺᴵⱽ Writing directly to these Christian wives *(your)*, Peter
took particular note of their concerns. These women wanted to be
attractive. As is the case today, society's focus was on *outward*

adornment. The word for "adornment" refers to what a woman uses to make herself attractive to others. Although there were no television stars and magazine models setting the standards for beauty, worldly beauty was achieved in the same way—hairstyle, jewelry, and clothes. But Peter contrasted putting beautiful "things" on the outside to make oneself beautiful, versus revealing the natural inner beauty that a Christian woman should have because of Christ (see 3:4).

This passage is teaching that women should not count on their beauty coming from outward adornments, not that women can't braid their hair or wear gold jewelry or nice clothes. (Paul wrote almost the exact words to the women in the Ephesian church; see 1 Timothy 2:9-10.) Christian women should not be obsessed by fashion or overly concerned with their outward appearance. On the other hand, neither should they be so unconcerned that they do not bother to care for themselves. Hygiene, neatness, and grooming are important, but even more important are a person's attitude and inner spirit. Beauty and adornments have their place, but they must be kept in proper perspective. True beauty begins inside.

MAKE YOUR STATEMENT

Should Christians, as an act of obedience, refuse to use deodorant (body odor is natural, after all) or lipstick (lips have a natural tint, you know) or hair spray (let wind do its natural work)? Should Christians make efforts to look plain, as do the Amish, who forbid zippers and other clothing features?

Peter does not get specific, but the Bible everywhere counsels moderation, dignity, and propriety. Always, inner beauty of soul provides the true measure of a person's charm and grace.

So be a "Number 10" in gentleness, generosity, wit, wisdom, and compassion. Don't worry if models in TV ads turn more heads. You turn their hearts!

3:4 Rather, let your adornment be the inner self with the lasting beauty of a gentle and quiet spirit, which is very precious in God's sight.[NRSV] Instead of only adorning themselves on the outside, Christian women should let their *adornment* (the center focus of their beauty) *be the inner self.* In other words, their beauty should come from inside—the inner nature and personality, the attitudes, thoughts, and motivations that are revealed in words and actions. For believers, this inner self has been transformed by the Holy Spirit.

While styles and fashions change, hair becomes gray, jewelry

tarnishes, and clothes wear out, there is a beauty that is *lasting*.
The Greek word for "lasting" is used elsewhere in the New Testament to describe heavenly realities that will remain for eternity.
The only kind of beauty with that quality, Peter wrote, is the
beauty of a gentle and quiet spirit. One's "spirit" here refers to
the disposition or frame of mind. To be
"gentle" means showing humility, consideration of others, not insisting on
one's own rights, not being pushy or
overly assertive (see also Galatians
5:23). To be "quiet" refers to the same

> God's fingers can touch
> nothing but to mold it
> into loveliness.
> *George MacDonald*

attitude as that described by "gentle," also focusing on not causing dissensions with inappropriate words or gossip.

   Not only is such a spirit a blessing to people around, especially
these women's husbands, it is also *very precious in God's sight.*
God is pleased when his followers act with Christ as their example. As Christ suffered wrongly but bore it patiently, so believers
are to be patient in suffering for the faith (2:20). As he was gentle
and quiet (also translated "meek," see Matthew 5:5; 11:29; 21:5),
so believers are to have a gentle and quiet spirit.

LOUD AND CLEAR
A changed life speaks loudly and clearly and is often the most
effective way to influence a family member. Peter instructs
Christian wives to develop inner beauty rather than being
overly concerned about their outward appearance. Their
husbands will be won over by their love rather than by their
looks. This does not mean that Christian women should be
dowdy and frumpy; it is good to be cheerful and attractive.
But their priorities should be virtue and moderation. Live your
Christian faith quietly and consistently in your home, and your
family will see Christ in you.

**3:5-6 It was in this way long ago that the holy women who hoped in
God used to adorn themselves by accepting the authority of
their husbands. Thus Sarah obeyed Abraham and called him
lord.**NRSV *It was in this way* refers back to being adorned with a
gentle and quiet spirit (3:4). Peter explained that *the holy women* of
the past were both holy and beautiful, not because they lived perfect lives and had perfect looks, but because they *hoped in God.*
Another ancient writer understood this: "Charm is deceptive, and
beauty is fleeting; but a woman who fears the Lord is to be praised"
(Proverbs 31:30 NIV). These women trusted in God and knew how

to submit to the authority God had established, *by accepting the authority of their husbands* (as described in 3:1-2 above).

Peter used the plural *women,* referring to many Old Testament holy women, but then he used one woman in particular as an example: Sarah. Sarah was submissive to her husband, Abraham. She *obeyed* and *called him lord.* The verb tenses indicate a continuing pattern of conduct, not just one particular incident. The Bible records a few incidents in which Sarah disobeyed (Genesis 16:2, 6; 18:15) and even doubted and ridiculed Abraham (Genesis 18:12); obviously her acts of disobedience were not to be imitated. Instead, Peter commended her attitude of obedience and submission, hanging his argument on Sarah's use of "lord." Sarah's submission certainly wasn't slavish. She insisted that Hagar and Ishmael (Abraham's other wife and first son) be sent away. Abraham didn't like it, but went along with her request. Apparently God approved of Sarah's request as supported by his answer to Abraham, "Listen to whatever Sarah tells you" (Genesis 21:10, 12).

Why did Peter use Sarah as an example? Because Sarah was considered the mother of God's people (as Abraham was the father, according to God's covenant promises, Genesis 12:1-3). The prophet Isaiah wrote, "Look to Abraham, your father, and to Sarah, who gave you birth. When I called him he was but one, and I blessed him and made him many" (Isaiah 51:2 NIV). Not only was Sarah an example to be followed because of her faithfulness to God and to her husband (she did submit to Abraham to have the child), but also because she was the mother of all believers—under the old covenant, the mother of the Jewish nation; under the new covenant, the mother of all who believe (see Galatians 4:22-26).

You have become her daughters as long as you do what is good and never let fears alarm you.^{NRSV} Peter saw Christians (in this case, Christian women) as true *daughters* of Sarah, and thus true children ("daughters") of God. To be Sarah's "daughter" was to be an heir of God's promises given to her and Abraham. All Jews drew their basic identity from being "children of Abraham." To be a daughter of Sarah also would be held in high regard.

Finally, Peter called upon Christian wives to *do what is good* (as described above) and to *never let fears alarm* them. A Christian woman's faith in God would help her not to be afraid. In context, this could refer to their not fearing the physical harm that might come to them from their husbands, not fearing the result of submitting to their husbands, or not fearing what might happen if they had to disobey their husbands because their husbands asked them to do wrong or evil acts. It could also refer to the theme of persecution throughout this letter, recommending that these women not be afraid of anything that might come upon them or their families. But in this context, their fear and hope in God (3:5) allowed them both to reverence (3:2) and not fear (3:6) their husbands.

LEAVE FEAR BEHIND
Peter counseled family peace, but with a limit. The first priority of a woman married to an unbeliever was always God. Peter knew how tough that faith would be on some women, who at that time had no legal redress against abuse.

Peter's word of hope to women (and to everyone who takes a beating for faith) is trust in God. This does not mean that God expects women to accept physical abuse in marriage. Women who live with men who show a pattern of physical abuse should seek professional help. They should withdraw to a safe place and seek to protect other family members from harm. An abusive person will never be helped or "saved" by appeasement or giving in to the abuse. Breaking the cycle of abuse can only start when the abused person gets help. A battered woman or child needs lots of love to recover their confidence and sense of value before God. They need support to overcome their fear of backlash.

Whatever bully you live with, whatever threat you face or pain you feel for walking with God, know that your prayers are heard. God will bring you through.

3:7 Husbands, in the same way be considerate as you live with your wives, and treat them with respect as the weaker partner.NIV In 3:1-6, Peter taught Christian women to be submissive to their non-Christian husbands. As explained above, the Bible does not require wives to be slaves for their husbands—that is not what the Bible means by "submission." The wife should submit to the husband's authority, but the Christian husband must use his authority with consideration and respect for his wife. He must not be a tyrant, faithless, unloving, or impatient. Likewise, the wife should not be rebellious, subversive, or contradicting.

Just as the wives were to accept authority, so the husbands *(in the same way)* were to be considerate as they lived with their wives. The phrase *be considerate as you live with your wives* is literally translated "living together according to knowledge." That a husband should *be considerate* implies more than just a kind attitude; it goes deeper, implying that his consideration of his wife is based on his knowledge of her needs, desires, gifts, and abilities. A husband who acts on his knowledge of his wife will greatly enrich her life, as well as his own. This is the explicit message of Paul in Ephesians 5:25-27.

Peter explained that a husband must also *respect* his wife *as the weaker partner.* The word for "weaker" is *asthenestero*; in this context, it refers to physical weakness, not to moral, spiritual, or intellectual inferiority. Peter used the term not to diminish women, but to build a case for respecting them. The men were not to bully their wives physically or sexually. Women had less authority in the marriage, so the husbands were encouraged to use their authority with respect for their wives. Their authority did not excuse abuse of power. The husband should not thunder and thump to get his way! While the woman may be "weaker," she is also a "partner," implying a side-by-side relationship of working together. A man who respects his wife will protect, honor, and help her. He will stay with her. He will respect her opinions, listen to her advice, be considerate of her needs, and relate to her both privately and publicly with love, courtesy, insight, and tact.

> A man said, "I don't understand my wife. She has everything she could want—a dishwasher, a new dryer, a nice house. I've been faithful and I don't drink. But she's miserable. I can't figure out why." His love-starved wife would have traded everything for a single expression of genuine tenderness from her unromantic husband. Appliances do not build self-esteem; being somebody's sweetheart most certainly does. *James Dobson*

Since they too are also heirs of the gracious gift of life—so that nothing may hinder your prayers.[NRSV] Some women have chafed under the biblical assertion that they are "weaker" and that they are to submit to their husbands. But these women need to remember that they are equal with men in God's eyes. Even though God gave husbands authority in the marriage and family, wives are equal to their husbands in spiritual privileges and eternal relationships. Both men and women who are believers are *heirs of the gracious gift of life*—eternal life. The actual word means "joint heirs" and signals equality. Paul had written to the Galatians, "There is no longer Jew or Greek, there is no longer slave or free, there is no longer male and female; for all of you are one in Christ Jesus" (Galatians 3:28 NRSV). (See also 1 Corinthians 11:2-12; Ephesians 5:22-33; Colossians 3:18-19.)

Peter added the admonition to husbands that if they were not considerate and respectful to their wives, their prayers would be hindered. The word *your* refers to the husbands' prayers, for

Peter was addressing husbands specifically in this verse. A living relationship with God depends on right relationships with others. Jesus said that if you have a problem with a fellow believer, you must make it right with that person before coming to worship (Matthew 5:23-24). This principle carries over into family relationships. If men use their position to mistreat their wives, their relationship with God will suffer. A man should not expect to have a vital ministry in life or prayer if he is mistreating his wife in any way.

BREAK THE MOLD
In Peter's day throughout Greco-Roman culture, men regarded women as confused, ignorant, and uneducable. Peter urged that Christians break the mold.

What stereotypes affect your relationships? Despite "political correctness," what prejudices color your regard for a race or gender?

The Bible urges that we see everyone as God does, abandoning stereotypes and showing the world a different way of treating each other. Marriages, friendships, and neighborly relations all take a new turn in light of God's Good News.

SUFFERING FOR DOING GOOD / 3:8-22

Peter knew that the believers would soon face persecution. Peter reminded these believers that they would need unity, and love and support from one another. Peter also assured the believers that no matter what sufferings they might have to face, God would vindicate them and punish their enemies. Rather than fear our enemies, we are to quietly trust in God as the Lord of all. We must believe that Christ, not our enemies, is truly in control of all events. When Christ rules our thoughts and emotions, we cannot be shaken by anything our enemies may do.

3:8 Finally, all of you, live in harmony with one another; be sympathetic, love as brothers, be compassionate and humble.[NIV] In saying *finally,* Peter was obviously not concluding the epistle; rather, he was summing up a series of exhortations concerning submission (which began in 2:18). After speaking to slaves (2:18-25), wives (3:1-6), and husbands (3:7), Peter next turned back to *all of you,* referring to his audience of all believers (1:1-2; 2:11).

Peter listed five building blocks for unity as Christians lived in their pagan culture. These blocks will build relationships among any group of believers.

1. *Live in harmony,* also translated "have unity of spirit," refers to working together for the common goal of spreading the gospel, having common attitudes and ideas. While there were many types of Christians from many types of backgrounds in Peter's audience, Peter knew that harmony would be possible. Just as different notes form chords to make beautiful harmonies, so different people can live and work together for God. (See also Romans 12:16; 15:5; Philippians 1:27; 2:2.)

2. *Be sympathetic* means being willing to share in others' needs and being responsive to their feelings, having sensitivity and compassion toward others. The believers to whom Peter wrote, although scattered across the world and unknown personally to one another, lived and worked in "sympathy"; that is, they understood and appreciated one another because of their mutual relationship with Jesus Christ. (See also Romans 12:15; 1 Corinthians 12:26; Hebrews 4:15.)

> When iron is rubbed against a magnet it becomes magnetic. Just so, love is caught, not taught. One heart burning with love sets another on fire. The church was built on love; it proves what love can do. *Frank C. Laubach*

3. *Love as brothers* means loving fellow Christians (brothers and sisters in Christ). The Greek word is *philadelphos,* referring not only to family love, but to the special love that should draw all Christians together. (See also 1 Thessalonians 4:9-10.)

4. *Be compassionate,* like "sympathy" (above), means to be conscious of others' needs but includes a drive to alleviate the need in some way. The Greek word *eusplagchnos* comes from *splagchna,* literally the internal organs, and refers to one's deepest feelings. Believers ought to be deeply touched and moved by the hurts, pain, needs, and joys of fellow believers and then act to help them. They should be affection-ate and sensitive, quick to give emotional support (Matthew 11:29).

5. *Humble* means having an honest estimate of oneself before God. Humility does not negate one's own worth or abilities, nor does it inflate them. Instead, a humble Christian can honestly view his or her characteristics and abilities with thankfulness to God. Humble people can encourage one

another and rejoice in each other's successes. (See Matthew
11:29; Ephesians 4:2; Philippians 2:3-8.)

Peter developed the qualities of compassion and humility the
hard way. In his early days with Christ, these attitudes did not
come naturally to his impulsive, strong-willed personality (see
Mark 8:31-33; John 13:6-9 for examples of Peter's blustering).
But the Holy Spirit changed Peter, molding his strong personality
to God's use and teaching him compassion and humility.

LIVING EVIDENCE
Where is God? How can we know God is real? Who says the
Bible is any better than other holy books?
To answer these questions, God sent his Son, Jesus Christ,
as living evidence. God also chose Peter and others to show
what a difference true faith makes in the real world. So here the
once rash, belligerent, domineering, and arrogant Peter bears
witness to a life of harmony, compassion, love, and humility.
What a difference God makes.
You, too, are God's witness to skeptical people. Let your life
be evidence of God's truth. Let your pride become humility and
your insensitivity give way to genuine affection for others.

**3:9 Do not repay evil with evil or insult with insult, but with bless-
ing, because to this you were called so that you may inherit a
blessing.**^{NIV} After describing how Christians should act toward
one another, Peter described how they should act toward those in
the pagan culture—a culture that would soon (if it hadn't already)
become very hostile toward them. While it would be most natural
to *repay evil with evil* and to return *insult with insult,* Jesus had
taught and exemplified otherwise: "But I say to you, Do not resist
an evildoer. But if anyone strikes you on the right cheek, turn the
other also. . . . Pray for those who persecute you" (Matthew 5:39,
44 NRSV). The word "insult" can also be translated "revile" or
"abuse" and refers to derisive speech. When Jesus "was abused,
he did not return abuse" (2:23), so believers should follow his
example, not repaying abuse for abuse or insult for insult. Peter
had already encouraged his readers to follow Christ's example:
"For to this you have been called, because Christ also suffered
for you, leaving you an example, so that you should follow in his
steps" (2:21 NRSV). Believers were not to retaliate, but were to do
good, even to those who harmed them.

The words are similar to Paul's recommendations for how
believers should act when persecuted for their faith (all verses
quoted from NIV):

- "Bless those who persecute you; bless and do not curse" (Romans 12:14).

- "Do not repay anyone evil for evil. Be careful to do what is right in the eyes of everybody" (Romans 12:17).

- "When we are cursed, we bless; when we are persecuted, we endure it" (1 Corinthians 4:12).

- "Make sure that nobody pays back wrong for wrong, but always try to be kind to each other and to everyone else" (1 Thessalonians 5:15).

Instead, evil and abuse ought to be repaid *with blessing*. How would these believers "bless" their enemies? Believers' speech should always be characterized by blessings, never curses, but "blessing" refers to more than words of kindness. The spiritual sense of the word refers to believers offering the gospel to those who persecute them.

The phrase *because to this you were called* has puzzled scholars. Some suggest that Peter was referring to his previous words about believers being called to nonretaliation, to repaying their persecutors with gracious words instead of cursing. Thus Peter was saying that believers should bless their persecutors because they were called to do so by Christ. Then it is the persecutors who inherit a blessing. Other scholars, however, explain that "to this you were called" refers forward to "inherit a blessing." They believe Peter was saying that believers should bless their persecutors because the believers have been called to inherit a blessing. They bless because God blessed them. Both options are appropriate in this context.

Finally, *so that you may inherit a blessing* has also caused discussion. What does "blessing" mean? Was Peter referring to eternal life, the final and most important "blessing" of all, or was he referring to blessings in this life?

Some commentators favor the first option, using the word "inherit" to refer to believers' heavenly inheritance: "an inheritance that can never perish, spoil or fade—kept in heaven for you" (1:4 NIV). The word translated "inherit" *(kleronomeo)* can be used to describe the inheritance that Christians look forward to—eternal life with God.

But the word *kleronomeo* can also mean to obtain or inherit something in this life (see Hebrews 12:17). Believers already know that they have the inheritance of eternal life. If they will live peacefully, however, as Peter recommended, their right actions will produce blessings in this life. Scholars who support

this view point to the following quotation of part of a psalm (see
3:10) that focuses on God's blessings for those who live righteously. Yet it must be understood that these blessings do not
assume freedom from persecution. Believers still may be persecuted, but they can depend on God's blessings, whether physical
or spiritual.

GETTING BACK
Peter says not to retaliate, but a child's first impulse is to hit
back, especially when the aggressor is a sibling. Adults do their
hitting back in more sophisticated ways, by shunning or
gossiping or making backroom deals. But retaliation is not the
Bible's way.
 Do you have a complaint? Have you been hurt? Has a com-
mittee colleague been bad-mouthing your work? Notice the
Bible's way to respond: Show cordial respect; give the opponent
the benefit of the doubt; then figure how to boost your antag-
onist's social stock by being gracious. It's such a radically
positive way of getting back that everyone will assume that you
have an ulterior motive. And that gives you the opportunity to
witness to the motive God has given you!

**3:10 For "Those who desire life and desire to see good days, let
them keep their tongues from evil and their lips from speaking
deceit."**NRSV Verses 10-12 are a quotation of Psalm 34:12-16. (Peter
also quoted from this Psalm in 2:3.) The theme of Psalm 34 is that
God hears and helps those who are afflicted or in trouble—a perfect psalm considering the theme of this letter. Peter quoted these
verses as his "proof text" for his words in 3:8-9, thus he began
verse 10 with the word *for.*

 The phrase *those who desire life and desire to see good days*
may refer to people who trust God and who are (or want to be)
enjoying their earthly lives no matter what the outward circumstances. These people have found contentment in God and can
live "good days" no matter how bad their situations might
become. The words "life" and "good days" also can refer to eternal life (depending on how 3:8-9 are interpreted). In any case, the
answer to such contentment and enjoyment is found in living
righteously, as suggested by both the psalmist and the apostle.

 In order to do so, watch what you say. People who desire life
and good days *keep their tongues from evil and their lips from
speaking deceit.* As reported by James, people who don't keep
their tongues under control can cause all kinds of problems (see
James 3:3-12). The word "evil" could refer to any type of speech
that is displeasing to God; "deceit" means to deliberately trick or

mislead by lying. Thus Peter was telling the believers not to
return insult for insult (3:9), and to rid themselves of malice,
deceit, and slander (2:1).

3:11 "Let them turn away from evil and do good."^{NRSV} People's
words are connected to their actions. Those who "keep their
tongues from evil and their lips from speaking deceit" (3:10
NRSV) have turned *away from evil.* Their God-honoring speech is
then accompanied by action—they then can *do good.* Thus Peter
called upon the believers to be sympathetic, compassionate, and
humble (3:8) and to return good for evil (repay evil and insults
with blessing, 3:9). Peter emphasized good works in 2:12, 14-15,
20; 3:1. This verse sums up that emphasis. He repeats it in 3:13.

"Let them seek peace and pursue it."^{NRSV} Peace means more than
simply the absence of conflict, and peacemaking requires an active,
not a passive, role. Effective peacemakers must *seek peace and pursue it.* They build good relationships, knowing that peace is a by-
product of commitment. They anticipate problems and deal with
them before they occur. When conflicts arise, peacemakers bring
them into the open and deal with them before they grow unmanage-
able. To "desire life and desire to see good days" (3:10), one must
actively seek peace. This also pleases God, for Jesus said, "Blessed
are the peacemakers, for they shall be called sons of God" (Matthew 5:9 NKJV). Thus Peter was calling upon the believers to live in
harmony and to love one another (3:8), as well as to accept and submit to authority (2:13-20; 3:1-7).

KICK BACK
Do we always respond peacefully? In this fallen world, it is
deemed acceptable by some to tear people down verbally
or to get back at them if they have hurt us. Peter, remembering
Jesus' teaching to turn the other cheek (Matthew 5:39),
encouraged his readers to respond to wrongs by praying for
the offenders. God considers revenge to be unacceptable
behavior, as is insulting a person, no matter how indirectly
it is done. Rise above retaliating against those who hurt you.
Instead of reacting angrily to these people, pray for them.

**3:12 "For the eyes of the Lord are on the righteous, and his ears
are open to their prayer."**^{NRSV} Those who do not retaliate, as
described in 3:10-11, can rely on God's protection. The righteous ones are God's people. *The eyes of the Lord are on the
righteous* means that God not only sees them but also that he
watches over them for their good. God sees all their difficulties

and persecutions. Nothing happens to God's people that he has
not allowed for some purpose. Whatever happens, God's people
know that his promises of blessing—whether in this life or in
the life to come—are certain.

Not only are the Lord's eyes open and
watching, but his *ears are open to their
prayer.* He listens when his people call to
him. He knows all their needs. He hears
their prayers in suffering. These words
would have been a great comfort to these
suffering Christians. Not only were they
seen, heard, and ultimately protected, but
those who hurt them would be judged.
**"But the face of the Lord is against
those who do evil."**NRSV This warning
implies a drastic threat of imminent judgment, not just God's disapproval. Leviticus 17:10; Psalm 34:16; and Ezekiel 14:8
refer to the most severe judgment God
could have on humanity. Therefore, believers are not to retaliate; instead, they must
trust that God will avenge the wrongs his
people have suffered.

In these verses, the scattered and persecuted Christians learned that those
who trust God and live righteously have
no reason to fear. God will reward his
followers with blessings (both in this life
and in the life to come) and will punish
those who have hurt them.

> The storm was raging.
> The sea was beating
> against the rocks in
> huge, dashing waves.
> The lightning was
> flashing, the thunder
> was roaring, the wind
> was blowing; but the
> little bird was sound
> asleep in the crevice of
> the rock, its head tucked
> serenely under its wing.
> That is peace: to be able
> to sleep in the storm!
> In Christ we are relaxed
> and at peace in the midst
> of the confusions, bewil-
> derments and perplex-
> ities of this life. The
> storm rages, but our
> hearts are at rest. We
> have found peace—at
> last! *Billy Graham*

**3:13 Now who will harm you if you are eager to do what is
good?**NRSV Up to this point in the letter, the theme of the persecution facing these young churches has been in the background.
At this point, however, it becomes a prominent theme in this
letter. After describing the attitudes and actions that should
characterize God's people (3:8-12), Peter began to explain how
the believers should live in an evil world in the face of persecution. The word for *harm (kakoun)* plays off of the word
"evil" *(kaka)* in 3:12. This is a rhetorical question—common
sense tells people that if they do good, they will be protected
from punishment or harm. It is usually much wiser for believers to do what is good and to follow the authorities and laws
so that they won't be persecuted unnecessarily. Peter was not

indicating that if the believers behaved well, they would escape persecution and ill treatment. He had already stated that they might do good and still suffer ill treatment (2:20). The next verse repeats the possibility.

IN HARM'S WAY
The answer to Peter's question, "Who will harm you if you are eager to do what is good?" is "Only a fool," of which there are many in the world, then and now. That's why Peter offered no guarantees about the pain any given day might bring. Life is not foolproof.

Only one guarantee is bona fide and tamperproof: the Lord Jesus Christ walking with us through the trouble. No matter how jagged your day, God promises peace, comfort, and joy.

Who can harm you for doing good? Today, the heartless and cruel. But tomorrow is all yours, by God's promise. "If God is for us, who can be against us?" (Romans 8:31 NIV). Trust in him to protect you.

3:14 But even if you do suffer for doing what is right, you are blessed.^{NRSV} Usually people were safe if they lived lawfully and carefully, but that was not always the case. Persecution comes for a variety of reasons. Christians who were living more morally and lawfully than many of their fellow citizens in the Roman Empire still might suffer. The phrase *even if you do suffer* contains a verb form used to speak of an event that was considered highly

> I believe that in the end the truth will conquer.
> *John Wycliffe*

unlikely. The atmosphere was charged with suspicion and hostility toward Christians. Thus, even though Peter thought that the possibility of persecution was remote, he still considered it possible and wanted to tell the believers how they should react. In 4:12-15, he would warn them more directly. They might have to suffer even though they were *doing what is right.* This phrase is also translated "for righteousness' sake." The Greek word *dikaiosune* is used in 2:24 telling believers to "live for righteousness" (NIV). In Romans 12:14-21, Paul gives guidelines for Christians living in a fallen world. When believers absorb the full cost and hurt of being mistreated by unbelievers, they are suffering for doing what is right.

Even though it may not seem like it from a worldly point of view, these believers who suffered for doing what was right, who suffered for righteousness' sake, were *blessed,* meaning "highly privileged," but not necessarily delighted. If the believers were living righteously and continued to be persecuted, no one would be able to harm them spiritually or change God's promises to them. Jesus had said, "Blessed are those who are persecuted for righteousness' sake, for theirs is the kingdom of heaven" (Matthew 5:10 NKJV).

"And do not be afraid of their threats, nor be troubled."NKJV Alluding to Isaiah 8:12-13, Peter counseled the believers to not be afraid of persecution. Evil people's threats were empty because they could not harm the eternal souls of God's people. The Greek word for *troubled* means shaken up or disturbed and refers to emotional turmoil (note its use in Matthew 2:3; 14:26, for example). Rather than fear their enemies, the Christians were to quietly trust in Christ (3:15) as the Lord of all, believing that he was truly in control of all events. When the Lord ruled their thoughts and emotions, they could not be shaken by anything their enemies might do. God alone is to be feared. When people respect and honor him, they have nothing else to fear. Peter remembered Jesus' words, "Do not be afraid of those who kill the body but cannot kill the soul. Rather, be afraid of the One who can destroy both soul and body in hell" (Matthew 10:28 NIV).

BOLDNESS
Peter gave us the antidote for dealing with fear—"in your hearts set apart Christ as Lord." Peter had seen the glory of Christ on the Mount of Transfiguration, and he had seen the glory of the resurrected Lord. He knew Christ had the full glory of God. Once we know and love Christ, opposition and persecution hold no terror for us. But this high regard of Christ in our heart includes—but requires more than—mental assent to his deity. We must love him with all our heart's devotion. To do this we must

- regard his prior claim to all we possess or desire
- place our future totally in his hands for safekeeping
- regard his teaching as superior to all earthly wisdom
- let obedience to him dictate our conduct
- set aside our personal agenda when asked to do his service

Praise Christ as the Lord of all, and your fear of what people can do will melt away.

3:15 But in your hearts set apart Christ as Lord.NIV Instead of being afraid of people, believers are to focus on Christ himself. This is also translated "reverence Christ as Lord" or "sanctify the Lord Christ in your hearts." The "heart" was considered a place of deep emotions—that's where fear would dwell. But Peter wanted these

believers to replace fear with faith and reverence. By acknowledging Christ as Lord and Savior, they would recognize his holiness and be able to rest in him. There would be no room in their
hearts for fear. This alludes to words from the prophet Isaiah: "But
the Lord of hosts, him you shall regard as holy; let him be your
fear, and let him be your dread" (Isaiah 8:13 NRSV). When believers have *set apart Christ as Lord,* regarding him as holy and rever-
encing him in their hearts, they know that he is in control of events,
that he is the reigning king, and that all powers and authorities ultimately must answer to him.

**Always be prepared to give an answer to everyone who asks
you to give the reason for the hope that you have. But do this
with gentleness and respect.**[NIV] When believers have Christ set
apart in their hearts, the courage he
gives them ought to make them *always*
ready to testify about him. Peter called
upon the believers not to fear, but he
didn't stop there. Their faith should be
active, ready to speak out—*prepared to
give an answer to everyone who asks.*
While Peter may have been thinking

> Only he who can say,
> "The Lord is the strength
> of my life" can go on
> to say, "Of whom shall
> I be afraid?"
> *Alexander MacLaren*

about believers speaking in a court, he seems also to have had in
mind the everyday informal inquiries that might be directed at
the believers—from either hostile or friendly neighbors. The
words "an answer" can also be translated "a defense" and usually
refer to responding to an accusation (see, for example, Acts 22:1;
25:16; 1 Corinthians 9:3; Philippians 1:7, 16). Thus, these may
refer to formal charges or informal accusations. Under any circumstances, the believers were to be ready to testify, explaining
the reason for the hope that they had.

The believers would be persecuted for their faith alone because
unbelievers would have no charges to bring against them except to
question them on their "hope." Unbelievers can see that Christians
have something different; only "hope" gives us strength and joy in
hardships and persecutions. Unbelievers will ask about it; believers
must be ready to tell them. Christians need not worry about what
they should say if accused, for they could prepare their defense
ahead of time! Even in a hostile situation, believers can witness for
Christ; their words might cause an accuser to come to faith. Paul certainly took advantage of every situation, no matter how hostile (read
Acts 22:1-21; 24:10-24; 26:1-23). All Christians must be ready and
able to give a reasonable defense of their faith. They need not be
apologists or theologians, but every Christian ought to be able to
clearly explain his or her own reasons for being a Christian. Some

Christians believe that faith is a personal matter that should be kept
to oneself. It is true that we shouldn't be boisterous or obnoxious in
sharing our faith, but we should always be prepared to give an
answer, gently and respectfully, when asked about our belief, our
lifestyle, or our Christian perspective.

Christians' words and manner of speaking
to an accusation should align with their
lifestyle. Peter had already said they
should be sympathetic, tender, loving, and
humble (3:8); he had explained that they
were not to return insult for insult (3:9).

> He who can tell men
> what God has done for
> his soul is the likeliest to
> bring their souls to God.
> *Robert Leighton*

Thus, if the believers were called upon to testify for their faith, they
must do so *with gentleness and respect.* Believers were not to be
arrogant, rude, or overly aggressive. They were to trust God for the
outcome of any hostile situation, and they were to trust the Holy
Spirit to work quietly in the hearts of their listeners. Thus, their manner of speaking ought to reflect an attitude of meekness and gentleness (neither of which implies weakness), remembering their
responsibility to always show respect (also translated "reverence")
for God.

GET READY
Here's how ordinary people can be ready to witness (make a
defense for their hope) without needing to become theological
scholars:

- Pray, read the Bible, and review God's promises every day.
  Then you'll be ready to explain why you're hopeful.
- Make praising Christ your daily practice. If you focus on his
  power and glory, you will be fortified and courageous to
  speak to others.
- Be as natural in witnessing as you are in conversation. Talk
  like you, not imitating anyone else. Find the clues in your life
  that help explain God's Good News to others. If you are a
  plumber, talk about God's love like running water. If you are
  a doctor, portray God's love as a healing force.
- Respond with care. Trust God to melt stony hearts. "A gentle
  answer turns away wrath, but a harsh word stirs up anger"
  (Proverbs 15:1 NIV).
- Listen to your audience. Where are their heads and hearts?
  What burdens them? Listen long and hard. Frame your witness
  in the words and at the level your audience will understand.

3:16 Keeping a clear conscience.[NIV] As believers' outward actions
should be above reproach, so should their inner life. A *clear
conscience* refers to one's personal integrity before God alone,

as he or she lives consistently with their knowledge of God. Unbelievers also have consciences that ought to guard their morality and actions (Romans 2:14-15), but a Christian's conscience has been transformed by God. The Holy Spirit helps each believer know and understand God's will, and sensitizes his or her conscience to God's desires. All believers should keep clear consciences.

How can believers follow Peter's advice to keep a clear conscience? We can treasure our faith in Christ more than anything else and do what we know is right. We can avoid willful disobedience. If we do disobey, we should stay in constant communication with God, repenting and asking forgiveness. Each time we deliberately ignore our conscience, we harden our heart. Over a period of time our capacity to tell right from wrong will diminish. As we walk with God, he will speak to us through our conscience, letting us know the difference between right and wrong. By being sure to act on those inner tugs so that we do what is right, our conscience will remain clear. Paul wrote (all verses quoted from NRSV):

- "Brothers, up to this day I have lived my life with a clear conscience before God" (Acts 23:1).

- "Therefore I do my best always to have a clear conscience toward God and all people" (Acts 24:16).

- "I am speaking the truth in Christ—I am not lying; my conscience confirms it by the Holy Spirit" (Romans 9:1).

- "Indeed, this is our boast, the testimony of our conscience: we have behaved in the world with frankness and godly sincerity, not by earthly wisdom but by the grace of God—and all the more toward you" (2 Corinthians 1:12).

- "I am giving you these instructions, Timothy, . . . so that by following them you may fight the good fight, having faith and a good conscience. By rejecting conscience, certain persons have suffered shipwreck in the faith" (1 Timothy 1:18-19).

- "I am grateful to God—whom I worship with a clear conscience" (2 Timothy 1:3).

We should remember that some Christians' consciences are so sensitive that they feel they can do nothing right. We should refer them to Hebrews 9:14: "How much more, then, will the blood of Christ, who through the eternal Spirit offered himself unblemished to God, cleanse our consciences from acts that lead to

death, so that we may serve the living God!" (NIV). This will
show them that Christ's death removes the guilt they bear. They
can have God's help to retrain their consciences based on the freedom they have in Christ instead of on self-condemnation.

SELF-CONSCIOUS SAINTS
What happens when a Christian becomes so worried over
"what other people think" that a clear conscience becomes
confused with pride of perfection? It's a sorry sight. Since
perfection is impossible, such people chase windmills fero-
ciously and religiously. To these people Jesus says, "My yoke is
easy and my burden is light" (Matthew 11:30). Keeping a clear
conscience is the delight of walking with God without hidden
sin. Pride of perfection is the burden of imagining God with a
clipboard putting ticks next to your name. If you must suppose
that God carries a clipboard, be assured that Jesus has erased
all your ticks and always will. In gratitude, walk with him
honestly and gladly.

**So that those who speak maliciously against your good behav-
ior in Christ may be ashamed of their slander.**[NIV] Why is there
all this concern about right living and clear consciences? Because
the believers lived in a hostile world. Just by being Christians,
they could find themselves facing persecution; they ought not
supply their enemies with ammunition by also breaking laws or
acting and speaking in an evil way. If the Christians' lives were
above reproach, unbelievers would end up *ashamed of their slander* when they *speak maliciously against* them. They would realize that they had done nothing more than slander *good behavior*
(also translated "conduct," see 1:15), an action that should make
anyone ashamed. The word "slander" means to speak evil of
another in order to destroy his or her good reputation.

That the believers should have good behavior *in Christ* refers
to their relationship with their Lord and Savior. The only way to
have a completely clear conscience and to live a life that is above
reproach is to trust Christ and be transformed by the Holy Spirit.

This verse is much like 2:12, where Peter urged believers to act
honorably before unbelievers. In 2:12, Peter wrote that if the unbelievers see the "honorable deeds" of the believers, they might end up
glorifying God. In this verse, however, the reaction of the accusing
unbelievers is quite different. Instead of glorifying God when they
see the good behavior of believers, they persist in their slander.
Thus, these evil people will be ashamed (or "put to shame"), refer-

ring to disgrace before God. They will be defeated, but will refuse to admit it; they will be wrong, but will refuse to turn to God.

ABOVE CRITICISM
You may not be able to keep people from slandering you, but you can at least stop supplying them with ammunition. As long as you do what is right, their accusations will be empty and will only embarrass them. Helping your neighbors and contributing your service to the community will silence the detractors and keep your conduct above criticism.

3:17 It is better, if it is God's will, to suffer for doing good than for doing evil.NIV Peter referred to the advice he had given servants in 2:19-20, suggesting that if Christians were to suffer, it should never be for wrongdoing. Here he expanded the teaching to all believers: If they had to suffer at all, they should suffer only for *doing good,* not for *doing evil.*

Why would it be *better* to suffer for doing good than for doing evil? Peter gave the answer in the next verse. Because Christ suffered unjustly so that people might be saved, so believers ought to patiently endure unjust suffering because such an attitude is a powerful witness that could lead unbelievers to Christ. Those who deservedly suffer for wrongdoing can hardly witness to unbelievers. Peter wanted his readers to know that no matter what happened to them, they should keep their integrity, their faith, and their clear consciences. In the end, God would bring them to glory and punish their enemies.

3:18 For Christ died for sins once for all, the righteous for the unrighteous, to bring you to God.NIV The results of Christ's innocent suffering confirm Peter's point in 3:13-17 that unjustly persecuted believers can consider themselves blessed. Christ suffered, died, and although he seemed to have been defeated, he rose again to great glory. The believers could be confident and trust God for the outcome of their suffering. The word *for* at the beginning of a verse sometimes indicates that the writer was going to quote from a well-known hymn or liturgy.

Some Greek manuscripts say that Christ "suffered" for sins (using the word *pascho*), which makes the connection between this verse and 3:17 even more obvious; other manuscripts use *apothnesko* (died), as here. In any case, Christ's suffering resulted in his death *for sins.* Christ paid the penalty for the sins of every person. Jesus Christ, God's Son, *the righteous* one ("righteous" is singular), died for the sins of *unrighteous* people ("unrighteous" is plural). Peter had previously quoted from Isaiah 53:9, that Christ "committed no sin, and no deceit was found in his mouth" (2:22 NIV). Only because Christ was perfect and righteous could he be an acceptable sacrifice for our sins. Only by paying the penalty that sin deserved could Christ *bring* sinners *to God.* Only by having our penalty paid can we sinners approach the holy God. Only by Christ's sacrifice can unholy people have a relationship with the holy God. Presently believers have spiritual access into God's very presence; in the future, we will actually dwell in God's presence.

> The holy walk, the devoted life of our Lord Jesus Christ could not avail to put away sin. It was life poured out in death that saved. Apart from his death, his life could only bring out in bold relief our exceeding sinfulness. But his blood shed for us was life given up, poured out in death that we might live eternally. *H. A. Ironside*

Christ's death was *once for all.* His sacrifice was sufficient. No one else will have to die for people's sins; Christ will not have to die again. The words "for all" do not refer to people, but rather are a translation of the Greek word *hapax* (once) and thus mean that Christ died "once for all time."

He was put to death in the flesh, but made alive in the spirit.NRSV But Christ's death for sins was not the end of the story. While he had been *put to death in the flesh,* he was afterward *made alive in the spirit.* Scholars have suggested various interpretations for these words. For example, the NIV translates the last phrase as "made alive by the Spirit." This phrase translates the Greek word *pneumati,* a word that could refer to the Holy Spirit or to Christ's divine spirit, in contrast to his human flesh (or "body" as in NIV). Not everyone agrees as to whether or not "spirit" should be capitalized, referring to the Holy Spirit. Part of the answer depends on whether the Greek preposition *en* should be understood as "in" or "by."

To follow the NIV rendering of this verse, Christ's body died, but he was brought back to life by the Holy Spirit. Some scholars suggest, however, that the sentence should be grammatically parallel. Thus it would not read, "in the body . . . by the Spirit," but instead would read, as above, "in the flesh . . . in the spirit." These scholars look to similar references in other New Testament books to prove their points. However, the problem still remains because the Greek word *pneuma* can be translated "spirit" or "Spirit" (referring to the Holy Spirit).

Some scholars explain the contrast to death in the flesh and life in the Spirit this way: Christ died to his former mode of life ("flesh") but lived on in another mode. His spirit did not die and have to be brought to life again; rather, although he had lived and died fully as a human, he began to live a spiritual "resurrection" life. This verse, then, speaks of two modes of existence: first, life in the flesh ended by death on the cross; second, a resurrected state of being, called "in spirit." But this view should be rejected because it separates Christ's human and divine nature.

Other scholars correctly emphasize that Jesus Christ was both human and divine throughout his life (see Luke 3:31; 2 Timothy 2:8). Maintaining a clear emphasis on both Christ's human nature and his divine nature is important for a complete understanding of the gospel. In Christ's humanity, we see his identification with us and his excellent moral example. In Christ's divinity, we have one capable to take our place, to receive the punishment for sin that is due us. Christ's divinity and humanity cannot be separated into modes. This last view maintains that Christ's "flesh" and his "spirit" are not different parts of Christ or different "times" of his existence; rather, they regard Christ from different perspectives or spheres. This is the view we will take. Christ's "flesh" died, yet his flesh was made alive again in a glorified state. His being made alive "in the spirit" refers to the paradox that, although he died as a man, his eternal spirit and glorified body were restored to life by God's power. He came back to life not as a spirit without a body. He had a body, but one that was not hindered by normal human limitations.

Christ now lives in the spiritual realm—the realm of permanence and eternity. Christ lives "in the spirit" because of his death and resurrection. In that state, he brings us to God. He opens the way and ushers us into God's presence.

3:19-20 **In which also he went and made a proclamation to the spirits in prison.**NRSV The words *in which also* form a break in thought here and refer back to "in the spirit" in the previous verse. The meaning of making *a proclamation to the spirits in prison* is not completely clear, mainly because the word translated "spirits" *(pneumata)* can be used to refer to human spirits, angels, or demons (the singular *pneuma* is also used to refer to God's Holy Spirit). The passage further indicates that these "spirits in prison" are those **who disobeyed long ago when God waited patiently in the days of Noah while the ark was being built. In it only a few people, eight in all, were saved through water.**NIV This passage has been tackled by many scholars over the years and given a variety of interpretations. Three main questions arise: (1) Who were the "spirits" to whom Christ made his proclamation? (2) When did Christ make this proclamation? (3) What was the content of this proclamation? Following are the main interpretations of Peter's words:

(1) Some explain that between Christ's crucifixion and resurrection, he went to the realm of the dead, to hell or hades. There he preached to "the spirits in prison"—meaning either all the people who lived before him who had died and gone to hell, or the fallen angels who had sinned by marrying human women before the Flood (a view highly dependent on apocryphal literature). The content of Christ's proclamation may have been to offer the sinful people a second chance at salvation (this is most unlikely because nowhere in Scripture does God offer a "second chance"), or to tell the sinful people and/or fallen angels that their condemnation was final and eternal. Still others say that Christ was preaching to all those who had repented before they died in the Flood. They had been "in prison" awaiting their release by Christ into heaven. They say that Christ, between his death and resurrection, announced salvation to God's faithful followers who had been waiting for their salvation during the whole Old Testament era.

(2) During Noah's building of the ark (120 years), Christ's "spirit" was in Noah preaching to all the unbelieving people. First Peter 1:11 refers to the "Spirit of Christ" residing in the Old Testament prophets, and 2 Peter 2:5 describes Noah as "a herald of righteousness" (NRSV). This view takes Christ's reference to Noah literally and holds that the "spirits" were humans (rather than angels or demons). Christ spoke through Noah to the people for 120 years as Noah was building the ark (Genesis 6:3). During that time, God was waiting patiently for any to repent of their sins. But none did. These unbelievers on earth were the "spirits in prison" who were imprisoned by their sin, or they were the souls of the evil human race of that day that are now "in prison," hades (they died long ago in the Flood), awaiting God's final judgment at the end of the age. Those who consider this to be the correct meaning of Peter's words consider that Noah and his family were a righteous minority among a huge majority of evil people. Just as Noah faced unjust persecution, so Peter's readers were also facing unjust persecution. Just as Noah had no converts, they might not either. Just as Noah knew that judgment would come soon, so Peter's readers knew that God would soon judge the world. Ultimately, as Noah and his family were saved from the floodwaters, so those who believe will be saved from eternal death.

(3) Between Christ's death and resurrection, or after Christ's ascension, he preached the triumph of his resurrection to the fallen angels. The verb "made a proclamation" most likely means "proclaiming" or "heralding," and not preaching the gospel (as it is used in 4:6). It is likely that Christ was simply making the announcement of his finished work on the cross and, by so doing, declaring his victory. (See Colossians 2:15, where Paul discusses disarming and making public display

of demonic forces.) The "prison" was an abyss near heaven, a kind of "storage place" for the evil angels. His declaration confirmed the testimonies of Enoch and Noah. By doing this, it confirmed the condemnation of those who had refused to believe, while assuring the salvation of Noah and believers. The spirits are fallen angels typified by those who instigated gross immorality in the days of Noah—such are the "sons of God" spoken of in Genesis 6:2. Many scholars favor this view because 2 Peter 2:4-5 and Jude 6 link "the angels that sinned" with the judgment of the Flood by God in the days of Noah. According to these verses in 2 Peter, these angels of God were cast into hell, literally Tartarus, a place of confinement prior to their judgment. Tartarus, therefore, is the prison mentioned here. Sometime after Christ was "made alive in the spirit" he made a proclamation to these fallen angels. (See discussion of Tartarus in 2 Peter 2:4.)

Therefore, to answer the three key questions noted above: the fallen angels were the spirits; the time of the proclamation is not known for certain, but either it was between Jesus' death and resurrection or at the time of his ascension; the content of Christ's message was to proclaim his victory to the fallen angels.

BIBLE MYSTERIES

After our best effort to figure what some Bible verses mean, we have to sit back and say, "We're not sure. We've got some ideas, but we're not certain which is right. We just don't know."

Some Bible passages, and this is one, puzzle portentous theologians and baffle bespectacled textual scholars. Yet certain truths about these mysteries can help us today:

- God's character is love, not malice or deceit. Whatever is happening here, God is reaching out to lost creatures, for whom he cares deeply.
- God speaks. While we puzzle over what, where, and how this happens, we can see that God is not focused on himself in some odd meditational stupor. God communicates.
- God triumphs. Christ victoriously preached to the spirits, indicating his power, control, and transcendence over all spiritual beings and authorities.
- God saves us. That's his business. We need it and God does it. God exerts himself to rescue the needy.

Bible mysteries tell us this much, and sometimes that's enough.

The passage shows that Christ's glorious reign extends over all the evil authorities and fallen angels that had wreaked havoc on the earth in Noah's day and were still doing so in Peter's time. Yet Peter offered his readers a vision: While the forces of evil could not yet be completely silenced (in fact, they actively continued to work against

believers), the believers could rest assured that Christ had already
won the battle. One day this will be evident to all, and the forces of
evil will receive their final judgment. Even today, believers must not
be surprised by suffering because Jesus himself was put to death in
the flesh before he was made alive in the spirit. Christ became the
true victor over what seemed apparent defeat. In our suffering, we
are blessed, because our defeat is not final. The purpose of this reference to disobedient spirits is not to identify these spirits directly with
the slanderers and accusers of Christians in the Roman Empire in
Peter's time. Instead, Peter wrote to reassure the readers that if
Christ can "subdue" the fallen angels, how much more easily can he
deal with their persecutors. In Jesus, we have the assurance of final
victory.

**3:21 And this water symbolizes baptism that now saves you also—
not the removal of dirt from the body but the pledge of a
good conscience toward God.**[NIV] Speaking of water led Peter to
explain that Noah's salvation was "through water" (3:20). The
Greek word *dia* can indicate "by" water or "through" water.
Scholarly argument has gone both ways, but most likely Peter
had a double meaning in mind. The waters of the Flood buoyed
the ark to rescue Noah and his family, but they also destroyed the
evildoers.

And this water symbolizes baptism. When dealing with sym-
bols in the Bible, we must always ask, What is being symbol-
ized? Otherwise, we lose ourselves in analysis. It was neither
the ark nor the water that "saved" Noah, but the power of God
conveyed in a promise. The Greek word for "symbolizes"
(antitupon) means "antitype" or "that which is prefigured"
(NRSV). It refers to a person, event, object, or act that antici-
pates or foreshadows a more perfect fulfillment of the essential idea. So the floodwaters convey some meaning and point
toward baptism. Peter may have intended a double meaning:
Baptism was both a sign and seal of salvation, and it was also
a solemn oath made before God (thus it was a warning not to
take baptism lightly). The Flood came as a judgment upon evil
people, but for Noah it brought deliverance from their mockery and sin, ushering him into a new life. In baptism, believers
identify with Jesus Christ, who separates us from the lost and
gives us new life. Baptism is a sign of the new covenant, identifying the person baptized with the people of God, the Christian community. It is not the ceremony, the water, nor *the
removal of dirt from the body* (referring not to physical cleansing but to a spiritual cleansing) that saves. The water of baptism does not "wash away sin" literally, although that picture

is inviting. Instead, baptism is the outward symbol of the inner transformation that happens in the hearts of those who believe (Romans 6:3-5; Galatians 3:27; Colossians 2:12). Baptism does not save anyone, but the belief it represents results in salvation. Its efficacy comes from the power of Christ's resurrection (see the box on baptism).

Peter explained that this "baptism that now saves you" results in a *pledge of a good conscience toward God.* This "pledge" *(eperotema)* is a technical word for the signing of a contract. The Holy Spirit convicts the person's mind and heart of sin, calling for a response or pledge of faith. This pledge is confirmed outwardly and tangibly in baptism. This pledge toward God implies that baptism conveys believers' desire to please God and therefore ask God for help to live out the reality of that inner transformation in their daily lives through repentance and forgiveness. By identifying themselves with Christ through baptism, Peter's readers could resist turning back, even under the pressure of persecution. Public baptism would keep them from the temptation to renounce their faith.

BAPTISM
God's promise to save us through the victory won by Jesus Christ provides the basis for Christian baptism.

Baptism means more than just a spiritual bath. It is not a magic moment that stands apart from the rest of God's message to us. It is a sign, seal, and sacrament that reminds us, objectively and before our Christian family, that God saves us in Jesus Christ.

In baptism we say, "Yes, God, we believe the promise. We identify with your people. We establish your leadership in our homes and lives. We join with others who love and trust you."

All who claim this promise are saved and receive a clean conscience, a new start, an eternal hope.

Some church traditions have taken these verses to support "baptismal regeneration." This belief ties the new birth (being "regenerated") and receiving the Holy Spirit to the moment when baptism is experienced. Some go to the extreme of claiming that salvation takes place even when the repentance and faith of the person don't take place or haven't yet taken place. Protestants view baptism not merely as the moment of contact with water, but the entire process of repentance, faith, and commitment culminating in the act of initiation into the church. The water of baptism has no spiritual power in itself; the rite of baptism does not automatically save anyone who is baptized regardless of faith. It is not merely external, as if the experience could convey salvation. Colossians 2:12 says, "Having been buried with him in baptism and raised with him through your faith in the power of God, who raised him from the dead" (NIV). Paul emphasized that it is our faith and the resurrection of Christ that bring salvation.

It saves you by the resurrection of Jesus Christ.^{NIV} Continuing from his thought above, Peter explained that baptism *saves you* (as used above, in evidence of salvation) only because Jesus Christ has made that salvation available. Paul explained how believers are baptized into Christ's death and resurrection:

- *We died to sin; how can we live in it any longer? Or don't you know that all of us who were baptized into Christ Jesus were baptized into his death? We were therefore buried with him through baptism into death in order that, just as Christ was raised from the dead through the glory of the Father, we too may live a new life. If we have been united with him like this in his death, we will certainly also be united with him in his resurrection. For we know that our old self was crucified with him so that the body of sin might be done away with, that we should no longer be slaves to sin—because anyone who has died has been freed from sin. Now if we died with Christ, we believe that we will also live with him. For we know that since Christ was raised from the dead, he cannot die again; death no longer has mastery over him. The death he died, he died to sin once for all; but the life he lives, he lives to God. In the same way, count yourselves dead to sin but alive to God in Christ Jesus. (Romans 6:2-11 NIV)*

3:22 Who has gone into heaven and is at God's right hand— with angels, authorities and powers in submission to him.^{NIV} Peter now entered into an exaltation of Christ and his victory over all opposition, whether attacks of Satan or the cruel treatment of the government. Peter himself had been an eyewitness. He saw Jesus "lifted up, and a cloud took him out of their sight" (Acts 1:9 NRSV). Jesus had *gone into heaven,* a place beyond the clouds, beyond our human sight. When Jesus ascended, he went to be with God. Throughout the New Testament, this is described as "heaven" (Mark 16:19; Ephesians 1:20; Hebrews 4:14; see also Psalm 110:1). There Jesus *is at God's right hand.* In ancient cultures, to sit at a sovereign's "right hand" indicated a position of great favor and authority.

At God's right hand, Christ has royal power and dignity as a result of his resurrection (Matthew 22:44; Mark 12:36; Acts 2:34; Romans 8:34; Colossians 3:1; Hebrews 1:13). Christ's authority includes *submission to him* of *angels, authorities and powers.* In this context, these words refer to all spiritual beings in the universe, both good and evil. Everything on earth and heaven is already subject to Christ. One day in the future, when he comes to judge, his power and authority will be made known to everyone.

1 Peter 4

Peter wrote a great deal about the way believers' lives should differ from the ordinary pattern of the world. The use of their God-given abilities is one of those ways. God has given every person special skills or abilities. Each time these skills are used to serve others, God is glorified. How can you use your gifts and abilities to serve others and glorify God?

4:1 Since therefore Christ suffered in the flesh, arm yourselves also with the same intention (for whoever has suffered in the flesh has finished with sin).^{NRSV} In 3:17-18, Peter explained that Christ had suffered and died for sins, once for all, and that believers should be ready to suffer. In 3:17, he explained that if they had to suffer, it should be for doing good, not for doing evil, in order to be a good witness to unbelievers. Here the point is slightly different. Believers ought to be ready to suffer as Christ suffered—not simply to be a good witness to others, but in order to stay away from sin.

The phrase *arm yourselves* is a military metaphor. With what were they to arm themselves? *The same intention,* the same courageous attitude and mind-set that Christ had toward suffering. This does not mean that believers should actively seek martyr-dom—the next verse describes how the believers are to live the rest of their earthly lives. Nonetheless, they should arm themselves for death if necessary. If believers suffer, it ought to be for living the Christian faith; they ought to suffer courageously, knowing that God will ultimately be victorious. Those who are armed with this intention have an unswerving resolve to do God's will in every situation; those so armed will be able to stand strong in the face of any persecution. They can persevere because of their personal relationship with Jesus Christ (see John 15:20-21).

For what purpose should believers arm themselves "with the same intention"? Peter explained that *whoever has suffered in the flesh has finished with sin.* The question arises, if the believers were to arm themselves to suffer in order to stay away from sin, how could that be suffering as Christ suffered? How did Christ's suffering accomplish his being "finished with sin"? Taken alone, this phrase sounds as though Peter was saying that suffering cleanses people from sinning. We know that is not the case, however, because many people have suffered for the Lord, yet are not completely cleansed of sin, for no person can be without sin (see 1 John 1:8). We will not be sinless until Christ returns. In addition, Jesus did not need to be cleansed from sin by suffering, for he was without sin in his nature and never sinned in his behavior.

One interpretation explains that "whoever" refers not to believers in general, but to Christ himself (see the first part of the verse). That Christ suffered and thus "finished with sin" could mean that Christ, through his suffering and death, conquered sin.

A second interpretation contends that those who suffer for doing right and continue to willingly obey God, despite suffering, have made a clear break with sin. In other words, such people have shown that obeying God, not avoiding suffering or hardship, is the most important motivation for their actions. This strengthens them and sets firmly into their lives a pattern of obedience.

The third and most likely interpretation is that Christians, having died in Christ, are one with him and are legally free from the penalty of sin. They are in union with Christ, so they regard themselves as dead to sin. Believers are no longer bound by sin's penalty; they must strive, in practice, to be free from its power. Suffering can be helpful in that area. Just as Christ's sufferings led to death and resurrection, so our suffering can help us put sin and selfishness behind us and enter more fully into a new life of service to God.

Christ's suffering made him victorious over Satan; believers' suffering, if they follow Christ's example, can strengthen their faith and solidify their obedient lifestyle. Believers ought to "arm" themselves with a resolve to be like Christ when they face suffering.

CLEAN BREAK
Suffering helps us be like Christ, yet people will do anything to avoid pain. Followers of Christ, however, should be willing and prepared to do God's will and to suffer for it if necessary. We can overcome sin when we focus on Christ and what he wants us to do. Pain and danger reveal our real values. Anyone who suffers for doing good and still faithfully obeys in spite of suffering has made a clean break with sin.

4:2 So as to live for the rest of your earthly life no longer by human desires but by the will of God.[NRSV] When believers have so armed themselves (4:1), their strengthened faith and resolve to obey will cause them to live *no longer by human desires but by*

the will of God. This describes the difference between believers'
lives without Christ and their new lives with him. Before conversion, they lived only to satisfy their human desires; after conversion, they are concerned with living by God's will, not their own.

First Peter 4:1 describes believers
who have suffered as being "finished
with sin" because their suffering caused
them to obey God more faithfully. This
verse describes how they can continue
to live for God with an even deeper

> Whatever your heart
> clings to and confides
> in, that is really your
> God. *Martin Luther*

resolve. Human desires are still present in believers, but can be
put aside in order to seek out and follow the will of God.

"Human desires" is used here in a negative sense. These are
the desires that war against their souls (2:11). These desires are
merely "human" and in opposition to "the will of God." What is
the will of God? Peter's answer is that the believers should:

- do good (2:15)

- act toward others with respect and love (2:17)

- revere God (2:17)

- be prepared to suffer for doing good (3:17)

- be finished with sin (4:1)

- reject evil human desires (4:2)

- reject the shameful actions of the Gentiles (4:3)

**4:3 You have already spent enough time in doing what the Gen-
tiles like to do, living in licentiousness, passions, drunkenness,
revels, carousing, and lawless idolatry.**NRSV Peter urged the
believers to no longer live as they had in the past because they
had *already spent enough time* doing so. In a sense, Peter was
saying, "You spent more than enough time in sin. Your old way
of life must be set aside. Let's move on." These believers had
new lives in Christ, so they were to spend the rest of their earthly
lives putting aside their sinful human desires and following
God's will (4:2). Peter reminded them of the shameful activities
of their past when they lived like pagans *(the Gentiles).* In his letters, Peter often used the word "Gentiles" to refer to non-Christians. Jews often referred to the pagan world as "Gentiles."

Peter's list of evil activities resembles Paul's in Romans 13:13.
These are examples of what does not please God: actions, activities, and attitudes that belong to the darkness. These have no
place in believers' lives.

■ *Licentiousness* ("debauchery" NIV) is open and excessive indulgence in sexual sins. A licentious person has no sense of shame or restraint. Licentiousness is the outworking of sexual immorality and impurity.

■ *Passions* ("lusts") are sinful human desires. Unbelievers pattern their lives after their desires, following where those desires lead, for they are unable to control them (see also 1:14).

■ *Drunkenness* refers to excessive use of wine and strong drink.

■ *Revels* (also translated "orgies") are drunken parties often filled with sexual promiscuity. These were often associated with festivals of some pagan gods.

■ *Carousing* is one's active involvement in the above-mentioned revels—getting drunk and out of control.

■ *Lawless idolatry* is actually plural, referring to idolatrous acts. Peter culminated his list with these words, indicating that many of the above acts were associated with the worship of pagan gods.

SPIRITED DISCUSSION
Peter warned against drunkenness. Some Christians consider the mere taste of fermented beverage a sin that stokes the fires of hell. Others enjoy fermented beverages at parties, socials, and family celebrations. Which lifestyle is right?

Christian prohibition is part of a heritage that wants to say no to worldly excesses and customs. It wants to say, "We're different."

Christian enjoyment of fermented beverage is part of a tradition that goes back to Cana (John 2) and Timothy (1 Timothy 5:23) and nearly every Bible character except Samson (Judges 13:14) and John the Baptist.

Peter counseled against drunken loss of control, not against fermented beverage itself. He warned against the lifestyle that abandons all restraint in the pursuit of pleasure. Let each Christian follow the Bible's counsel first, then respect community customs and guard conscience, without second-guessing another's choice.

4:4 They think it strange that you do not plunge with them into the same flood of dissipation, and they heap abuse on you.NIV
When a person becomes a Christian, sometimes his or her lifestyle changes drastically. This was especially true for first-century believers who had come out of the morally corrupt pagan world. Many of Peter's readers were Jewish Christians, but, as 4:3 indicates, many also had come from a pagan background. Former Jews would have

at least led a morally upright life, while former pagans had been involved in the activities that Peter had just listed (4:3). The word *they* refers to the "Gentiles" (unbelievers) in 4:3. Christians no longer desire to *plunge . . . into the same flood of dissipation.* Peter's words picture people without God diving into all kinds of human desires and passions, desperately trying to find real pleasure or fulfillment. Without hope in Christ for life in eternity, all they can do is live for self-gratification. "Plunge with them" is also translated "join them" or "run with them"—referring to the Christian's former group of friends and their common activities. This pictures the incomprehensible act of deliberately jumping into a raging torrent to one's death. "Flood of dissipation" is also translated "wild profligacy" or "unrestrained indulgence." In other words, these friends had sought pleasure by denying themselves nothing. Together, they did it all.

THE 180-DEGREE TURN
Christians are an odd bunch. They don't plunge into every party. They go to church when other good people play sports, enjoy the sunshine, or catch up on sleep. They give money away when other fine people struggle along to maximize investment potential. They pray about matters that normal, reasonable, levelheaded people would gladly sue over. They poop out when the party heats up. They seem satisfied with monogamy. How quaint!

A person whose life changes radically at conversion may experience contempt from his or her old friends. He may be scorned not only because he refuses to participate in certain activities, but also because his priorities have changed and he is now heading in the opposite direction. His very life incriminates their sinful activities. Mature Christians should help new believers resist such pressures of opposition by encouraging them to be faithful to Christ.

As Peter had explained in 4:3, that was "enough." Believers no longer wanted to be involved in these activities and said so to their friends. Not only did these former friends *think it strange* that the Christians had suddenly stopped joining them, but they also became the persecutors. *They heap abuse on you* describes the reaction of people who love darkness when they become confronted by the light. This is the process of peer pressure. The four steps are: (1) We don't do it, (2) they're surprised, (3) they mock us, (4) we are tempted even more to give in to sin (implying the sins listed in 4:3). A believer's refusal to participate in an activity is a silent condemnation of that activity. Unbelievers then react with hostility, often because they want to justify their actions or silence their own consciences. The "abuse" is verbal—slander, lies, and malicious comments.

ALL RISE FOR THE JUDGE

Matthew 12:36	"But I tell you that men will have to give account on the day of judgment for every careless word they have spoken" (NIV).
Acts 10:42	"He commanded us to preach to the people and to testify that he is the one whom God appointed as judge of the living and the dead" (NIV).
Romans 14:9	"For this very reason, Christ died and returned to life so that he might be the Lord of both the dead and the living" (NIV).
2 Timothy 4:1	"In the presence of God and of Christ Jesus, who will judge the living and the dead, and in view of his appearing and his kingdom" (NIV).
Revelation 20:11-15	"Then I saw a great white throne and him who was seated on it. Earth and sky fled from his presence, and there was no place for them. And I saw the dead, great and small, standing before the throne, and books were opened. Another book was opened, which is the book of life. The dead were judged according to what they had done as recorded in the books. The sea gave up the dead that were in it, and death and Hades gave up the dead that were in them, and each person was judged according to what he had done. Then death and Hades were thrown into the lake of fire. The lake of fire is the second death. If anyone's name was not found written in the book of life, he was thrown into the lake of fire" (NIV).

4:5 They will give an account to Him who is ready to judge the living and the dead.^{NKJV} Unbelievers who live immorally (4:3) and who "heap abuse" on Christians (4:4) will one day *give an account* of their actions and words to the one whom they are ultimately slandering—God himself. This gives believers great relief and confidence—they will receive justice. Scripture makes clear the certainty of judgment (see the chart): All will give an account to God, including believers, so we must be ready. We have no reason to taunt those who are in line for judgment because this final judgment will be universal. Those who have died will rise again to join those still alive to meet God for reward or punishment. Unbelievers, whether alive or dead at the time of Christ's return, will receive the punishment they deserve. God is *ready to judge*; that is, judgment may come at any moment.

We base our salvation on our belief in Jesus (Acts 16:31), and God bases our judgment on how we have lived. Those who inflict persecution are marked for punishment when they stand before God. Believers need not fear eternal punishment, however, because Jesus will be the final Judge (John 5:22). Peter's argument in 3:13–4:5 is that God will protect and reward his people who suffer, and he will hold their persecutors accountable on the Day of Judgment.

4:6 **For this is the reason the gospel was proclaimed even to the dead, so that, though they had been judged in the flesh as everyone is judged, they might live in the spirit as God does.**^{NRSV} *For this is the reason* refers back to the subject of 4:5, the final judgment. Peter's words that *the gospel was proclaimed even to the dead* have caused debate among scholars, resulting in four main views:

1. Some tie this verse back to 3:18-20 and Christ's proclamation of salvation to the unbelievers who lived before he came. But an understanding of a "second chance" after death in this verse argues against everything else in Scripture, as well as how unhelpful that would be to Peter's readers, who were being encouraged to persevere in suffering.

2. Others look back also to 3:18-20, but say that Christ was preaching salvation to those Old Testament people who had believed in God in the time before Christ preached on earth, offering them the gift he brought—eternal life.

3. Still others say that this verse refers to the gospel proclaimed by the apostles to those on the earth who were physically alive but spiritually dead.

4. Most likely, however, Peter was referring to those dead at that time of his writing who had heard and accepted the gospel. Many people in the early church had concerns about life after death. In Thessalonica, Christians worried that loved ones who died before Christ's return might never see Christ (1 Thessalonians 4:13-18). They wondered if those who died would be able to experience the promised eternal life. Peter explained that these believers, *though they had been judged in the flesh as everyone is judged*—that is, they died physically as everyone dies physically—will still one day *live in the spirit as God does.*

Perhaps some of the "abuse" heaped on the believers (4:4) included unbelievers' scoffing that it meant nothing to be a Christian because the Christians simply died like everyone else. Peter's readers needed to be reminded that the dead (both the faithful and their oppressors) would be raised from the dead—the faithful to eternal reward, the unfaithful to eternal punishment. God's judgment will be perfectly fair, Peter pointed out, because even those dead from ages past had heard the gospel. The Good News was first announced when Jesus Christ preached on the earth, but it has been operating since before the creation of the world (Ephesians 1:4), and it eternally affects all people, the dead as well as the living.

4:7 The end of all things is near. Therefore be clear minded and self-controlled so that you can pray.^{NIV} This verse gives us the vertical component (how we relate to God) to help us overcome the pressure to sin. Verses 8 and 9 give the horizontal component (how we relate to other people). The fact that God is "ready to judge" (4:5) means that *the end of all things is near.* These early Christians who faced persecution took great comfort in the fact that their suffering would one day end and that the evil ways of the wicked would be judged. The Lord is ready and waiting, desiring that the gospel should be preached to all the nations before he returns. Peter, like the other apostles, was always aware that Christ could return at any moment (see Romans 13:11-12; 1 Corinthians 7:29; 1 Thessalonians 4:13–5:3; 1 John 2:18). Likewise, believers today must always remember that "the end of all things is near," for Christ can come at any time.

The warning rings clear throughout the New Testament: The approach and suddenness of Christ's return challenge believers to be watchful and morally upright (see, for example, Matthew 24:36–25:13; Romans 13:13-14; 1 Corinthians 15:58; Hebrews 10:25; James 5:8). Peter explained that the shortness of time remaining should motivate believers to *be clear minded and self-controlled.* "Clear minded" is the opposite of insanity and of drunkenness. "Self-controlled" refers to sobriety and restraint. We are to have a clear head; we are to take Christ's return seriously. Persecution and suffering battle against clear-mindedness; self-control is difficult when one faces injustice. Peter reminded his readers that the time was short and their reward was

> God does not mind your stumbling and faltering phrases. He is not hindered by poor grammar. He is interested in your heart.
> *Billy Graham*

sure, so they must keep clear minds and maintain self-control so that they could pray intelligently and appropriately (see 1 Thessalonians 5:6). Certainly Peter remembered the Lord Jesus' words to him in the Garden of Gethsemane: "Watch and pray so that you will not fall into temptation. The spirit is willing, but the body is weak" (Matthew 26:41 NIV). Peter also knew from experience how weak a believer could become when faced with severe temptation without being grounded in prayer. Peter had proclaimed loyalty to Christ, but instead of praying in the Garden with Jesus, he had slept. When the time of trial had come, Peter had betrayed his Lord. Peter did not want his followers to face the same weakness, but to be ready and strengthened through prayer.

The meaning for today calls for self-discipline when we pray. Rather than merely a quick blessing on our food or a three-minute devotional, we should reserve extended times for sober, direct communication with God. Lack of prayer will render us unprepared for the end times.

A GOOD INVESTMENT
We should live expectantly because Christ is coming. Peter gives six admonitions for how to prepare for the end times.

1. Live each day as though Christ could return at once (4:7).
2. Keep a clear head, not getting carried away by self-indulgence (4:7).
3. Stay disciplined and alert for prayer (4:7).
4. Make active expressions of love a priority (4:8).
5. Be faithful in the stewardship of your gifts, investing your time and talent where they will make an eternal difference (4:10).
6. In everything, praise God as the source of your energy and the reason for your service (4:11).

4:8 Above all, love each other deeply, because love covers over a multitude of sins.[NIV] The words *above all* indicate that love would help these Christians face suffering. The mutual love, support, and encouragement would be a great defense. *Deeply* means sustained, eager, earnest; in other words, keep your love at full strength. (The same word was used in 1:22.) No Christian is an island; no one is alone. When believers experience deep love from the fellowship, they have the human network of support that can help them through any crisis. Jesus said, "'Love the Lord your God with all your heart and with all your soul and with all your mind and with all your strength. . . . Love your neighbor as yourself.' There is no commandment greater than these" (Mark 12:30-31 NIV); Paul had explained that believers should have faith, hope, and love, "but the greatest of these is love" (1 Corinthians 13:13 NKJV); John also wrote, "This is the message you heard from the beginning: We should love one another" (1 John 3:11 NIV; see also John 13:34; 15:12-17).

The same thought as *love covers over a multitude of sins* is found in Proverbs 10:12: "Hatred stirs up dissension, but love covers over all wrongs" (NIV). Peter may have been quoting from this or from a proverb of his day that was based loosely on this verse. This does not mean that love ignores, overlooks, or tries to hide sin. Instead, Peter probably was thinking back to his words in 4:1-2 that the believers should live the rest of their lives according to God's will and not human desires. As believers, they were "finished with sin." The "covering of sins," then, is the ability that believers have to forgive one another because Christ has forgiven them. Love works as a shock absorber, cushioning and smoothing out the bumps and irritations caused by fellow believers.

> If our hospitality is to minister, to impart to each who crosses our threshold something of the presence of Christ—if it is to transcend the human and deal with the supernatural—there must be an agony of growth, a learning, a tutoring at the hand the the Holy Spirit.
> *Karen Burton Mains*

LOVE AS ANTIDOTE
Life needs strong soap to wash away the buildup of hurt and grief. What's the better soap—love or hate—when

- your friend forgets a breakfast meeting that you lost sleep to get to?
- your teenager has a fender bender, distracted by a song on the radio?
- your church passes a budget with expenditures you believe. are frivolous?
- your spouse is in a cantankerous mood?
- the renter above you likes her music loud?
- some potbellied loudmouth on the first-base side is talking about your son's pitching?
- your mom is on the phone again?
- your boyfriend is seen with someone else?

As Christians, we should forgive the faults in others' lives because we have experienced God's gracious forgiveness in our own.

4:9 Be hospitable to one another without complaining.NRSV Being *hospitable* is different from social entertaining. Entertaining focuses on the host—the home must be spotless; the food must be well prepared and abundant; the host must appear relaxed and good-natured. Hospitality, in contrast, focuses on the guests. Their needs— whether for a place to stay, nourishing food, a listening ear, or acceptance—are the primary concern. Hospitality can happen in a messy home. It can happen around a dinner table where the main dish is canned soup. It can even happen while the host and the guest are doing chores together. Believers should not hesitate to offer hospitality just because they are too tired, too busy, or not wealthy enough to entertain. Hospitality is a strong expression of love, which Peter already commanded the believers to show (4:8).

The early Christian church depended on hospitality. There was not a network of motels and wayside restaurants for travelers as we would picture today. Traveling preachers and teachers depended on Christians to give them a place to stay, and churches needed homes in which to meet. Also, hospitality draws people together and allows them to get to know one another. The young church needed this interdependence. Jesus had counted on this for his disciples (Mark 6:10; see Romans 12:13, Hebrews 13:1-2, and 3 John 5-8 for more commands regarding hospitality).

The addition of the words *without complaining* gives a tinge of realism to the well-known command to be hospitable. Hospitality can be hard work: Some guests will be more difficult than others, and there may be times when it is more of a duty than a joy. In any case, Peter recommended that the believers not complain but serve their guests as though serving the Lord himself, "As you did it to one of the least of these who are members of my family, you did it to me" (Matthew 25:40 NRSV).

THE WELCOME MAT
Why would anyone complain about being hospitable? Well . . .

- Guests eat up the cupboard. Hospitality is expensive. Food isn't cheap.
- Guests eat up emotional energy. They talk about themselves, their aches and pains, their relatives' aches and pains. It gets tedious.
- Guests eat up time. You've got a fix-it list a mile long, a phone-back list that stretches the length of the refrigerator, and there's that new computer program you wanted to learn.

But the Bible advises us to invest in people and to let the rest take its course. Budgets are flexible, emotions replenishable, and there will never be an end to fix-it or learn-it chores. When guests arrive, focus on them generously. Your time and cupboard are God's anyhow. Build bonds of friendship by treating guests like royalty.

4:10 Each one should use whatever gift he has received to serve others, faithfully administering God's grace in its various forms.NIV Each person has received one or more spiritual gifts from God. A spiritual *gift* is a talent or ability empowered by the Holy

Spirit and able to be used in the ministry of the church. Spiritual "gifts" help God's people to serve and love one another (4:8) and continue the work of spreading the gospel. Paul wrote, "Just as each of us has one body with many members, and these members do not all have the same function, so in Christ we who are many form one body, and each member belongs to all the others. We have different gifts, according to the grace given us" (Romans 12:4-6 NIV). Different types of gifts given to God's people are listed in Romans 12:6-8; 1 Corinthians 12:4-11, 27-31; and Ephesians 4:11-12—these lists are different and are by no means exhaustive. When believers humbly recognize their partnership in the body of Christ, their gifts can be used effectively. Only then can they also appreciate one another's gifts. God gives his people various spiritual gifts so they can build up his church. The gifts were not meant for self-aggrandizement; instead, each believer has *received* at least one gift from God in order *to serve others.*

When believers use their gifts in humble service to others, they are actually *faithfully administering God's grace in its various forms.* The gifts God gives believers are as varied and many-faceted as are the believers themselves. As God's grace varies in its dealings with people, so God's gifts (given because of his grace) are varied in their administration of his grace as Christ's body on earth. To be "faithful" means not to hide the gifts, but to use them as they were meant to be used—serving and building up the body of Christ.

A GIFT FOR YOU
Our abilities should be faithfully used in serving others; none are for our own exclusive enjoyment. Some people, well aware of their abilities, believe that they have the right to use their abilities as they please. Others feel that they have no special talents at all. Peter addresses both groups in these verses. Because each believer has been given a way to minister, we should find our way to serve and do it. Most importantly, when we see a need in the church, we should meet it the best way we can. If it's possible to serve by way of our gift, that's great. But if there remains a need, even though it may not be perfectly matched to our gift we still should help. We should never withhold our ability to minister.

4:11 **Whoever speaks must do so as one speaking the very words of God; whoever serves must do so with the strength that God supplies, so that God may be glorified in all things through Jesus Christ.**NRSV Scholars differ on Peter's focus here. Some say *whoever speaks* refers not just to those speaking publicly (preachers and teachers), but to the speech of all believers in the worship setting, including speaking in tongues. Speaking in tongues was usually regarded more as prayer than proclamation (see 1 Corinthians 14:2, 28). The words *speaking the very words of God* set this apart from everyday conversation. All believers, when conversing with one another in a worship context, ought to speak God's words, meaning that everything they say should be spoken seriously and after careful study and prayer so that they are speaking God's truth. (Others say that Peter was not speaking to everyone, but only to the preachers and teachers. They explain that as the apostles divided the ministry of the church into two categories—preaching and serving, see Acts 6—so Peter was dividing the church's body into two groups—teachers and servers—although admittedly, these overlap. However, the text does not support this interpretation.) Peter encouraged the believers to use their gifts (4:10). Men and women with gifts that required speaking must be responsible with what they said.

Likewise, those gifted with abilities that centered on serving also have a responsibility—to serve not in their own strength but *with the strength that God supplies.* If believers serve in their own strength alone or in order to look good to others, they will begin to find serving a wearisome task. But to serve with God's strength is to be able to go above and beyond, and to do so for one purpose: *so that God may be glorified in all things through Jesus Christ.* When believers use their gifts as God directs (to help others and build up the church), others will see Jesus Christ in them and will glorify him for the help they have received. Peter may have been thinking of Jesus' words, "Let your light shine before men, that they may see your good deeds and praise your Father in heaven" (Matthew 5:16 NIV).

WHOSE POWER?
We need God's strength to do God's work. A vital church requires lots of serving—and that means work. Typically, much of the work falls on a few shoulders. Those people need the strength that God supplies. How do active people get help from God's supply cabinet? Often they get it through your efforts. They need your prayers, cooperation, and an occasional sabbatical. Offer to pitch in, to provide relief, and to shoulder a load.

All who serve must trust in God for the joy to do the work cheerfully. When your batteries run low, take a break for prayer and meditation. Work is lighter when it's shared, and easy when you feel God's joy in it.

To him belong the glory and the power forever and ever. Amen.NRSV This is a brief doxology. *To him* refers directly back to Jesus Christ. God is glorified in all things, but to Christ also belongs *the glory and the power forever and ever,* for God raised Christ from the dead and gave him lordship over all creation. It is through Jesus Christ alone that believers have a relationship with God that allows them to receive gifts from a gracious God and use those gifts to serve others. *Amen* means "so be it" (see also Romans 1:25; Galatians 1:5; Philippians 4:20; 1 Peter 5:11).

SUFFERING FOR BEING A CHRISTIAN / 4:12-19

The early Christians must have wondered why they were targeted with such abuse and hatred when they were living peacefully and striving to do God's will. However, Jesus himself suffered, and he warned his followers that they too would face suffering. Christians should not be surprised by suffering, for this is what Jesus had said to Peter and the other disciples at the Last Supper, "If they persecuted me, they will persecute you also" (John 15:20 NIV). A participant in the Last Supper, the apostle John, later wrote, "Do not be astonished, brothers and sisters, that the world hates you" (1 John 3:13 NRSV). Peter offered this warning to his readers as well.

4:12 Dear friends, do not be surprised at the painful trial you are suffering, as though something strange were happening to you.NIV As he had done at 2:11, Peter again addressed his readers as *dear friends,* emphasizing the unity of all believers, even though he had not met most of those to whom he wrote. Unbelievers may be surprised at Christians' behavior (2:12; 3:9, 16; 4:4); Christians ought *not be surprised* at unbelievers' behavior and the trials they inflict upon believers. The word for "surprise" means a bewildering astonishment. Like Christ, Christians should expect to face persecution.

The question arises, Why was Peter seemingly speaking of a singular *trial,* and how could that jointly affect the believers scattered across the Roman province of Asia? We must remember that the gospel faced opposition from the very beginning; the book of Acts records persecution and even martyrdom of the believers who witnessed for Christ. Therefore, it is reasonable to think that such persecution was not the exception but the rule, wherever the gospel went. The period of persecution under Emperor Nero stood out for its organization and horrible intensity. Peter's admonition that the believers not be surprised at "the painful trial" should be seen as a general term—varying degrees of persecution occurring at different times in different places. "Whatever trial your church might be facing at this time should not come as a surprise," Peter was saying. "This is not *something strange*—persecution has followed the gospel from the time of Jesus' crucifixion." We should expect persecution and suffering because they are part of God's plan to perfect Christians. Even Christ was not spared from persecution (Romans 8:32).

The words "painful trial" are also translated "fiery trial" or "fiery ordeal." In 1:6-7, Peter had described the various trials believers face as a means of purifying their faith in the same way that fire purifies metals. The thought is the same here. By its very nature, a trial is "painful." But Peter had already challenged them to rejoice in trials (1:6), and he repeated this admonition in the next verse.

NO PAINFUL SURPRISES
Weather forecasters are in the business of "surprise reduction." They tell us what's coming so we can prepare. Obstetricians are in that business, too, along with travel agents and economists.

Peter creates no illusions for Christians under his care. God's plan for your life often but not always includes pain and hardship. When trouble comes, don't be surprised, he writes. It's normal. God will help you through it.

The Christian life holds plenty of wonderful surprises—friendship, intimacy, heaven itself—but about pain and struggle we are forewarned. It's coming. Trust God and be encouraged. Your trial will test and refine your faith.

4:13 But rejoice that you participate in the sufferings of Christ, so that you may be overjoyed when his glory is revealed.NIV Instead of being bewildered by trials, Peter exhorted the believers to *rejoice*. The reason? Because when they suffered for their faith in Christ, they were actually "participating" in Christ's sufferings. To suffer for the faith proves that we truly belong to Christ. Jesus said, "'Servants are not greater than their master.' If they persecuted me, they will persecute you" (John 15:20 NRSV). The book of Acts records how Peter and the apostles, after being flogged for teaching about Christ, "rejoiced that they were considered worthy to suffer dishonor for the sake of . . . the Messiah" (Acts 5:41-42 NRSV). Believers, as servants of Christ, must expect to participate in his sufferings as well as in his future glory. Paul wrote to the Romans: "We are children of God, and if children, then heirs, heirs of God and joint heirs with Christ—if, in fact, we suffer with him so that we may also be glorified with him" (Romans 8:16-17 NRSV). If we suffer, it shows our identification with Christ and it shows that our faith is genuine. Since Christ was persecuted, we also will be persecuted and, thereby, participate in his suffering. If we persevere, we will enjoy our future inheritance with him. Servants who know the suffering of Christ will *be overjoyed when his glory is revealed.*

This does not mean that all suffering is the result of good Christian conduct. Sometimes a person will grumble, "He's just picking on me because I'm a Christian," when it's obvious to everyone else that the person's own unpleasant behavior is the cause of his or her problems. It may take careful thought or wise counsel to determine the real cause of our suffering. We can be assured, however, that whenever we suffer because of our loyalty to Christ, he will be with us all the way.

4:14 If you are insulted because of the name of Christ, you are blessed, for the Spirit of glory and of God rests on you.^{NIV} Peter offered a specific example of the type of suffering the believers might face. To be *insulted* means to face verbal abuse, to be reviled, ridiculed, or slandered. Peter brought to mind Jesus' words: "Blessed are you when people insult you, persecute you and falsely say all kinds of evil against you because of me" (Matthew 5:11 NIV). Not only will suffering believers find great joy when Christ returns (4:13), but they would also be *blessed* in this world (see also 3:14, 16). That blessing takes the form of *the Spirit of glory and of God* (that is, the Holy Spirit) resting on them. Christ will send his Spirit to strengthen those who are persecuted for their faith.

Peter built upon Isaiah 11:2 when encouraging the oppressed. God's "glory" refers to his glorious presence, which resided in the pillar of cloud in Old Testament times (Exodus 33:9; 34:5). "Glory" is one of God's greatest attributes (Acts 7:2; Ephesians 1:17); God revealed his glory in Jesus (John 1:14, 18). In Revelation, special regard is given to martyrs (Revelation 6:9; 20:4). So not only would the Holy Spirit be with believers who are persecuted, but they were already participating in final glory to be revealed (2 Corinthians 3:18).

When Stephen became the first martyr for Christianity, the Bible tells us that he was "a man full of faith and of the Holy Spirit," whose "face was like the face of an angel," and who, upon his death, "looked up to heaven and saw the glory of God, and Jesus standing at the right hand of God" (Acts 6:5, 15; 7:55 NIV). While all believers have the Holy Spirit, Peter here indicated that those who suffer for Christ receive an even greater measure of the Spirit, strengthening them, empowering them, and giving them peace.

TAKING THE HEAT
How should we deal with insults? Does Peter really mean we should give back blessings when we're insulted? God turns everything upside down. Normally, if you receive an insult, revenge is in order, expected, and anticipated. People who fling an insult are daring you to punch back.

God wants those insults received because of your allegiance to him to witness to his grace and love. If you hit back, what's so different about God? If you love back, perhaps the offender will wake up and realize that God really does make a difference.

When you take an insult for God today and the fist clenches up, remember Peter. He would have hit back, too, before Jesus took charge of his life. But he grew stronger, sturdier, and more confident in God. You can respond the same way.

4:15 But let none of you suffer as a murderer, a thief, an evildoer, or as a busybody in other people's matters.^{NKJV} Peter has made the point that not all suffering results in blessing: "If you endure when you are beaten for doing wrong, what credit is that?" (2:20 NRSV). If believers must suffer, it must be because of their faith, for that alone results in blessing. They ought not be counted among those who murder, steal, do evil, or meddle in other people's matters. Such people deserve the punishment and suffering they receive, and there is no blessing in such suffering.

DON'T STEAL AWAY
Have you ever picked up a waitress's tip? filled your gas tank without paying? swiped a donut from a table set for another party?

Peter warns against dishonesty, lest little thefts lead to prosecution. What an embarrassment for someone who claims that God will supply all needs to be caught stealing. Don't take what isn't yours. Trust God for what you need.

4:16 Yet if any of you suffers as a Christian, do not consider it a disgrace, but glorify God because you bear this name.^{NRSV} Peter reminded his readers that it was not shameful to suffer for being Christians. No one wants to suffer, and there is a certain amount of disgrace in any sort of public suffering. But to be insulted publicly for one's faith, to be put in jail or hurt physically for being *a Christian,* should not be considered a *disgrace.* In other words, those who suffer shouldn't be ashamed. While they ought not seek out suffering, neither should they try

to avoid it. Instead, Peter admonished them to keep on doing
what was right regardless of the suffering it might bring. In that
suffering they could *glorify God* because they bore his name.
As bearers of Christ's name, Christians are his representatives
on this earth; therefore, in everything they do, including what
might seem like shameful suffering, they can glorify God.

Peter used the term "Christian" to describe the believers, those
who followed Christ. This name first came into use in Antioch:
"The disciples were called Christians first at Antioch" (Acts
11:26 NIV).

**4:17 For the time has come for judgment to begin with the house-
hold of God; if it begins with us, what will be the end for
those who do not obey the gospel of God?**^{NRSV}This *time . . . for
judgment* refers both to final judgment and also to God's refining
discipline (Hebrews 12:7). In 1 Peter 1:17, Peter warned that God
judges all people according to their deeds. He also disciplines
and judges his people (all believers, *the household of God*) in
order to refine them, as Peter has
explained in 1:6-7. This judgment purifies and strengthens believers, readying
them for God's kingdom.

> There is no fear of
> judgment for the man
> who judges himself
> according to the Word
> of God.
> *Howard G. Hendricks*

Some commentators read this phrase
as judgment beginning "from the house
of God" and explain that Peter was metaphorically describing the imminent
destruction of the temple in Jerusalem (as described in Ezekiel
9:6-7; Zechariah 13:7-9; Malachi 3:1). Peter may have had the
judgment scene in Ezekiel 9 in mind as he described the judgment of God beginning either in Jerusalem at the temple, or in
the church, the new "temple" (dwelling place) of God on earth.

NO CHANCE
God often allows believers to sin and then experience the
consequences. He does this for several reasons:

- to show us our potential for sinning
- to encourage us to turn from sin and more constantly depend
  on him
- to prepare us to face other, even stronger temptations in the
  future
- to help us stay faithful and keep on trusting him

For believers, God's actions refine like fire to turn them away
from sin. We who believe must learn to recognize and accept
God's correction even if it comes from painful circumstances.

This fire will also spread to *those who do not obey the gospel of God,* but for them it will not be a refining fire; rather, it will be a fire of judgment. Peter asked a rhetorical question, "If this fire is difficult for us believers, who know its reason and our future, what will it be like for unbelievers, especially those who are actively hostile toward Christians?" The inescapable response: It will be terrible. (See 2 Thessalonians 1:5-10.)

4:18 And "If it is hard for the righteous to be saved, what will become of the ungodly and the sinners?"NRSV Reinforcing his rhetorical question in 4:17, Peter continued by quoting from Proverbs 11:31. If the *righteous* ones (the believers) experience difficulty in their refining process, how much more horrible will be the great disaster experienced for eternity by *the ungodly and the sinners* who chose to reject Christ.

The phrase *it is hard* means "with difficulty" not "just barely." Peter was not introducing uncertainty to the believers' assurance of salvation because in 1:4-5 he referred to the inheritance kept in heaven for us. Instead, he was talking about the difficult road believers must travel. It is not easy to be a Christian; we must count the cost.

The phrase *to be saved* refers not to God's work in salvation, nor to the initial step of coming to faith (new birth), but to the entire process of salvation with specific emphasis on persevering to the end.

4:19 Therefore, let those suffering in accordance with God's will entrust themselves to a faithful Creator, while continuing to do good.NRSV With the word *therefore,* Peter drew a conclusion to his words in the previous verses. Peter consistently encouraged his readers that their suffering was all under God's control. If they suffered for the faith, they were *suffering in accordance with God's will.* Their suffering was not because God had lost control; rather, all that happens to believers is according to his will. While it is difficult to accept that one's suffering is part of God's plan, we can find comfort in understanding that, as part of God's will, suffering has a reason, a goal, and an end. For believers, suffering is a purifying process to draw us closer to God.

Thus, in times of suffering, believers must *entrust themselves to a faithful Creator.* The word "entrust" means to give over to someone for safekeeping. Jesus used the word on the cross when he said, "Father, into your hands I commit my spirit" (Luke 23:46 NIV). This also follows Christ's example (2:23). If the believers entrusted their lives to the one who created them, they would have nothing to fear.

Even in suffering, as Peter had admonished throughout his letter, the Christians must continue *to do good.* Peter often recommended doing good works as a response to being persecuted (see 2:12, 15, 20; 3:1-2, 13, 17). Paul also recommended this response (Romans 12:14-18; Titus 3:1, 14). In the early days of the church, doing good would have been a tremendous boon to believers and a counteragent for the hostility they faced in society. If Christians were leading productive lives and helping in society, the necessity of their contribution would make it difficult for the government or society to ostracize or persecute them. This could well be a strategy for our own times, whether dealing with a community or neighbors who are either hostile or skeptical toward Christians. Those whose careers provide a visible service (education, medicine, child care, feeding the hungry) would be regarded as indispensable. Others can serve or volunteer. When others see our valuable help, they will not be able to use our "religion" as a wedge against us. They will be glad for our help. If the believers would "do good" even in the face of injustice, they would reveal that they truly had entrusted themselves to God, that they were suffering for their faith alone, which is commendable before God (2:20), and that their attitude toward suffering might draw others to faith as well (2:12).

God created the world, and he has faithfully ordered it and kept it since the creation. Because we know that God is faithful, we can count on him to fulfill his promises to us. If God can oversee the forces of nature, surely he can see us through the trials we face. We must never doubt his loving concern for us or his ability to rescue us.

TRUST
Everywhere the Bible counsels that we trust God—in good times and bad, during sunny skies and thunderclouds, when we have a pocket full of change and a pocket full of sawdust. How does trust work?

- *Trust overcomes fear.* Genuine trust in God says, "Whatever mess I'm in, my heavenly Father will lead me."
- *Trust overcomes depression.* This common malady would grow like a weed, were God not the gardener.
- *Trust overcomes hate.* When careless or cruel people hurt you, sometimes irreparably, you can hate forever or trust, but you can't do both.

God is there to steady even the worst situation—always with a promise, always with hope. Commit your life to him for safekeeping. Rely on him when you face your worst circumstances.

---

1 Peter 5

Peter wrote this letter just before Emperor Nero began cruelly persecuting Christians in Rome and throughout the empire. About thirty years earlier, Peter, fearing for his life, had three times denied even knowing Jesus (John 18:15-27). Since then, having learned how to stand firm in an evil world, Peter encouraged other Christians, who were facing pressure to deny their faith. Peter believed and lived what he wrote in this letter—later he was executed by the Romans for believing in and preaching Christ. In this section, Peter addressed three groups: elders, younger men, and the church as a whole. Those who stand for Christ will be persecuted because the world is ruled by Christ's greatest enemy. But just as the small group of early believers stood against persecution, so we must be willing to stand for our faith with the patience, endurance, and courage that Peter exhibited.

5:1 To the elders among you, I appeal as a fellow elder, a witness of Christ's sufferings and one who also will share in the glory to be revealed.^{NIV} This continues the thought in 4:12-19. Since God's judgment will "begin with the household of God" (4:17), then the *elders* of those congregations carry great responsibility. This thought is paralleled in the book of Ezekiel, where judgment is said to begin with "the elders who were in front of the temple" (Ezekiel 9:6 NIV). In Peter's day, elders provided supervision, protection, discipline, instruction, and direction for the other believers. Modeling the role of elders in the Jewish synagogue, these "elders" were the appointed leaders in the churches (see Acts 14:23; 20:17; 1 Timothy 5:17, 19; Titus 1:5-6) and were to lead the churches by teaching sound doctrine, helping believers mature spiritually, and equipping believers to live for Jesus Christ despite opposition. This letter is addressed to all believers, but Peter included a special message for the elders among the people. "Elder" simply means "older." Both Greeks and Jews gave positions of great honor to wise older men, and the Christian church continued this pattern of leadership. Elders carried great responsibility, and they were expected to be good examples.

Peter appealed *as a fellow elder,* thereby identifying with the other church leaders, although he had authority as one of the apostles (as he had identified himself in 1:1). Since God's judgment of sin would begin with the believers (4:17), Peter could speak from personal experience. These fellow elders knew Peter's story—how he had denied his Lord three times. Yet Peter had been forgiven and empowered to serve. Peter knew that the elders needed to deal with sin in their lives before the time of God's judgment.

Peter had been a *witness of Christ's sufferings.* Actually he did not witness Jesus' crucifixion because he had denied and deserted Jesus; the word "witness" in this verse does not mean "eyewitness." Neither he nor all these elders had been eyewitnesses; however, they had all been called to "witness" (testify or bring news about) Christ's sufferings to those under their charge. As witnesses, they could also share in those sufferings, personally "witnessing" those sufferings in their own lives.

But they share in even more, for Peter described himself as *one who also* (along with the other elders, as well as all believers) *will share in the glory to be revealed.* Peter and the believers shared in Christ's glory at present, and they would also share that glory when it would be revealed at the last day (the Second Coming).

5:2-3 Be shepherds of God's flock that is under your care, serving as overseers.[NIV] Peter's command that the elders *be shepherds of God's flock* echoed Jesus' words to Peter himself, "Take care of my sheep" (John 21:16 NIV). The same Greek word is used in both places: *poimaino,* meaning "to shepherd," "to tend," or "to take care of," "to pastor." The "flock" is the believers; elders had charge over individual churches and thus over a certain part of God's "flock." Elders were to be like shepherds who lead, guide, and protect the sheep under their care. Believers would need good leaders as they faced persecution.

The phrase *serving as overseers* is not in some Greek manuscripts. The words "shepherds" and "overseers" are most likely interchangeable, referring to leadership positions in the church. The word "overseer" referred to almost any kind of overseeing responsibility over others. Like a "shepherd" or "pastor," an overseer was concerned for the well-being of the those under his care. We must be careful not to read into the word "overseer" twentieth-century overtones of management, administration, and supervision.

If Peter had been thinking of Ezekiel's message (see the notes on 5:1), then he may have also been considering Ezekiel 34:1-16 and the message God had given to the "shepherds of Israel" (34:1). These shepherds realize they are caring for "God's flock," not their own. They should never take pride in numbers or names, but always remember that the church is not theirs, but God's. (Throughout Ezekiel 34:1-16, God refers to the flock as "my flock.")

Peter, as Jesus' disciple, became a pillar of the Jerusalem church. But writing to the elders, he identified himself as a fellow elder, not a superior. He asked them to be shepherds of God's flock, exactly what Jesus had told him to do (John 21:15-17). Some have taken Peter's reference to himself as an elder as a sign that he didn't write 1 Peter. They explain that he would have referred to himself as an apostle. But Peter's experience with Jesus, where Jesus plainly told Peter, "Feed my sheep," would cause Peter to think of himself as an elder or pastor first. Peter was taking his own advice as he worked along with the other elders in caring for God's faithful people. His identification with the elders is a powerful example of Christian leadership, where authority is based on service, not power (Mark 10:42-45).

CREDENTIALS
Academic credentials, administrative skills, or even ability to speak do not automatically qualify a Christian leader as a successful pastor. Then what does it take?

■ A heart for people. Helping others grow strong in faith must delight you.
■ A humble spirit. Fatal to a pastor's work is the ego that comes with leadership. A realistic appraisal of yourself is crucial.
■ A growing faith in God.

Others in your church will become wealthy, some politically powerful, and a few may court fame. But not you. Your life, each day, depends on God's supply of money, energy, and maturation. Good shepherds get to know the Good Shepherd very well.

Not because you must, but because you are willing, as God wants you to be; not greedy for money, but eager to serve; not lording it over those entrusted to you, but being examples to the flock.^{NIV} This passage describes three possible problems that elders might face and how they should respond:

1. Wrong motivation. *Not because you must, but because you are willing, as God wants you to be.* Elders must lead out of willingness and eagerness to serve, freely choosing to take

on the responsibility and not leading out of obligation. The motivation to serve must also be pure, not colored by social pressure or self-gratification. Elders should serve out of love for God. Peter called upon them to make God's will their own, eagerly seeking to please God in it. (In Ezekiel 34:2, the evil shepherds were asked, "Should not shepherds take care of the flock?" NIV.) Pastors and elders should serve willingly in churches today. Too often a slate of elders becomes hard to fill because of unwillingness by people in the congregation to serve.

2. Wrong goals. *Not greedy for money, but eager to serve.* In many of the churches, elders were paid for their services; however, that remuneration alone probably would not make an elder rich. This temptation to be greedy probably arose because the church's finances (the money collected for the poor, etc.) usually were entrusted to the elder or overseer. The opportunity to abuse the trust was very real. Thus, both Peter and Paul explained that elders were to be paid adequately and were to be trustworthy with money (see 1 Timothy 3:8; 5:17-18; Titus 1:7, 11). Instead of money, elders were to focus on serving. The word for "eager" is very strong in the Greek, expressing great zeal and enthusiasm. Today only pastors receive pay for serving, but pastors can fall prey to the greedy desire for money. Not having money can lead to as much preoccupation with funds as having a lot of money.

3. Wrong methods. *Not lording it over those entrusted to you, but being examples to the flock.* Elders lead by example, not force. "Lording it over" means "forcefully domineering or subduing." Elders also must fight the temptation to abuse their authority and hurt "those entrusted" to them (the church under their care). The formula Jesus used was always that those who led were to be the best servants (Mark 10:42-45). The leaders were to be examples of humility and servant-hood. Such leaders always seek the good of their congregation. Today "my leadership style" or "my gifts" can be an excuse for a pastor or church leader to manipulate or spiritually strong-arm others to get his way. Even when they know they're right, leaders must not bully or steamroll people.

5:4 And when the Chief Shepherd appears, you will receive the crown of glory that does not fade away.NKJV Peter had already referred to Jesus Christ as a Shepherd in 2:25. Here he calls him the *Chief Shepherd*. Elders were to be shepherds of God's flock, but they were answerable to the Chief Shepherd (also called "the

Good Shepherd" in John 10:11, 14 and "great Shepherd" in
Hebrews 13:20). The word *appears* refers to Christ's second coming, when he will return to judge all people. At that time, the
elders (along with all believers) *will receive the crown of glory.*
This is a proper motivation for service. Elders were not to expect
to become rich or to be greedy for gain (5:3), but they could
expect to receive great reward at the return of Christ.

CHURCH LEADER
What gets you out of bed in the morning? Peer approval, habit,
commissions, a schedule someone else has set for you? Most
adults relate well to earning a living, doing a job, and getting
ahead.
    A church leader, however, has a different motivation. Church
leaders don't earn commissions and shouldn't find "making a
living" the reason they get to work. A pastor, elder, or deacon
needs to wake up with people in mind, people who need a
word of hope, encouragement, comfort, or challenge.
    Want to be a leader in the church? Pray for a heart that really
wants people to know and love God.

The "crown of glory" refers not to a literal crown that each faithful person will wear (both the words "crown" and "glory" are singular), but to a common glory that all will share, both distinguished
servants and those who persevered through suffering. All believers
will receive this "crown of glory" for doing what God has called
them to do. Other passages describe a "crown" to be received as a
reward for suffering and endurance. Paul spoke of receiving the
crown of righteousness (2 Timothy 4:8); James wrote of believers
receiving the crown of life (James 1:12), as did John (Revelation
2:10). The "crown," while metaphorical, pictures the laurel-wreath
crown that was given to winners in the Greek and Roman athletic
games. A symbol of triumph and honor, this was the most coveted
prize in ancient times. All believers will receive such a crown, only
theirs will *not fade away.* The laurel-wreath crown will eventually
fade, dry up, and wither, but the glory believers will receive is eternal, unending, unchanging. What better motivation for selfless service! What better motivation for keeping the faith in the face of
suffering and temptation. All believers will be declared winners and
will receive a wonderful, everlasting reward. This could be their
source of strength and encouragement in times of trial.

**5:5 In the same way, you who are younger must accept the
authority of the elders.**NRSV Peter's words *in the same way* focus
on motivation, not the exact action (as used in 3:1, that wives

serve "in the same way" as servants). As Peter had presented the best plan for household relationships, so here he described the best plan for church relationships. Those who were *younger must accept the authority of the elders.* To accept the authority of the elders means to submit to their decisions and to treat them respectfully (unless, of course, they lead people into sin).

BIG BONUS
God is pleased with those people who give up wealth and prestige to serve his kingdom, and with all those who serve faithfully, remaining loyal under persecution. To all his followers, God promises a huge bonus when finally their race is run. But Christ gives the crown of glory on *his* terms, not ours. It comes from him, not from people. It's given at his proper time.

What's the crown really like? What benefits does it represent? The Bible tells us that it will not fade away, but not much beyond that. The "crown" is a metaphor; each person doesn't receive a laurel wreath or a jewel-studded diadem. But the "glory" is real, referring to the shared glory we have as children of the King. By faith, we believe that God's rewards are truly satisfying, generous, and well worth waiting for.

It's worth working and serving for God's approval, even when your efforts go unnoticed or unappreciated in this life. Christians do not serve God *because of* a reward at the end. Instead, the reward is God's way of saying, "Well done. I am pleased."

Scholars are divided over whether Peter was referring to those who held the church office of "elder," to those who were simply older (and thus were "elders" as opposed to those who were "younger"), or to more experienced church leaders. Most likely, Peter was referring to those holding the office of elder. In any case, Peter continued his theme of right relationships for the purpose of glorifying God in a hostile environment.

And all of you must clothe yourselves with humility in your dealings with one another, for "God opposes the proud, but gives grace to the humble."[NRSV] Here Peter stressed the horizontal application of humility *(one another),* while he stressed the vertical application in 5:6 *(under . . . God). All of you,* whether young or old, church leader or not, had a responsibility in the congregation. Peter told both young and old to be humble in their dealings with one another. The Greek word here *egkombosasthe* is derived from *egkomboma,* an apron a servant wears while working. Thus to *clothe yourselves*

> Where there is patience and humility, there is neither anger nor vexation.
> *St. Francis of Assisi*

with humility means to put on the apron and go to work, humbly
serving one another. Humility means being able to put others'
needs and desires ahead of one's own (see Philippians 2:3-4).
Young people should follow the leadership of the older people
(especially those who have been put in authority over them as
elders). The elders, in turn, should lead by example. All should
actively serve one another. No doubt
Peter remembered how Christ clothed | No man ruleth safely but
himself with humility as he washed the | he that is willingly ruled.
disciples' feet (see John 13:1-17). | *Thomas à Kempis*

Peter quoted from Proverbs 3:34 to
make his point. The believers must deal with one another in
humility because *"God opposes the proud, but gives grace to the
humble"* (see also James 4:6). Not only does pride keep people
from listening to or following God, it also can keep older people
from trying to understand young people and young people from
listening to those who are older. Humble people receive God's
"grace," giving them the ability to live faithfully on earth with
the promise of a glorious eternity with him. The verbs are in the
present tense—God continually opposes those who are proud and
think they do not need to listen to God or God's servants; God
continually gives grace to those who humbly listen, love, and
serve, especially in the face of mounting threats and persecutions.

SUBMISSION
Accepting authority and clothing ourselves with humility sounds
like the dark ages to modern readers. If you want to appear
"out of sync" with modern culture, talk about the virtue of submission to authority.

Granted, submission has often been a convenient cover for
perpetuating racism, physical abuse, or political injustice.

Biblical submission, however, assumes that authority is given
by God to leaders in a church. These leaders, under God's
care, nurture the church by establishing priorities, maintaining
order, evaluating curriculum, judging moral dilemmas, resolving
conflicts, and interpreting the Word of God for today. That's a
big responsibility, and it requires teamwork. True leaders—
humble servants of God whose hearts are strong with faith—
deserve our support and cooperation.

Submission or accepting authority has become distasteful to
our society; instead, many have made gods out of autonomy
and independence. But God has a prior claim to our lives that
is more binding than the Bill of Rights. In his church, we are to
show respect and accept authority. Do you despise authority?
Maybe you should check to see who controls your life.

5:6 **Therefore humble yourselves under the mighty hand of God, that He may exalt you in due time.**NKJV *Therefore,* because God opposes the proud and gives grace to the humble (5:5), Peter admonished the believers to *humble* themselves. This would be an act of the will; humility does not come naturally. But when the believers humbled themselves *under the mighty hand of God,* they were actually submitting to his care and protection. The reference to God's "mighty hand" was often used in the Old Testament to describe God's power (as when he delivered Israel from slavery in Egypt; see, for example, Exodus 13:3, 9, 14, 16; Deuteronomy 9:26; Job 30:21; Psalm 32:4; Ezekiel 20:34). To truly humble themselves, believers need to accept life's struggles as part of God's providence (see 5:7). They must humble themselves even in the face of persecution because God would *exalt* them. Being "exalted" refers to a reversal of past misfortunes and troubles, triumph over their oppressors, and participation in Christ's glory. The exalting may be in this life or in the next. In any case it will be *in due time;* that is, in God's perfect time. Most likely, Peter was thinking of that last day, when the Chief Shepherd would appear (5:4) and all those who have faithfully followed would be exalted and given eternal glory.

We often worry about our position and status, hoping to get proper recognition for what we do. But Peter advises us to remember that God's recognition counts more than human praise. God is able and willing to bless us according to his timing. Humbly obey God regardless of present circumstances, and in his good time—either in this life or in the next—he will lift you up. Let us remember that Jesus humbled himself completely when he died on the cross (see Philippians 2:6-11) and that God exalted him to the highest heaven.

5:7 **Casting all your care upon Him, for He cares for you.**NKJV This verse explains what it means for believers to humble themselves (5:6). It is not negative and reactive; believers are not abandoned to the arbitrary will of God. Rather, it is positive and active: *Casting all your care upon Him, for He cares for you.* Peter explained that the believers who continued to carry their worries, anxieties, stresses, and daily struggles by themselves showed that they had not

> Worry does not empty tomorrow of its sorrow; it empties today of its strength.
> *Corrie ten Boom*

trusted God fully. It takes humility, however, to turn everything (literally, "throw your anxieties") over to God and trust that he cares. God is not indifferent; he knows what he's doing in our lives. Sometimes we think that struggles caused by our own sin

and foolishness are not God's concern. But when we turn to God
in repentance, he will bear the weight even of those struggles.
Letting God have your anxieties calls for action, not passivity.
Don't submit to circumstances, but to the Lord who controls circumstances. Peter wanted the believers facing persecution and
suffering to remember to give their troubles to God and that he
cared. Peter surely remembered Jesus' words, "Come to me, all
you who are weary and burdened, and I will give you rest" (Matthew 11:28 NIV; see also Psalm 55:22; Matthew 6:25-34; 10:29-
31; Philippians 4:6-7).

CARE-CASTING
How do we cast all care upon God? Try this simple prayer:
  "Heavenly Father, you know what problems I face today. You
know where I will meet discouragement, and where I may feel
too weak to go on. You know that most of my anxiety is over
worldly pursuits that won't matter when I am with you in eternity.
Today I will trust you each hour for the strength, wisdom, and
love to make this day worthwhile. In all my busyness today, let
me feel all your joy. Amen."

**5:8 Be self-controlled and alert. Your enemy the devil prowls
around like a roaring lion looking for someone to devour.**[NIV]
At the same time that believers can cast all their cares on God,
they must still *be self-controlled and alert.* These words are also
translated, "Pay attention! Wake up!" urgently commanding the
believers, for the warning must be heard. Peter had given the
same admonition in 4:7 regarding
prayer: "The end of all things is near.
Therefore be clear minded and self-controlled so that you can pray" (NIV). Likewise, Paul urged the Thessalonians to
"be alert and self-controlled" (1 Thessalonians 5:6 NIV). Both words refer to not
being lazy in one's faith, but maintaining discipline and steadfastness.

> The safest road to Hell
> is the gradual one—the
> gentle slope, soft under-
> foot, without sudden
> turnings, without mile-
> stones, without sign-
> posts. *C. S. Lewis*

   As soldiers wait and watch, so believers must be constantly
alert for the enemy. All of the persecution facing believers ultimately comes down to one source: *your enemy the devil.* The
devil has other names—Satan, Accuser, Beelzebub—but he is the
source of all evil in the world. He hates God and is God's archen-
emy; thus he also hates God's people and is their enemy as well.
While Satan has no power against God, he does what he can to
harm God's people. Peter described him as prowling *like a roar-*

ing lion looking for someone to devour. Lions attack sick, young, or straggling animals; they choose victims who are alone or not alert. Lions prowl quietly, watching and waiting, suddenly pouncing when their victims least suspect it. They use fear caused by their roar to drive their prey into the jaws of another lion.

Peter warned believers to be alert for Satan, especially in times of suffering and persecution, for he walks up and down the earth (Job 1:7) seeking whom he or his demons can attack and defeat. (For more on demons, see Mark 1:23-26 and Ephesians 6:12.) When believers feel alone, weak, helpless, and cut off from other believers, they can become so focused on their troubles that they forget to watch for danger. In those times, believers are especially vulnerable to Satan's attacks, which come in various forms, often at a person's weakest spot—temptation, fear, loneliness, worry, depression, persecution. Therefore, Peter and Paul urged the believers to always be alert for Satan's tricks.

SATAN'S TACTICS
How does Satan work today? How can we be ready for his attacks?

- He attacks the sick, the weak, the isolated. Be alert to support and surround with prayer those who face illness, who are weakened with pressure and stress, and those who are on the fringes.
- He attacks the newborns. Be especially watchful over new Christians. Help them face doubts and temptations that will weaken their defenses.
- He attacks those who pull away from the church. Go after those whose participation in church has dropped off. They may be especially vulnerable.
- He attacks the unwary. Make sure that teaching and preaching give clear warning about Satan's strategies.
- He attacks using fear. Today's climate of economic, social, and political problems makes us afraid. Beware lest fear drive us to doubt God or abandon his call to love and service.

Many have seen a reference to the horrors of persecution of Christians under Nero when Christians were supposed to have been thrown to lions. We have no documentation of this happening, but in the second century, the Roman historian Tacitus wrote that under Emperor Nero Christians were sewn into animal hides and attacked by wild dogs. Paul used a similar image to Peter's in 2 Timothy 4:17 where he wrote that he had been "rescued from the lion's mouth" (NRSV). Most likely, both men were using a common biblical metaphor describing deliverance from extreme danger (see, for example, Psalm 22:21; 57:4; Ezekiel 22:25).

5:9 Resist him, steadfast in your faith, for you know that your brothers and sisters in all the world are undergoing the same kinds of suffering.^{NRSV} James wrote that if the believers resisted the devil, he would flee from them (James 4:7). Once we have identified the devil as our enemy, we need to understand who he is and how he operates in order to effectively *resist* him. Satan is the leader of angelic beings who revolted against God and were banished from heaven. His primary purpose now is to separate people from God. Destined for destruction, Satan wants to take as much of creation with him as he possibly can. We desperately need God's grace because we are locked in mortal combat with a superior enemy; we need God's help to resist this enemy, Satan. We need to realize, however, that Satan's power over us is only as strong as the illusion that he is more powerful than God's help and care (5:7). We must trust that "the one who is in you is greater than the one who is in the world" (1 John 4:4 NIV). The word "resist" is a term of defense rather than attack. The best way for believers to resist Satan is to remain *steadfast in [their] faith.* The word "steadfast" in Greek is used in Isaiah 50:7 (in the Greek version of the Old Testament—the Septuagint): "I have set my face like flint," referring to rocklike resolution. Like Peter who became the "rock" for the church, we are to set our resolve to resist Satan. But we must trust in Christ our cornerstone (2:6) for our toughness, not in our own human effort. This means trusting in Christ, who has already defeated Satan and will ultimately destroy him. Paul described the "armor" that believers must wear in Ephesians 6:10-18.

FAMILY

Becoming a Christian is like being adopted into a family with so many sisters and brothers that you could never learn all their names, spread around so widely you could never visit them all, in so many countries you could never learn all their languages. But they are family.

Peter reminds us that often the family members suffer. Christian missions scholars say that more Christians have died for their faith in the last fifty years than in the previous two millennia. Two-thirds of Christians live in countries where government is hostile or repressive to Christianity. Because we do not feel the persecution does not mean that it has stopped. Sometimes the best we can do for these persecuted family members is pray that the evil they face be restrained; sometimes we can offer personal help. But always our hearts should be soft toward the pain our big family feels. Today, do something for a sibling in distress. Gather a group to pray, write a check, send a letter.

These believers were encouraged also to remember that they were not alone in their suffering. *For you know that your brothers and sisters in all the world are undergoing the same kinds of suffering.* Other believers scattered all over the world were suffering for the faith; this fact should give them strength. All of this, of course, was under God's control and was accomplishing his purposes.

5:10 **And after you have suffered for a little while, the God of all grace, who has called you to his eternal glory in Christ, will himself restore, support, strengthen, and establish you.**^{NRSV} When we are suffering, we often feel as though our pain will never end. Peter gave these faithful Christians the wider perspective. In comparison with eternity, their suffering would last only *a little while.* This repeats what Peter said in 1:6. Some of Peter's readers would be strengthened and delivered in their own lifetimes. Others would be released from their suffering through death. All of God's faithful followers are assured of eternal life with Christ where there will be no suffering (Revelation 21:4).

God is described as *the God of all grace.* God supplies grace to believers sufficient for every situation they face. While their suffering will be only for a little while, their *glory in Christ* will be *eternal* (see also Romans 8:18; 2 Corinthians 4:16-18). Peter's final words promise victory and vindication, perhaps in this life, but certainly in the next. Not only does God care and give grace, but he promises to *restore* (set right what has gone wrong, put in order, complete), *support* (by admonition and guidance), *strengthen* (give you courage no matter what happens), and *establish* (build on a "rock," set upon a firm foundation, as in Matthew 7:25, therefore being unmovable). In life or in death, God's purposes will be accomplished and his promises to believers will be fulfilled because believers have been *called* into God's eternal glory. God called—this was his initiative; therefore, he will do as he promised.

JUST A LITTLE WHILE
For believers, suffering will not last forever. If you're under stress, if food is scarce, if disease is spreading, God promises that suffering will last "just a little while more."

No matter what trouble you face, hard as it is, God has stamped your life "temporarily out of order," with emphasis on "temporarily." A day is coming when the Great Repairman will wrench evil from the world and restore your life so that it works as God intended. You will be in mint condition, guaranteed to function as God designed.

Many times all we can do is trust God and look forward to Jesus' return, when God will restore us. Our hope is in him!

5:11 To him be the power forever and ever. Amen.NRSV Unlike the
doxology in 4:11, here Peter attributed the *power forever and
ever* to "the God of all grace" (5:10) rather than to Jesus Christ.
Praise is given to the Son and also to God, who alone holds ultimate power forever and ever.

PETER'S FINAL GREETINGS / 5:12-14

Many of the letters in our Bible close with the writer's personal
greetings to friends and colleagues in the letter's destination. In
this case, Peter's letter would be carried along to various
churches, so Peter greeted no one in particular, but rather sent
greetings from those with him in Rome. No doubt the letters of
Peter, Paul, James, John, and Jude offered great comfort to the
Christians scattered across the world. Believers realized a unity
in Christ, a bond of love, and a common future together that
could help them survive whatever the world might bring. The
worldwide Christian family is a continual blessing to believers
who find they have Christ in common, even if they live in different cultures.

**5:12 With the help of Silas, whom I regard as a faithful brother, I
have written to you briefly, encouraging you and testifying
that this is the true grace of God. Stand fast in it.**NIV Silas (also
called Silvanus in some versions) apparently served as the secre-
tary to Peter, writing this letter as Peter dictated it. He may then
have carried this letter to the churches of Asia Minor. More
likely, he took it to the first church, from which it was sent along
by messengers from one church to another, perhaps along the
route implied in 1:1.

Silas was *a faithful brother* to Peter and to other church leaders
as well. Silas was one of the men chosen to deliver the letter from
the Jerusalem Council to the church in Antioch (Acts 15:22). He
accompanied Paul on his second missionary journey (Acts 15:40–
18:11), was mentioned by Paul in the salutation of his letters to
the Thessalonians (1 Thessalonians 1:1; 2 Thessalonians 1:1),
and ministered with Timothy in Corinth (2 Corinthians 1:19).

Peter described the reason for his brief letter—to encourage
believers and to testify that the glory they would soon enter was
the true grace of God. They could rely upon it as fact. The
troubles they faced should never make them doubt; instead, they
should *stand fast* in that grace. Grace would help them stand fast,
and by standing fast, they would receive the reward of that
grace—glory with Christ.

WHEN YOU DOUBT
Some of Peter's readers, like some of us, might pause to
wonder if the Christian life really works, given all the trouble we
face. Maybe it's just a mirage. Perhaps the skeptics are right.
When suffering or oppression cause you to doubt, remember:

- Everybody asks questions, including questions about faith.
  We are not robots, and good questions are normal.
- Good questions raise issues about what is true and what
  isn't. God gave us the capacity to reflect on truth, to probe
  for truth.
- God meets each of us personally, and he listens to the good
  questions we raise about our Creator. God does not reject
  your questions.
- Truth is God's character; it radiates from his Word and pene-
  trates our whole being, mind, and emotions. You can count
  on the fact that your questions will find answers in God.

Explore, wonder, and believe. Take your questions to God,
and you will find the true grace of God.

5:13 **She who is in Babylon, chosen together with you, sends you
her greetings, and so does my son Mark.**[NIV] *Babylon* has been
broadly understood by believers to be a reference to Rome (see
the introduction to 1 Peter, under "Setting," for further discussion). Most scholars suggest that Peter was in Rome when he
wrote this letter and was sending greetings from the church there,
the church being *in* Babylon and *chosen together with* the believers to whom Peter wrote. Peter may have been disguising his
location to protect both himself and the Roman church in this
time of persecution, or he may have been comparing the nation
of Israel's past captivity in Babylon to the Christians' (the new
Israel's) exile in a foreign land, the Roman Empire. The power
and might of Babylon, as well as its sinfulness, could be compared to Rome. In Revelation 14:8, the name "Babylon" was the
name of both an evil city and an immoral empire, a world center
for idol worship. Babylon ransacked Jerusalem and carried the
people of Judah into captivity (see 2 Kings 24–25 and 2 Chroni-
cles 36). Just as Babylon had been the Jews' worst enemy, the
Roman Empire was the worst enemy of the early Christians.
John, who wrote the book of Revelation, probably did not dare
speak against Rome openly and applied the name "Babylon" to
this enemy of God's people. Peter may have been doing likewise.

Mark, also called John Mark, was known to many of this letter's readers because he had traveled widely (Acts 12:25–13:13;
15:36-41) and was recognized as a leader in the church (Colos-

sians 4:10; Philemon 24). Mark was probably with the disciples
at the time of Jesus' arrest (Mark 14:51-52). Mark knew Peter
well, and Peter looked on him as a "son," a close associate in
Christ's service. Tradition holds that Peter was Mark's main
source of information when Mark wrote his Gospel. Paul had
mentioned that Mark was with him at an earlier time in Rome
(Colossians 4:10), so it is likely that he returned there at one time
and was with Peter at the writing of this letter.

**5:14 Greet one another with a kiss of love. Peace to all of you who
are in Christ.**[NRSV] This *kiss of love* was a cultural form of greeting that the Christians used for one another. It expressed the love
and unity among the believers. Peter wanted his readers to
express their love and unity to one another, for they would need
those for strength in the days ahead. (Compare Paul's closing
words in Romans 16:16; 1 Corinthians 16:20; 2 Corinthians
13:12; 1 Thessalonians 5:26.)

Thus Peter ended as he began, with peace (1:2). Peter's final
words, *peace to all,* underscore what was most needed by the
Christians: peace in the middle of turmoil. They could not count
on worldly peace, for it was not to be. Instead, they would find
peace within, by resting in God's grace. Only those who are *in
Christ* can have such peace.

Christians today would do well to demonstrate their love and
unity, perhaps not through a "kiss of love," but through kind
actions and gentle, caring words. Such attitudes and actions bring
peace to the fellowship. Peace among the members allows the
church to move out and beyond in order to bring the life-changing message of the gospel to those who need it.

CHRISTIAN GREETINGS
One sure way to tell others that you are halfhearted, dull witted,
and tuned out is to limply shake hands upon greeting, to
mumble "hello," and never meet eyes. By word and deed you
are a certified deadbeat.

Better, Peter knows, to demonstrate your enthusiasm at
seeing a beloved brother or sister in Christ with joy and good
cheer.

Pep up your Christian greetings. If it's to be a handshake,
double pump and add a big smile. If it's hugging, do it like you
mean it. Observe local customs on how to conduct yourself, but
show a whopping-full portion of enthusiasm. Let your love for
this person show through your action.

2 PETER

INTRODUCTION TO 2 PETER

Who taught you how to read? ride a bike? shoot a basketball? solve algebraic equations? repair an appliance? prepare a meal? understand the political process? draw closer to God?

Whether parents, coaches, professors, pastors, or friends, we hold our teachers in high regard. They have opened our eyes, provided counsel, broadened our horizons, solved mysteries, and filled our minds. We have benefited greatly from their wisdom and expertise.

That's what makes *false* teachers so dangerous. Misusing their privileged position and betraying trust, for the sake of pride, reward, or ambition, they prey on the unsuspecting and lead many astray.

Knowing this powerful influence of teachers, the apostles and other church leaders continually warned against those who would twist the truth and lead believers astray. That was the purpose of 2 Peter. Written to strengthen the church to resist the internal challenge to their faith, this brief letter warns of false teachers who deny Christ and scoffers who mock his return. Believers are to beware and to keep their focus on Christ.

Our world is filled with cult leaders, religious scams, and others who would lead people astray. Estimates of the number of cults worldwide run as high as ten thousand. Some of these cults and many false teachers have even infiltrated the church. Read 2 Peter and determine to grow in your faith and to reject every type of false teaching.

AUTHOR

Peter: apostle of Christ, one of the original twelve disciples, outspoken leader, and courageous preacher.

Second Peter has less external, historical evidence for its genuineness than any other New Testament book. That is because it is so short, contains very little new information, and is not addressed to a specific individual or church. But the writer identifies himself as

Simon Peter and alludes, accurately, to events in Peter's life. These include the Transfiguration (1:16-18) and Jesus' prediction of Peter's death (1:12-14; see also John 21:18). Actually, this letter sounds as though it was authored by Peter.

Through the years, however, many scholars have doubted Peter's authorship. In fact, 2 Peter is probably the most widely doubted New Testament book. One reason for this skepticism arises from the fact that there is little evidence that the church universally accepted 2 Peter as an inspired book of the New Testament until the fourth century. Origen, who lived at about A.D. 185–254, wrote that its genuineness was "disputed," although he accepted it, as did Jerome. In the next century, Eusebius (A.D. 265–340) recognized only 1 Peter as having been written by the apostle, although he admitted that most accepted 2 Peter as Peter's. Eventually, 2 Peter was included in the Festal Letter of Athanasius in A.D. 367, which affirms the 27 books of the New Testament we now have; and this was ratified by the Council of Carthage in A.D. 397.

Internal evidence cited by those who question Peter as the author of this letter includes the following:

The Parallels with Jude. Second Peter and Jude are very similar at certain points. Compare, for example, chapter 2 with Jude 4-18. If the writer borrowed from Jude, so the argument goes, this would rule out apostolic authorship.

This is not a valid conclusion, however. Whether or not Peter borrowed from Jude or vice versa is irrelevant. A number of New Testament writers may have used other sources. In the opening to his Gospel, for example, Luke admits that he checked a number of sources to be certain of the accuracy of his account: "Many have undertaken to draw up an account of the things that have been fulfilled among us, just as they were handed down to us by those who from the first were eyewitnesses and servants of the word. Therefore, since I myself have carefully investigated everything from the beginning, it seemed good also to me to write an orderly account for you, most excellent Theophilus, so that you may know the certainty of the things you have been taught" (Luke 1:1-4 NIV). In his Gospel, Mark may have relied on Peter's testimony, and Paul may have borrowed from a variety of sources. It is also possible that, instead, both Peter and Jude incorporated a common document that denounced the false teaching of their day.

The Relationship with 1 Peter. There is a marked difference in writing style between the two letters ascribed to Peter. This led many in the early church, and also scholars today, to doubt the authenticity of the second.

As early as Jerome, however, the suggestion has been made that Peter used two different amanuenses (secretaries) for writing the letters: Silas (Silvanus) with the first and perhaps Mark with the second. Of course, it is also possible that Silas assisted with the first letter, while Peter wrote the second completely by himself. Undoubtedly there are differences between the two books; however, they have been shown to have a linguistic similarity comparable to 1 Timothy and Titus, both written by Paul. Thus the presence of stylistic differences is not a compelling argument against Peter as the author of both letters.

First and Second Peter also seem to differ in doctrine, adding fuel to the fire: 1 Peter focuses on hope, while 2 Peter emphasizes knowledge. Critics charge that these differences point to different authors.

The emphasis of each letter, however, can be attributed to that letter's purpose. The first was written to Christians facing persecution. Thus, 1 Peter reviews the person and work of Christ and stresses comfort and hope. But 2 Peter was written to counter false teachers who had infiltrated the church. The best way to counteract false teaching is to know the truth and to be ready for Christ's return—the emphases of the second epistle.

Possible Anachronisms. Some scholars believe that some phrases in 2 Peter were common to mystery religions of the second century, thus suggesting a later date for this epistle. Phrases such as "participate in the divine nature" (1:4), "escape the corruption in the world" (1:4), and "eyewitnesses of his majesty" (1:16) are cited. But similar references in the writings of Philo and Josephus (and other discoveries) show that these phrases were common to the first century.

Another possible anachronism is the reference to the destruction of the world by fire (3:7), a common topic in the second century. But here we have the question of which came first. In other words, it is possible that the Christian belief in the destruction of the world by fire may have come from 2 Peter and not the other way around.

Some even have thought that the phrase in 3:4, "ever since our fathers died," refers somehow to the first generation of Christians. If so, this would lead to a late date for the letter. But the context of the verse seems to indicate that reference is to the Old Testament "fathers."

Finally, the reference in 3:15-16 to Paul's letters seems, to some, to imply that the author had all of Paul's writings, which would be rather unlikely for Peter, who died at about the same time as Paul, perhaps even a year earlier. The allusion to Paul's epistles, however, does not necessarily mean that Peter had all of them or that they had all been written. Peter was simply referring to the letters that he had come to know.

Conclusion. The case against Peter as the author of 2 Peter is very shaky at best. In fact, because the letter claims to have been written by the apostle and has been accepted by most of the church for many centuries as being the inspired Word of God and thus belonging in the canon of Scripture, we affirm that Peter is the author.

For more on Peter, see the introduction to 1 Peter.

SETTING

Written from Rome in about A.D. 67.

As was mentioned in the introduction to 1 Peter, the traditional view is that Peter was executed by crucifixion in Rome by Nero in A.D. 67. Thus this letter would have been written just before his death.

At age sixteen, in A.D. 54, Nero became the fifth Roman emperor. At first, his reign was peaceful, giving promise of a bright future. At this time, Paul had appealed to Caesar in the trial in Caesarea (Acts 25:10-11) and, consequently, had been brought to Rome to present his case (A.D. 61). We presume that Paul eventually went to trial and was cleared of all charges, for he was freed to resume his ministry. He used his new freedom to travel extensively. During this time (A.D. 62–67) Peter likely came to Rome and wrote 1 Peter (approximately A.D. 64). There is no evidence that Peter and Paul were in Rome together except during the time just before both were executed.

After he married Poppaea, Emperor Nero became brutal and ruthless, killing his own mother, his chief advisers Seneca and Burrus, and many of the nobility, in order to seize their fortunes. The downward spiral continued, fueled by Nero's lust for attention and excitement. He sponsored wild chariot races, combat between gladiators, and the gory spectacle of prisoners torn apart by wild dogs. Seeing Nero's insane path and sensing the increased persecution of the church, Peter wrote his first epistle to warn believers and to encourage them to be strong and to have hope during their suffering.

In A.D. 64, fire destroyed a large part of Rome. Nero is thought to have ordered the fire himself to make room for a new palace. Deflecting blame from himself, he accused the Christians. This devout religious group made a convenient scapegoat because they were a small minority and because they were popularly thought to engage in many wicked practices, including their refusal to worship the emperor. Thus began the pursuit, capture, and imprisonment of believers, leading to torture and execution. In A.D. 67, Peter wrote his final words in 2 Peter, urging believers to reject false teachers and to hold fast to the truth. Peter knew that he was about to die: "I think it is right to refresh your memory as long as I live in the tent of this body, because I know that I will soon put it aside, as our Lord Jesus Christ has made clear to me. And I will make every effort to see that after my departure you will always be able to remember these things" (1:13-15 NIV). With death in sight, Peter reminded his readers of their great heritage and urged them to look forward to the Day of the Lord. Soon thereafter, Peter fell victim to Nero's thirst for blood.

Eventually, during this time of intense persecution, Paul was arrested again and returned to Rome. In this prison experience, he was isolated and lonely, awaiting execution (2 Timothy 4:9-18). Paul was martyred in the spring of A.D. 68, just before Nero's death.

For more on Rome, see the introduction to 1 Peter.

AUDIENCE

The church at large.

Peter hints at his intended audience in 3:1: "Dear friends, this is now my second letter to you. I have written both of them as reminders to stimulate you to wholesome thinking." It seems, therefore, that the "strangers . . . scattered throughout Pontus, Galatia, Cappadocia, Asia and Bithynia" (1 Peter 1:1) also received this letter. However, a comparison of the opening of the first letter with the second ("To those who through the righteousness of our God and Savior Jesus Christ have received a faith as precious as ours"—1:1) seems to indicate that Peter was addressing a much wider group of believers.

Although a specific group of believers is not mentioned, the intended recipients of this letter were Christians who had been taught the basics of the faith (1:12-13, 16).

OCCASION AND PURPOSE FOR WRITING

To warn Christians about false teachers and to urge them to grow in their faith and in their knowledge of Christ.

Peter knew that he was about to die at the order of Nero and at the hands of a Roman executioner (1:13-15), so he wrote to remind believers to be strong in their faith after his departure (1:3-11, 19-21; 3:1-7).

Peter also had heard of "false teachers" who were twisting the truth, teaching for their own financial gain, and leading believers astray. Evidently these teachers were elevating themselves and their own ideas and interpretations ("stories they have made up" 2:3) above Christ (2:1). So Peter wrote to warn believers of these greedy men, exposing their heresies and predicting their punishment (2:1-22). Jude also warns of this heresy. (For more, see the introduction to Jude.)

This false teaching seems to be the idea that through knowledge a person can find his or her identity and relationship with God. Thus the false teachers were claiming to have special wisdom and insight—the inside track to finding God. This was an early version of Gnosticism, a heresy that would hit the church full force in the second century. Full-blown Gnosticism emphasized that special knowledge provides the way to spirituality. This knowledge was attained through astrology and magic and was available only to those who had been initiated into the Gnostic system. Another Gnostic belief, that all matter is inherently evil and only the spiritual and nonmaterial is of itself good, led to the idea that God could not have created the world and would have no contact with it. Therefore they taught that God, in Christ, never could have become a human person. If matter is evil, how could God ever be united with a human body? Thus they denied either the humanity or the complete deity of Christ (in their view, he couldn't have been both).

Peter concludes this brief letter by reminding his readers of the sure second coming of their Lord and urging them, in light of Christ's return, to guard their faith and to be ready (3:3-18).

MESSAGE

Diligence, False Teachers, Christ's Return.

Diligence (1:5-11, 19-21; 3:14-18). With his last words to the faithful followers of Christ, Peter urges them to continue to grow in their goodness, knowledge, self-control, perseverance, godliness, kindness, and love (1:5-7). Real faith is demonstrated by faithful behavior. Peter knew that believers who are diligent in Christian growth won't backslide or be deceived by false teachers.

Importance for Today. Just as babies and children need to grow and mature physically and mentally, so too Christians need to grow spiritually. Our growth began, by faith, at our spiritual

birth. The spiritual maturation process continues by faith and cul-
minates in love for others. To keep growing, we need to know
God, stay close to him, and remember what we have learned
from him. And we must faithfully obey him.

How's your spiritual maturity? Are you growing in your faith?

False Teachers (2:1-22; 3:3-5, 17). Peter warned believers to
beware of false teachers. These men were proud of their position,
promoted sexual sin, and advised against keeping the Ten Commandments. Peter countered these teachers by exposing their lies
(2:1-3, 10-11, 14, 18-19; 3:3, 16), predicting their eventual punishment (2:1, 3-10, 12-22; 3:16), and emphasizing the Spirit-
inspired Scriptures as the ultimate authority (1:16-21; 3:2, 15-16).

Importance for Today. Today, false teachers wrench Bible
verses out of context, entice believers down doctrinal tangents,
build large followings for their own power and profit, and exploit
the gullible and weak. Christians need discernment in order to
discover false teachers and courage to resist and refute their lies.
God will give us what we need if we read, study, and apply his
Word, the Bible. To reject error, we need to know the truth.

How well grounded are you in the basic doctrines of the Christian faith? How well do you know your Bible?

Christ's Return (3:3-14). The Day of the Lord will come. That's
when Christ suddenly will return, to rescue his own from this evil
world, to punish the ungodly—those who refuse to believe in
Christ—and to create a new heaven and earth where believers
will live forever. "Scoffers" mock the second coming of Christ
(3:3-4), but God's people know that it is sure. No one knows
when Christ will return; but when it happens, everyone will
know. Christians take hope in this promise.

Importance for Today. The cure for complacency, lawlessness,
and heresy is found in the confident assurance that Christ will
return. He has not come yet because God is still giving unbelievers time to repent of their sins and to turn to him. To be ready for
Christ's return, Christians must stay strong in their faith, trusting
God and resisting the pressures and temptations of the world.

What should you do to be ready for Christ's return? What can
you say to those who don't believe in the Second Coming
because it hasn't happened yet?

VITAL STATISTICS

Purpose: To warn Christians about false teachers and to exhort them to grow in their faith and in their knowledge of Christ

Author: Peter

To whom written: The church at large and all believers everywhere

Date written: About A.D. 67, three years after 1 Peter was written, possibly from Rome

Setting: Peter knew that his time on earth was limited (1:13-14), so he wrote about what was on his heart, warning believers of what would happen when he was gone—especially about the presence of false teachers. He reminded his readers of the unchanging truth of the gospel.

Key verse: "His divine power has given us everything we need for life and godliness through our knowledge of him who called us by his own glory and goodness" (1:3 NIV).

OUTLINE

1. Guidance for growing Christians (1:1-21)
2. Danger to growing Christians (2:1-22)
3. Hope for growing Christians (3:1-18)

2 Peter 1

GREETINGS / 1:1-2

First Peter was written just before the time that the Roman emperor Nero began to persecute Christians. Second Peter was written two or three years later (between A.D. 66 and 68), after persecution had intensified. First Peter was a letter of encouragement to the Christians who were suffering, but 2 Peter focuses on the church's internal problems, especially on the false teachers who were causing people to doubt their faith and turn away from Christianity. Second Peter combats the heresies by denouncing the evil motives of the false teachers and reaffirming Christianity's truths: the authority of Scripture, the primacy of faith, and the certainty of Christ's return.

1:1 Simon Peter.[NIV] In contrast to 1 Peter 1:1, this letter begins with the names *Simon Peter.* Peter comes from *petros,* the Greek translation of the Aramaic word *cephas,* meaning "stone." Jesus had given this name to Simon: "Jesus looked at [Simon] and said, 'You are Simon son of John. You will be called Cephas' (which, when translated, is Peter)" (John 1:42 NIV). In those words, Jesus identified not only who Simon was, but who he would become. That is why he gave him a new name. The Gospels do not present Peter as rock solid, but he became a solid rock in the days of the early church, as we learn in the book of Acts. By giving Simon a new name, Jesus introduced a change in Peter's character. Peter had been one of Jesus' twelve disciples and one of the three (with James and John) to whom Jesus had given special training. He often acted as spokesman for the disciples, sometimes being rebuked for not thinking before he spoke. The story of Peter's denial of Jesus and later restoration by him were well known to the early church.

Some Bible versions have Simeon Peter, or even Symeon Peter, which are transliterations from the Hebrew. Thus the debate over whether this letter was written by Peter begins at the first word. The use of "Simeon" has been viewed as either a mark of authenticity or an attempt by some writer to make the letter appear authentic. Some scholars attest that 2 Peter was written by someone else using Peter's name on Peter's behalf. Some have suggested Jude, who wrote the letter of Jude and then used most of his material in Jude to form this letter and expand upon it. Another theory contends that 2 Peter and Jude were composed by different people, perhaps colleagues who worked with Peter (e.g., the letter was approved by Peter and allowed to be sent out under his name). Another theory regarding 2 Peter is that a colleague wrote it on Peter's behalf after Peter's death, confident that he was being true to Peter's teachings. The letter reflects the concern that the church in Rome had for various churches located across the empire toward the end of the first century.

A final theory, which many scholars believe to be correct, is that the differences between 1 and 2 Peter occur from Peter using different writers (amanuenses) to record the letter, or a writer for one and not the other. Therefore, they take literally the name of Peter at the beginning of this letter as describing the true author of this letter. (For more about the questions of authorship, see the "Author" sections in the introduction to 1 Peter and in the introduction to 2 Peter.)

A servant and apostle of Jesus Christ.[NRSV] Peter identified himself first as a *servant,* then as an *apostle of Jesus Christ.* The word translated "servant" *(doulos)* means "slave," one who is subject to the will and wholly at the disposal of his master. Peter used the term to express his absolute devotion and subjection to Jesus Christ. Peter claimed that he belonged to Jesus because Jesus had purchased him from slavery (1 Peter 1:18-19; see also 1 Corinthians 6:19-20). The title "apostle" designated his apostolic position as leader and one of the twelve original disciples (see Matthew 10:2; John 20:21-23). It also designated authority to set up and supervise churches and discipline them if necessary. Even more than a title of authority, "apostle" means one sent on a mission, like an envoy or an ambassador. Peter and the other apostles (including Paul, see Romans 1:1) had been chosen, called, and given the authority and responsibility to evangelize the world.

To those who have received a faith as precious as ours through the righteousness of our God and Savior Jesus Christ.[NRSV] The words *those* and *ours* refer to those who were not apostles and to the apostles themselves (of whom Peter was one). Peter's salutation removed any concern that because many of the apostles had died, Christianity would die. All those believers who had *received a faith as precious* as the apostles' faith received it from the same source: *through the righteousness of*

our God and Savior Jesus Christ. The apostles had been eyewitnesses of Jesus' life, death, and resurrection. Some second-
and third-generation Christians may have been concerned that
somehow their faith was inferior ("faith" referring not to the
body of belief, but rather to the believer's action of trusting in
God). But Peter reassured them that their faith was equal to the
faith of the apostles; it was just as precious and just as sure, for it
was faith in God and in Jesus Christ.

Different forms of the word "value" or "precious" are used in
1 Peter 1:19 ("the precious blood of Christ"), 1 Peter 2:4, 6 (the
"precious" cornerstone), and 2 Peter 1:4 ("great and precious
promises"). In 1:1, it means "equal value" or "equally privileged." Both apostles and all readers have equal access to Christ.
The word "received" translates the verb *lanchano,* meaning "to
obtain by lot" (also used in Luke 1:9; John 19:24). Peter's use of
this word underscores his point that those who have received the
precious faith did so by God's sovereign choice and not for anything they did. The word "righteousness" (some versions say "justice") refers to the fairness and lack of favoritism that give equal
status and privilege to all believers. God's mercy and grace provide faith to us as his gift.

Scholars have debated the authorship of both 1 and 2 Peter, as
well as the audiences for each. We receive a clue in 3:1, which
states that this was "the second letter I am writing to you"
(NRSV), indicating that this letter was most likely intended for the
same audience described in 1 Peter 1:1-2, believers scattered
across the empire.

The phrase "our God and Savior Jesus Christ" has also caused
some debate. Scholars wonder if Peter was referring to two
beings (God, Jesus) or to Jesus Christ as God. Peter had clearly
heard Jesus say during his ministry on earth that Jesus and God
were one. Because only one definite article is used for both
nouns, the grammar strongly suggests that both references are to
one person, Jesus. Thus, Peter's theology is correct as he identifies God the Father and God the Son (as he does in 1:2), as well
as Jesus Christ being God himself.

**1:2 May grace and peace be yours in abundance in the knowl-
edge of God and of Jesus our Lord.**NRSV The first part of Peter's
greeting here is identical to 1 Peter 1:2. *Grace* is God's unmerited
favor; *peace* refers to the peace that Christ made between sinners
and God through Christ's death on the cross. The persecuted and
suffering believers may have been feeling very little grace and an
absence of peace. But Peter reassured them that both grace and
peace could be theirs *in abundance.* How? *In the knowledge of*

God and of Jesus our Lord. The Greek word *ginosko* is the normal verb for "know." When used with the prepositional prefix
epi, the meaning becomes "comprehend thoroughly, know
exactly." Though some scholars have taken this to mean deep and
thorough understanding of Jesus, most likely it means the knowledge of Christ that a person gains at conversion. By knowing
Christ when we become Christians, we begin the process of
receiving grace and peace in abundance.

Peter was concerned that the believers'
faith remain sound and steadfast. Only
knowledge of God and Jesus as Lord
could help them remain faithful in the face
of false teaching (a theme in this letter).
But knowledge must not remain static;
that is, believers must not have knowledge
for the sake of knowledge. Their knowledge must lead to changed behavior (or
"godliness"), as is explained in the next verse.

> There is nothing but
> God's grace. We walk
> upon it; we breathe it;
> we live and die by it;
> it makes the nails and
> axles of the universe.
> *Robert Louis Stevenson*

This verse seems to distinguish between God and Jesus Christ
(although some manuscripts read simply "in knowledge of our
Lord"). Believers must understand both, for their faith rests in
knowing who God is and who Jesus Christ is: "And this is eternal
life, that they may know you, the only true God, and Jesus Christ
whom you have sent" (John 17:3 NRSV).

HOW DOES OUR KNOWLEDGE GROW?
Psychologists who study faith development report that strong,
seasoned, vital faith passes through several stages in its move
from naïveté to maturity. Unfortunately, many churches stifle
believers who are developing, as if growth in knowledge were
a sign of apostasy. For example:

- The first time they raise a serious question, someone (whose
  growth ended years ago) will charge that they are being corrupted by "secular science."
- The first time they wonder about one of the many rules the
  church has created (quite apart from the Bible), someone will
  start to mourn their loss of piety.

"Precious faith" is not static, mechanical, rule bound, or
isolated from knowledge gathered by geologists and astrono-
mers. Precious faith grapples with doctrine, questions methods
and rules, and continues to love all the people in church who
worry about what's going on. Precious faith respects traditions
(while it seeks to change some of them) and yearns for close-
ness (conceptually and practically) to Jesus Christ, precious
Lord. Make sure that your faith grows this way.

GUIDANCE FOR GROWING CHRISTIANS / 1:3-21

1:3 His divine power has given us everything needed for life and godliness, through the knowledge of him who called us by his own glory and goodness.^{NRSV} The word *his* refers back to God and Jesus Christ (being one person, see 1:1). God's *divine power,* or the divine power that Jesus Christ shares with God, is the power well-known to believers, for it raised Christ from the dead. The word *us* refers to all believers—Peter, the other apostles, and all readers of this letter. Christ's power manifests itself in the lives of Christians. Christ *has given us everything needed for life and godliness.* The power to grow doesn't come from within us, but from God. Because we don't have the resources to live as he requires, God gives us everything we need for godly living (to keep us from sin and to help us live for him). "Godliness" means moral uprightness and honoring of God. Peter used the word here and in 1:6-7; 2:9; 3:11. When we were born again, God by his Spirit empowered us with his own moral goodness, enabling us to live for him. See John 3:6; 14:17-23; 2 Corinthians 5:21; and 1 Peter 1:22-23.

KNOWLEDGE OF HIM
We live in an era when religious studies are gaining popularity in universities, sociologists are interested in measuring and understanding religious life, and daily newspapers are expanding coverage of religion. Peter does not refer to those kinds of knowledge.

Peter refers not to information about religion, not cross-cultural seminars about differences between "faith" and "isms," but to genuine, honest, personal, solid, life-changing, dynamic eye-openness to the true God himself, "the knowledge of him." Such knowledge is more like opening a gift than attending a lecture. God wraps the gift and offers it; we open it, dazzled by its beauty and warmed by its love.

What's at the center of this knowledge? That Christ has come to fulfill God's promises. How do we grow in this knowledge? By a prayer that says, "Of all the important and exciting things to learn in my short life, from baseball statistics to computer protocol, I want most of all, and at the center of all, to know Jesus Christ, God's Son, my Savior. Dear God, lead me ever to him."

Not only do believers have grace and peace in the knowledge of God (1:2), but they also receive that divine power to live for God *through the knowledge of* his Son, Jesus Christ. An intimate knowledge of Christ gives believers power for life and growth. The phrase *who called us by his own glory and goodness* explains what attracts people to Jesus in the first place. Jesus' glory (the impact of who he is, his splendor) and his goodness (also translated "moral excellence") draw sinful, seeking people to him. When they come to Christ, they have access to the knowledge they need in order to live for him. "Called" means that believers are chosen (see 1 Peter 1:2, 15; 2:9, 21; 3:9; 5:10 for more on "chosen"). They are called to salvation and to live for God.

1:4 Through these he has given us his very great and precious promises, so that through them you may participate in the divine nature and escape the corruption in the world caused by evil desires.[NIV] Continuing from his thought in 1:3, Peter explained it was *through these* (through Jesus' glory and goodness) that Christ also has *given us* the power for life and godliness (1:3) and even more, as described in this verse. The Greek word translated "given" is *doreomai* (also used in 1:3), meaning "to bestow or endow," thus indicating the value of the promises Christ has given. To "us"—that is, all believers—Christ has bestowed *his very great and precious promises,* so that, through these promises, believers *may participate in the divine nature.* What are these promises? When Christ came, he made promises of the new messianic age. Peter referred to Christ's second coming (1:16; 3:4, 9-10, 12), the new heavens and earth (3:13), and the believers' welcome into Christ's kingdom.

> God's promises are like the stars; the darker the night the brighter they shine. *David Nicholas*

How can we "participate"? To believers, Christ's power has granted a portion of his goodness (moral excellence) in this life. That participation in the divine nature begins with our new birth and extends into eternal glory. How can we "participate"? This verse explains that the promises of Christ's coming and eventual glorification with him purify believers (see 1 John 3:3), and that believers are unified with Christ and share his nature (1 John 1:3). We have fellowship and unity in our relationship with God. But this fellowship does not grant us all divinity, as some have said, because verse 3 attributes the action to God's divine power. We are created beings, thus not divine in the way God is divine. Peter pointed to our future total transformation.

No wonder Peter called these "very great and precious promises"! In his first letter, Peter had written, "You have been born anew, not of perishable but of imperishable seed, through the living and enduring word of God" (1 Peter 1:23 NRSV). After our new birth, we begin to take hold experientially of all the things promised to us as children of God and heirs to the kingdom. There is no way to appropriate these all at once; it happens over time. The promises encourage us to take action to grow. (See also Romans 8:9; Galatians 2:20; 1 Peter 5:1; 1 John 5:1.)

Participation in the divine nature also enables believers to *escape the corruption in the world caused by evil desires.* Thus far in this letter, Peter had been using words that were infrequent in the New Testament, but common to Greek culture. Words such as *theios* (divine) and *arete* (goodness, virtue) were common in Greek but uncommon on the lips of a fisherman from Palestine. (This is another reason for the debate over this letter's authenticity.) However, we cannot presume to know what Peter had learned over the years. He may simply have been using the key terms of the false teachers in order to turn their arguments against them. He spoke their words, but he filled those words with Christian meaning.

Many first-century false teachers emphasized a secret "knowledge" of God; such people were called Gnostics (from the Greek word for "knowledge"). Gnosticism undermined Christianity in several basic ways: (1) it insisted that important secret knowledge was hidden from most believers; (2) it taught that the body was evil; (3) it contended that Christ only seemed to be human but was not. While these false teachers spoke about secret knowledge, Peter wrote of "knowing" Jesus Christ. Pagan philosophers puzzled over "godliness" and "goodness," deciding that these were impossible; Peter used those words to explain that the one true God's divine power imparts godliness and goodness to those who believe in him. Philosophers also discussed at length how people could escape "corruption" of the world and instead "participate in the divine nature" (divinity belonging to the spiritual world rather than the physical world). They concluded that people had to try to get away from the material world into the spiritual realm by keeping strict laws or refusing any type of pleasure. Peter used their language to explain that all their conclusions were incorrect; people escape corruption and partake in the divine nature as God's gift through Christ's death and resurrection.

1:5 For this very reason, make every effort to add to your faith goodness.NIV *For this very reason,* that is, because of God's great gift, their promised destiny, believers must *make every effort* for high moral living. The word translated "make every effort" is *pareisenenkantes*; another unique New Testament word, it means "to work alongside of." While Christ gives the power and the divine nature, believers must make use of that power by making every effort to set aside their sinful desires and actively seek the qualities Peter described below (in addition to others, such as the fruits of the Spirit outlined in Galatians 5:22-23). As Christians make every effort, they will continue to become more and more like Christ.

Believers are to use God's power and every ounce of determination *to add to [their] faith goodness.* The little word "add" is rich with meaning. Peter employed a form of the verb *epichorego* (from which

we get our words "chorus" and "choreogra-
phy") common to Greek culture. A wealthy
person called a *choregos* would pay the
wages for singers in his chorus, as well as
pay the expenses of lavish productions that
were put on in cooperation with a poet and
the state. Thus the word came to stand for
generous and costly cooperation. Here the
word describes the kind of generosity
believers must have in giving of their own
effort and in their cooperation with God in
appropriating the eight characteristics mentioned below.

> There is knowledge and
> knowledge; knowledge
> that resteth in the bare
> speculation of things,
> and knowledge that is
> accompanied with the
> grace of faith and love,
> which puts a man upon
> doing even the will of
> God from the heart.
> *John Bunyan*

HOW DO WE TEACH PETER'S PROGRAM?

Peter gives us a plan for moral development, but he gives us
few clues for how we should present these truths to others.
The only clue seems to be that the eight virtues are presented
in four pairs, indicating that one virtue develops out of the
other. So we know they are progressive and active. Some have
explained the relationship of these virtues to each other like
steps or rungs on a ladder. We must reach one in order to
progress to the next. Others see them as spokes of a wheel to
be developed simultaneously. Perhaps they are like Chinese
boxes where each contains a smaller box inside of the other.
This would indicate that to discover the next virtue, we must
realize and express the prior one. We simply don't know. But
we can be certain of these principles:

- We must fully cooperate with God, using all diligence in
  developing each characteristic.
- We can meditate and ask God for discernment for how we
  should understand and apply each one.
- In areas where we are weak, we can double our efforts to
  exemplify the virtue.

"Faith" is, of course, the first characteristic, for without it,
Christians are no different from the pagans in the world around
them. The faith Peter referred to is faith in Christ, faith that
brings them into the family of God. While people might have
some of the following characteristics by nature, those are worthless in eternity without being grounded in faith.

But Christians were not to stop at faith alone. Peter knew, like
James, that faith without works is dead (see the Life Application
Bible Commentary *James* on James 2:14-26). The believers had
work to do. The word *arete* (goodness) is also translated "virtue."
The Greek word is used only here, in 1:3 above, and in Philippians

4:8. In all cases, it signifies moral excellence, high moral standards that surpass those of pagans. While uncommon in the New Testament, this word was familiar to Greek moral philosophy. While the Greek philosophers discussed such excellence at length, Peter once again explained that true goodness could be found only in relationship with Christ. To their faith, believers were to add lifestyles that mirrored Christ's (1:3). Their motive for such high standards? The shining moral quality of Christ's life compels us to be our very best.

MAKE IT GROW
Faith must be more than belief in certain facts; it must result in action, growth in Christian character, and the practice of moral discipline, or it will die away (James 2:14-17). Peter lists several of faith's actions: learning to know God better, developing perseverance, doing God's will, loving others. These actions do not come automatically; they require hard work. They are not optional; all of them must be a continual part of the Christian life. We don't finish one and start on the next, but we work on them all together. God empowers and enables us, but he also gives us the responsibility to learn and to grow.

And to goodness, knowledge.[NIV] *Knowledge* was a word common in the Greek lists of virtues. Thus Peter included it here with a specifically Christian focus. "Knowledge" as used here refers not to the knowledge of God that leads to salvation; rather, here *gnosis* is that knowledge that leads to wisdom and discernment that enables believers to live godly lives (see Ephesians 5:17; Philippians 1:9; Hebrews 5:14).

GROWING CLOSE
Tired of boring, do-nothing religion—the kind that shuffles into a pew on Sunday and stays awake by thinking about what professional sports to watch that afternoon?

Peter has a deal for you. "Off the couch," he says. "Let's get shakin'." These eight qualities move us from couch-potato faith (lots of bulk, not much activity) to marathon faith (lean, mean, light, strong, and on the move).

The eight qualities (faith to love) are part of one seamless package, the total person. But you can work on them one at a time. Here's how: Pray about one of them, talk about it, practice it. Don't wait for perfection before moving to the next one. Plan to repeat the process soon. These are traits of growing faith, the only kind that matters.

1:6 And to knowledge, self-control.^{NIV} The word for self-control (*egkrateia*) is used only here and in Acts 24:25 and Galatians 5:23 (as one of the fruits of the Spirit). *Self-control* refers to mastery over sinful human desires in every aspect of life. This was another highly prized virtue for the Greeks. Their focus, of course, was entirely on self-effort, but the problem was that self-effort always fails in the long run because it may control the body but does not affect inward desires. We know from Romans 8:13 and Galatians 5:22-23 that Christians have the Holy Spirit's help to gain self-control. (See the discussion in Life Application Bible Commentary *Colossians* on Colossians 2:22-23.)

The false teachers were teaching that self-control was not needed because works would not help believers anyway (2:19). It is true that works cannot bring salvation, but it is absolutely false to think that works are unimportant. Peter explained that believers are saved so that they can grow to resemble Christ. God wants to produce his character in his people. But this demands discipline and effort. The believers' knowledge of Christ should naturally lead to self-control.

SELF-CONTROL
Whatever happened to self-control? Many books and speakers guide wandering souls to self-fulfillment, self-satisfaction, and self-awareness. Not many tackle self-control.

Self-control requires an honest look at your strengths and weaknesses, with emphasis on the latter. It means building the will to say no when a powerful appetite inside you screams yes.

- No to fatty food, choosing health instead.
- No to friends who will lead you away from Christ.
- No to casual sex, saving intimacy for marriage.
- No to laziness in favor of "can do" and "will do."

Self-control is a long, steady course in learning attitudes that do not come naturally, and channeling natural appetites toward God's purposes. Where are your weak points? Pray with a friend for God's help to redirect weakness into strength.

And to self-control, perseverance.^{NIV} The quality of self-control must then lead to *perseverance,* the ability to steadfastly endure suffering or evil without giving up one's faith. Perseverance is not a stoic indifference to whatever fate allows; rather, perseverance springs from faith in God's goodness and control over all that happens in believers' lives. This word is often used in the New Testament to refer to steadfastness in the face of adversity (see, for example, Romans 5:3-4; Colossians 1:11; 1 Thessalonians 1:3; 2 Thessalonians 1:4; James 1:3).

And to perseverance, godliness.^{NIV} To a steadfast character, believers are to add *godliness*. This is another word that is unusual to the New Testament, but common to Greek ethics lists of that day. Paul emphasized godliness in the Pastoral Epistles as being that virtue which should characterize the life and conduct of the believers (see 1 Timothy 6:6, 11; 2 Timothy 3:5; Titus 1:1; 2:12). Godliness *(eusebeia)* was the primary word for "religion" and referred to a person's correct attitudes toward God and people, usually referring to performing obligatory duties. Here in 2 Peter the word describes an awareness of God in all of life—a lifestyle that exemplifies Christ and is empowered by him (the same word is used in 1:3). Christians must have a right relationship with God and right relationships with fellow believers. The false teachers claimed such "godliness," but were sadly lacking in reverence toward God and in good attitudes toward others.

1:7 And to godliness, brotherly kindness.^{NIV} If godliness includes right attitudes toward others, then to godliness believers must add *brotherly kindness* (also translated "mutual affection" NRSV). In non-Christian circles, this word referred to affection between family members. Peter extended its meaning in this letter to include the family of believers. It is an especially intense love (see 1 Peter 1:22; Hebrews 10:24) that considers others as brothers and sisters. John explained the connection between godliness and brotherly kindness this way: "Those who say, 'I love God,' and hate their brothers or sisters, are liars; for those who do not love a brother or sister whom they have seen, cannot love God whom they have not seen. The commandment we have from him is this: those who love God must love their brothers and sisters also" (1 John 4:20-21 NRSV). This "brotherly kindness" *(philadelphia)* refers to a concerned caring for others.

And to brotherly kindness, love.^{NIV} While Christians must exhibit "brotherly kindness" in their dealings with others, their love must also go deeper. To brotherly kindness, they must add *love* that always puts others first, seeking their highest good. The Greek word *agape* refers to self-sacrificial love. It is the kind of love God demonstrated in saving us. Such love among believers allows for weaknesses and imperfections, deals with problems, affirms others, and has a strong commitment and loyalty. Such a bond will hold the believers together no matter what persecutions and suffering they may face.

1:8 For if these things are yours and are increasing among you, they keep you from being ineffective and unfruitful in the knowledge of our Lord Jesus Christ.^{NRSV} The eight qualities mentioned above *(these things)* ought to be part of every believer's life, but they are not static. Believers don't merely "have" these qualities; instead, they are *increasing* in these qualities. To grow in these qualities, we must practice them in the rough-and-tumble of daily life. As these characteristics increase, they keep believers from *being ineffective and unfruitful in the knowledge of our Lord Jesus Christ.* "Ineffective" means idle and slothful, literally "out of work," and parallels James 2:20, "Faith without works is dead" (NKJV). "Unfruitful" means barren, unproductive, and refers to the life crowded with pleasures and cares (see Matthew 13:22). The false teachers exemplified these qualities (see chapter 2 and Jude 11).

Believers "know" the Lord Jesus, but their knowledge must bear fruit in such qualities as those mentioned above; otherwise, the believers are "ineffective" and "unfruitful." This can happen when believers rest on past achievements, stagnate, and cease to grow, or when other priorities dampen our desire and service to Christ. The false teachers sought knowledge for its own sake, but Peter explained that we must go beyond knowledge. Our knowledge must bear fruit.

Our faith must go beyond what we believe; it must become a dynamic part of all we do, resulting in good fruit and spiritual maturity. Salvation does not depend on positive character qualities and good works; rather, it produces those qualities and works. A person who claims to be saved while remaining unchanged does not understand faith or what God has done for him or her. Faith in and knowledge of the Lord Jesus Christ that leads to growth in these qualities causes believers to make a difference in their world and persevere to the end.

FRUIT GROWERS
Bearing fruit was important to Jesus' teaching (see John 15:1-8). Fruit growing on a tree describes genuine disciples of Jesus. There's no fruit on broken branches, and there's no life without fruit. Fruit harbors the seed, which perpetuates the life of the species.

A true disciple has life flowing from Jesus, and his own character and power shape the disciple's attitudes and behaviors. True disciples become fruitful by God's power. Does your moral life result in fruitful impact on those around you? Is your spiritual knowledge producing greater moral integrity?

1:9 For anyone who lacks these things is nearsighted and blind, and is forgetful of the cleansing of past sins.NRSV In contrast to the believer who is increasing in the positive qualities Peter mentioned above, a believer who *lacks these things,* who is not growing in these qualities, *is nearsighted and blind.* Peter had harsh words for believers who refused to grow. The word "near-sighted" is also translated "shortsighted." Peter may have meant that believers who were not growing could see only as far as the world around them. Their shortsightedness left them *blind* to the big picture—the promise of eternity and the glory of becoming more like Christ. Thus they remained tied to earthly possessions and transient promises. The word *muopazo* (shortsighted) can also mean "to blink" or "to shut the eyes." Thus Peter may also have meant that these believers were intentionally closing their eyes to Christ's light, thus causing spiritual blindness. This second interpretation is most likely, for the phrase *is forgetful of the cleansing of past sins* pictures those who deliberately put out of their mind all that Christ had done in erasing the sins they committed before they were saved. The "cleansing" was a reminder of the believer's vows at baptism—the public show of faith and desire to live for Christ. At baptism, believers professed their cleansing from past sins and their break with old, sinful lifestyles. A believer who is "forgetful" of this and refuses to grow becomes unfruitful for God.

1:10 Therefore, brothers and sisters, be all the more eager to confirm your call and election.NRSV The word *therefore* ties this verse with the preceding passage (1:3-9):

■ therefore, because Christ has empowered believers through knowledge of him to live morally excellent lives (1:3),

■ therefore, because he has given believers great and precious promises so that we can participate in the divine nature and escape the corruption in the world (1:4),

■ therefore, because believers desire to increase in godly characteristics so that they do not become ineffective and unfruitful (1:8)—

then believers must *be all the more eager to confirm* themselves as God's children. The Greek word translated "all the more eager" (*spoudasate*) was also used in 1:5, "make every effort." Peter urgently called upon these believers to determine to live for God, no matter how difficult it might become, and to be growing in the virtues mentioned above. To *confirm your call and election* is also translated "make your calling and election sure." On one hand, the calling and election were already "sure" and "confirmed" because they were by God's initiative. However, the believers' behavior would "confirm" that call by their good qualities and good works. They were "confirming" their call and election not for God, but for themselves. Peter probably was making no distinction between the words "call" and "election" and was using them to emphasize God's initiative in salvation.

CALLED, ELECTED
Peter wanted to rouse the complacent believers who had listened to the false teachers and believed that because salvation is not based on good deeds they could live any way they wanted. If you truly belong to the Lord, Peter wrote, your hard work will prove it. If you're not working to develop the qualities listed in 1:5-7, you may not belong to him. If you are the Lord's—and your hard work backs up your claim to be chosen by God ("calling and election")—you will be able to resist the lure of false teaching or glamorous sin. What does your life say about your faith?

For if you do this, you will never stumble.NRSV The believers to whom Peter wrote were in danger of turning to the doctrine of false teachers who were teaching that immoral living incurred no judgment. These false teachers said that once people were "saved," they could live any way they pleased. Peter countered this teaching, explaining that Christians must match their calling and election with holy living. If they did this, they would *never stumble* (see Colossians 1:22-23; 2 Timothy 2:12-13). The word "stumble" means more than merely to "trip." It means to come to grief or ruin, referring to the Day of Judgment, when sin takes the unbeliever and rebel into eternal damnation.

1:11 And you will receive a rich welcome into the eternal kingdom of our Lord and Savior Jesus Christ.NIV Those who live fruitful and productive lives for God, who do not disastrously stumble along the path to *the eternal kingdom* (heaven) *will receive a rich welcome.* This pictures the type of welcome Stephen experienced as he was martyred, "'Look,' he said, 'I see heaven open and the Son of Man standing at the right hand of God'" (Acts 7:56 NIV). All believers will experience a wonderful welcome into their true home, the eternal kingdom of the Lord and Savior. Those who have been called and chosen, but have been unfruitful and have stumbled much along the way, will still reach the kingdom and receive their salvation, but it will be, as Paul wrote in 1 Corinthians 3:15, "only as through fire" (NRSV). Whether this welcome will be any different is unknown; but Peter encouraged his readers to confirm their calling and election (1:10) and to ensure a rich welcome by living to please God during their time on earth. Looking toward our future eternal life provides the motivation for right living now. We must be centered on heaven's priorities, not those of this world. We can face hardships and still be faithful to God because we know the bright future he has for us. How wonderful it is to contemplate that God wants, expects, and waits for us.

LIVING FOR THE FUTURE
God promises us a rich welcome. Unless God's promise of eternal life with him is true, morality makes no sense at all. We might as well get what pleasure we can each day until death does us in.

Everywhere the Bible points to history's culmination when all believers will live with God forever. God's character defines the future. God's love wants to share that future with you.

Today may have been tedious, humdrum, discouraging, or hurtful, but God promises a bright tomorrow when all his holiness will shine and all your devotion to him will be rewarded. You're almost there. Keep up the pace. Never even think about quitting. Jesus welcomes you at the finish line.

1:12 Therefore I intend to keep on reminding you of these things, though you know them already and are established in the truth that has come to you. Because of the glories awaiting the believers, Peter intended to *keep on reminding* them not to allow their salvation to become a license for immoral living, nor to rest content in knowledge of the gospel without obeying it and applying it to their lives. The times were difficult—persecution was increasing from without; false teachers were spewing evil doctrine from within. He encouraged the believers to continue to stand firm on the basics of their faith, to continue to remind themselves of these truths (even though they knew them already), and to reestablish themselves in the truth they had been taught.

REVIEWING THE BASICS
Outstanding coaches constantly review the basics of the sport with their teams, and good athletes can execute the fundamentals consistently well. Believers must not neglect the basics of their faith, even as they go on to study deeper truths. Just as an athlete needs constant practice, Christians need constant reminders of the fundamentals of our faith and of how we came to believe in the first place. Don't allow yourself to be bored or impatient with messages on the basics of the Christian life. Instead, take the attitude of an athlete who continues to practice and refine the basics.

Peter explained that he knew these believers were *established in the truth*. The word "established" translates the perfect passive participle, *esterigmenous*. Jesus used a form of the word when he told Peter, "But I have prayed for you, Simon, that your faith may not fail. And when you have turned back, strengthen *[sterizo]* your brothers" (Luke 22:32 NIV). Knowing (being established in) the truth is a source of spiritual strength.

1:13-14 **I think it is right to refresh your memory as long as I live in the tent of this body, because I know that I will soon put it aside, as our Lord Jesus Christ has made clear to me.**NIV Peter would continue to "remind" the believers (1:12) and *refresh* (literally "wake up" or "arouse") their memories regarding the basic truths of their faith as long as he lived. The phrase *as long as I live in the tent of this body* emphasizes the transitoriness of this life on earth (see Paul's use of the word "tent" in 2 Corinthians 5:1, 4). As nomads pack up their tents in order to move to a new location, so human beings one day will put aside their physical bodies in order to move into eternity—in the case of believers, to new and glorious bodies (1 Corinthians 15:42-44). Peter reminds us that the eternal realm matters, not the temporal.

MEMORY AIDS
An English professor, arriving for an eleven o'clock class, admitted to his students that he had left their quizzes in his car. The students insisted he get them. But walking back to the car, he began thinking about research projects and, forgetting the nature of his errand, he jumped into the car and promptly went home for lunch.

The professor needed memory aids, and so do we. That's why it's OK for sermons on Sunday or family devotions on Monday to emphasize regular, normal, well-rehearsed themes of God's Word: Jesus' coming, death, and resurrection; salvation by faith; prayer and repentance; heaven ahead of us and evil behind us.

Always take these reminders to heart. Listen carefully, even if it's for "the thousandth time."

Peter knew that he would die *soon*. Many years before, Christ had prepared Peter for the *kind* of death Peter would face, although the only timing Peter knew was that he would be "old" (see John 21:18-19). At the writing of this letter, Peter knew that his death was at hand. Scholars have discussed whether Peter had received some kind of revelation so that he knew his death was coming, or whether Peter simply thought he would die because of the intense persecution in Rome and his being a prominent Chris-

tian figure in the church. In any case, Peter was martyred for the
faith in about A.D. 68. According to some traditions, he was crucified upside down, at his own request, because he did not feel worthy to die in the same manner as his Master.

**1:15 And I will make every effort to see that after my departure
you will always be able to remember these things.**^{NIV} Christ
had told Peter about Peter's own death, and Peter carried this
knowledge through his years of ministry. Now, as an old man,
knowing he would soon die, Peter wrote of his coming *departure*
calmly and fearlessly. It would be merely a "departure" (the
Greek word is *exodos*), a moving on to another place. Peter was
prepared to leave the "body" (1:13) and move into the "eternal
kingdom" (1:11).

WILL GRANDCHILDREN BELIEVE?
How can we get future generations to remember Christ and
how important he is to us? Will the faith you hold precious
survive in your family after you're gone? Here are six things
you can do:

1. Talk with your grandchildren. Many grandparents fail to
   connect with younger ones, especially as grandchildren
   become teenagers. Talk about God. Keep it simple.
2. Start a scrapbook that tells the story of faith in your family.
   Include important dates and records (baptisms, funeral
   announcements, etc.).
3. Make an audio or video tape of the real you—your
   struggles and God's work in your life. Explain how you
   became a Christian.
4. Talk about God in your Last Will and Testament.
5. Plan your Christian funeral, so that everyone will know
   where your hope lay.
6. Demonstrate assurance that your future with God in
   heaven is a source of real happiness.

Peter again used the Greek word *spoudaso,* translated "make every
effort," to reveal his urgency and strong desire (see 1:5; 1:10). Peter
wrote that he would *make every effort* so that the believers would
always be able to remember these things. In other words, Peter wanted
to make sure that his teaching would be available to them after his
death. "These things" could refer to more than just Peter's words in
this letter. Some scholars suggest that Peter was referring to the Gospel
of Mark, for Peter is thought to have been Mark's major source. Some
believe Peter was describing future letters that he hoped to write before
his death. Some think he was referring to his labor to finish this letter
before his death. Those who take the view that this letter was written

by another author after Peter's death see this
phrase as the author revealing Peter's desire
that the teaching in 1:3-11 be his final "testament" (farewell sermon, last words) to the
believers, and that the believers would
"remember these things" after he died.

> I came from God, and
> I'm going back to God,
> and I won't have any
> gaps of death in the
> middle of my life.
> *George MacDonald*

It is not clear what written material
Peter had in mind, but it is clear that Peter
was concerned that the gospel teachings not be forgotten after the
deaths of the eyewitnesses to Jesus' ministry on earth (to which he
alludes in 1:16). The Christians were to carry on this message after
the apostles' departure from this world.

**1:16 For we did not follow cleverly devised myths when we made
known to you the power and coming of our Lord Jesus
Christ, but we had been eyewitnesses of his majesty.**[NRSV] Peter
explained that he and the other apostles *(we),* the original carriers
of the gospel message, had not been following *cleverly devised
myths,* nor had they taught such myths (the word could also be
translated "stories" or "fables"). Some scholars feel that Peter
was referring to the cleverly devised myths of the false teachers
or to fables about the gods or even allegories of Old Testament
figures (see 1 Timothy 1:4; 4:7; Titus 1:14). But most likely,
Peter was defending the gospel against accusations from false
teachers that the Incarnation, Resurrection, and Second Coming
were myths (see 3:4; 2 Timothy 2:17-18).

Peter and the apostles had been *eyewitnesses of [Jesus'] majesty.*
They knew who Jesus was because they had seen Jesus' majesty
with their own eyes. Peter was referring to the Transfiguration,
where Jesus' divine identity had been revealed to Peter and two
other disciples, James and John (see Matthew 17:1-8; Mark 9:2-8;
Luke 9:28-36). At the Transfiguration, the three disciples received a
foretaste of what Christ would be like in glory and what eternity
with him would be like. Thus all that the apostles taught and wrote,
even regarding the awesome *power* of Christ and the promise of his
second *coming,* was grounded in experience and fact, without embel-
lishment or speculation. The believers must always remember that
the truth they received was truth indeed, passed on by those who had
lived with and learned from Jesus.

Jesus had revealed some of his most unusual demonstrations
of "power" to his disciples alone. He had stood up in their partly
swamped boat and had taken command of the wind and the
waves. He had walked on water. He had given three of them an
incredible glimpse of his glory. The disciples later relied on what
they had seen and experienced. At first, most of it was hard to

understand. Even after the Transfiguration, Jesus had ordered the three amazed disciples "not to tell anyone what they had seen until the Son of Man had risen from the dead" (Mark 9:9 NIV). Everything became more clear after Jesus' resurrection and the coming of the Holy Spirit. The apostles made these demonstrations of Jesus' power known to the believers, and also made known Jesus' "coming," his return, when the kingdom would be displayed. Jesus' "power" will also be seen when he raises the dead (John 5:28), brings judgment (John 5:27), destroys the lawless one (2 Thessalonians 2:8) and his evil accomplices (Revelation 19:11-16), and consummates his kingdom (Revelation 11:15-18).

Verses 16-21 are a strong statement about the inspiration of Scripture. Peter affirmed that the Old Testament prophets wrote God's messages. He put himself and the other apostles in the same category because they also proclaimed God's truth. The Bible is not a collection of fables or human ideas about God. It is God's very words given "through" people "to" people. Peter emphasized his authority as an eyewitness as well as the God-inspired authority of Scripture to prepare the way for his harsh words against the false teachers. If these wicked men were contradicting the apostles and the Bible, their message could not be from God. Peter's affirmation "we did not follow cleverly devised myths" denies the charge from some liberal scholars that the Gospels are merely myth. Peter and the apostles staked their lives on the truth of those narratives.

1:17 For he received honor and glory from God the Father when that voice was conveyed to him by the Majestic Glory, saying, "This is my Son, my Beloved, with whom I am well pleased."NRSV Peter wrote what only an eyewitness to this event could have written. At the Transfiguration, Jesus had *received honor and glory from God the Father.* Because of Peter's mention that he, James, and John had been eyewitnesses (1:16), "honor and glory" most likely refers to what they saw—that is, Jesus' glorious appearance: "His face shone like the sun, and his clothes became as white as the light" (Matthew 17:2 NIV). "Honor" refers to Jesus' exalted status conveyed by the voice. It was God's public announcement of Jesus' sonship. "Glory" refers to Jesus' shining moral splendor as light radiating from his Person (see 1 Peter 1:7).

The Transfiguration was a brief glimpse of Jesus' true "glory from God the Father." This was God's divine affirmation of everything Jesus had done and was about to do. The Transfiguration assured the disciples that their commitment was well placed and their eternity was secure. Jesus was truly the Messiah, the divine Son of God. On earth, Jesus appeared as a man, a poor carpenter from Nazareth turned itinerant preacher. But at the Transfiguration, Jesus' true identity was revealed with the glorious radiance that he had before coming to earth (John 17:5; Philippians 2:6) and that he will have when he returns in glory to establish his kingdom (Revelation 1:14-15).

During the Transfiguration, a cloud appeared and enveloped the group on the mountain (Jesus, Elijah, Moses, Peter, James, and John). God's voice came *by the Majestic Glory,* singling out Jesus from Moses and Elijah as the long-awaited Messiah who possessed divine authority. The "Majestic Glory" is a name for God (see Exodus 16:10; Numbers 14:10) and means that God himself exalted Christ. As he had done at Jesus' baptism (Mark 1:11), God gave verbal approval of his Son. The voice spoke to the three disciples, saying, *"This is my Son, my Beloved, with whom I am well pleased."*

HONORING JESUS
Because God the Father honored Jesus at the Transfiguration, so should everyone else. But profane use of Jesus' name is so common that we often dismiss it as nothing. Motion picture tough guys use Jesus' name as an expletive; more and more television tough guys are following that example.

Christians should not even approach such profanity. Many are the "minced oaths" that come close to the phonetics and cadence of actual profanity. Why play with fire? Keep the minced and the real oaths far from your tongue. Reserve the name of Jesus for high honor and joyful praise.

1:18 And we heard this voice which came from heaven when we were with Him on the holy mountain.^{NKJV} Not only had the three disciples (*we* refers to Peter, James and John) seen Christ's honor and glory, but they also had *heard* about it as well—from God himself! Peter's testimony counters the heresy of the false teachers. They pointed to esoteric knowledge as the basis of salvation and holiness. Peter pointed to a heavenly origin of the voice, not earthly knowledge. The voice that spoke approvingly of the Son *came from heaven* while the disciples were with Jesus *on the holy mountain.* The words "holy mountain" were not meant to designate any particular site (such as Mount Sinai or even Zion, both considered holy sites). In fact, the location of the Transfiguration is uncertain. Mark wrote that the disciples went "up a high mountain" (Mark 9:2 NRSV); most likely this was either Mount Hermon or Mount Tabor. Mount Hermon, located near Caesarea Philippi, is over nine thousand feet high; thus it or a lower nearby mountain has been suggested. Others suggest Mount Tabor, a steep area in the Plain of Jezreel; however, it has a lower elevation than Mount Hermon.

The Transfiguration obviously had had a profound impact on Peter. As he prepared for his death, his last words of assurance to future believers focused on the reliability of the gospel. Peter knew that his eternal glory was sure, for he had seen it with his own eyes. Thus he could assure all believers that they too would one day share in this glory.

1:19 And we have the word of the prophets made more certain, and you will do well to pay attention to it, as to a light shining in a dark place, until the day dawns and the morning star rises in your hearts.[NIV] As Peter reflected on the assurances of the Second Coming—what he and the other apostles had seen, heard, and experienced—he was reminded of another assurance (*we* here could still refer to the apostles, or more likely Peter may have meant that all believers in general also have this assurance). He added the prophets to the mixture of evidence, showing the error of the false teachers. What God had said on the mountain made *the word of the prophets* (that is, the Old Testament Scriptures) even more *certain*. These words could mean that the Transfiguration verified and validated all that the prophets had foreseen—God would come to earth as a human; Jesus Christ was that person, human but glorious, who would save people from their sins. More likely, these words could mean that if the people were having trouble believing Peter, then they could go back to the Old Testament Scriptures; there they would find the same truth.

The Old Testament Scriptures were not set aside by Christ. Indeed, Christ himself said, "Do not think that I have come to abolish the Law or the Prophets; I have not come to abolish them but to fulfill them" (Matthew 5:17 NIV). Thus Peter strongly advised the believers, as they kept hold on the Scripture without veering from its truth (as he explained above), that they should also *pay attention to* the Scriptures as one would pay attention *to a light shining in a dark place*. The psalmist wrote, "Your word is a lamp to my feet and a light to my path" (Psalm 119:105 NKJV). This light illuminates the "dark place," referring to the world in its sin or the mind in its ignorance, but especially to these heretical teachings. The Old Testament Scriptures verify the gospel, making even more "certain" its truth. See Paul's use of the Old Testament as warning in 1 Corinthians 10:6, 11.

The believers were encouraged to continue in this manner *until the day dawns and the morning star rises in your hearts.* The "day" that will dawn refers to Peter's recurrent theme of the second coming of Christ. Christ is the "morning star," and when he returns, he will shine in his full glory. These words most likely alluded to Numbers 24:17, "A star will come out of Jacob" (NIV), a verse that was considered to be a prophecy of the Messiah. The Greek term *phosphoros* (literally meaning "light-bearer" or "morning star") was commonly used by Greek writers to describe Greek divinities and kings. Christ is the true deity and king because he is the unique bearer of light, "the light of life" (John 8:12). (For more on Christ as the morning star, see Luke 1:78; Ephesians 5:14; Revelation 2:28; 22:16.)

Until the day comes when Christ returns to dispel all darkness, believers have Scripture as a light and the Holy Spirit to illuminate Scripture for us and guide us as we seek the truth. But when Christ is completely revealed, Scripture will no longer be needed. The phrase "rises in your hearts" could mean that at Christ's return, believers will receive an illumination that will dispel all previous doubts and misunderstandings. There will be instant recognition of Christ when he returns (Mark 13:21-26).

1:20-21 **First of all you must understand this, that no prophecy of scripture is a matter of one's own interpretation, because no prophecy ever came by human will, but men and women moved by the Holy Spirit spoke from God.**NRSV Peter wrote here of revelation, the source of all Scripture. One's belief about revelation is foundational for faith. Christians must be able to rest on the infallibility of Scripture, or their faith is of no value. Hence Peter's words, *first of all you must understand this.* Perhaps the false teachers were denying Scripture by denying its divine origin, saying that the words were merely the writers' interpretations, not God's words.

Some commentators have thought that the expression "that no prophecy of scripture is a matter of one's own interpretation" refers to the reader's interpretation of the Scripture, and then said that this indicates that the reader must not

> There is only one real inevitability: It is necessary that the Scripture be fulfilled.
> *Carl F. H. Henry*

interpret the Scripture privately and/or the reader must not interpret any portion of Scripture by itself but by all of Scripture, so that Scripture can interpret Scripture. But the context of 1:21 indicates that Peter was not speaking of the reader of Scripture but of the speaker of Scripture, the prophet. This verse tells us that the Scripture (specifically the Old Testament prophecies) did not orig-

inate with any man nor was it interpreted by the prophets themselves as they delivered the message. False prophets produced
false prophecies from their own inspiration (see Ezekiel 13:2, 17
NASB), but genuine prophets did not interpret the message as God
gave it to them; they simply spoke what was spoken to them and
recorded the God-originated, Spirit-motivated words (see 1:21).

Peter reaffirmed the divine origin of Old Testament prophecy,
that the writers were *men and women moved by the Holy Spirit,*
speaking *from God.* Scripture did not come from the creative
work of the prophets' own invention or interpretation. The same
God who spoke to the disciples at the Transfiguration had spoken
to the prophets, guiding them in their writings. God inspired the
writers, so their message is authentic and reliable. God used the
talents, education, and cultural background of each writer (they
were not taking dictation); and God cooperated with the writers
in such a way to ensure that the message he intended was faithfully communicated through the words they wrote.

Peter was not prohibiting Bible study, personal devotions, interpretation, or application of the Bible. Instead, he was emphasizing the Bible's authenticity, its divine origin. The Bible is not a
collection of stories, fables, myths, or merely human ideas about
God. It is not a human book. Through the Holy Spirit, God
revealed his person and plan to certain believers, who wrote
down his message for his people. The process of "inspiration"
makes Scripture completely trustworthy because God was in control of its writing. The Bible's words are entirely accurate and
authoritative for our faith and for our lives. Through knowledge
of the Scriptures, believers would be able to recognize and stand
firm against false teaching; through the knowledge of the
Scriptures, believers would have all the tools and guidance they
would need to live for God.

2 Peter 2

This chapter includes severe warnings against the false teachers who had infiltrated the church and threatened to turn young believers away from the truth. (It contains parallels to Jude 4-16. See the introduction to 2 Peter for explanation.) Peter spared no words against these false teachers, explaining their evil characteristics and motives, the danger of their teaching, and the certainty of their fate.

The church has done a great deal to identify false teachers and cults today, so what dangers do we face? False teachers today may be the ones who ignore or leave out elements of scriptural teaching such as

- warnings about Christ's second coming

- dangers of cultural infiltration into our lifestyles through materialism and secularism

- pitfalls of sexual immorality and greed

Believers today would do well to heed Peter's warnings against false teachers; the danger is great.

2:1 **But there were also false prophets among the people, just as there will be false teachers among you.**^{NIV} The end of chapter 1 leads into the topic of his letter. Peter had explained that God had worked through humans to give his words to people (1:21). At the same time, however, evil was at work. The true prophets spoke and wrote God's words, but *there were also false prophets among the people.* In Old Testament times, false prophets contradicted the true prophets (see, for example, Deuteronomy 13:1-5; 1 Kings 18:19; 22:6ff.; Jeremiah 23:16-40; 28:1-17), telling people only what they wanted to hear. These "false prophets" did not speak God's words, and they brought messages to make the people and the kings feel good. Scripture explains that these false prophets would face God's judgment (Deuteronomy 18:20-22).

How can we distinguish "heresy" from "difference of opinion"? The term "heresy" applies to cardinal doctrines whose misinterpretation would be destructive to Christianity. "Differences of opinion" apply to issues that will never be fully solved. We've known the cardinal doctrines for fifteen hundred years (such as the deity of Christ, the Trinity, substitutionary atonement) while we will always "agree to disagree" on the others (Calvinism vs. Arminianism, infant baptism, roles of women in the church, etc.).

FALSE TEACHERS TODAY
Peter warned against false teachers. Many powerful speakers claim to have important ideas for Christians to hear. These speakers range from political reactionaries to extreme environmentalists. Add to the list those who present special angles on church doctrine coming from big denominations and small— and you have a dazzling array of choices. How do we separate the good (teaching that leads to Christ), the bad (off-center but benign ideas tacked onto the gospel), and the ugly (false teaching, much to be avoided)?

It's a complicated problem, but the following safeguards will help along the way:

- *Use condemnation sparingly.* An off-center idea may be way out but is not necessarily heresy. A sincere but misguided teacher may not be a "false" teacher. None of us understands God perfectly, so we must be generous and helpful long before we condemn and cast someone out.
- *Pay attention to the teacher's ethical and moral behavior.* The Bible stresses that false teachers will have immorality in their lives. Watch how they treat people and money. Don't excuse or cover up bad behavior.
- *Choose your church carefully.* Is the living Christ at the center of your church's ministry? Do leaders pray? Is the Bible honored and taught? Is God at work there? "False" churches may be very busy, but their teaching reveals the void when Christ and the Bible are pushed to the side. If that is the case, go somewhere else.

Just as there were false prophets in Old Testament times, Peter explained, *there will be false teachers among you.* The words "among you" indicate the origin of these teachers. Just as the false prophets arose from God's people, Israel, so the false teachers will come out from among the believers and from the church. Jesus had told the disciples that false teachers would come:

- "Beware of false prophets, who come to you in sheep's clothing but inwardly are ravenous wolves. You will know them by their fruits" (Matthew 7:15-16 NRSV).

- "And many false prophets will arise and lead many astray" (Matthew 24:11 NRSV).

- "False messiahs and false prophets will appear and produce signs and omens, to lead astray, if possible, the elect. But be alert; I have already told you everything" (Mark 13:22-23 NRSV).

Very shortly, these words began to come true. False teachers infiltrated the early churches just as the gospel message was spreading. Like Peter, the apostle Paul was aware of the dangers of the false teachers:

- "I know that after I have gone, savage wolves will come in among you, not sparing the flock. Some even from your own group will come distorting the truth in order to entice the disciples to follow them" (Acts 20:29-30 NRSV).

- "For such boasters are false apostles, deceitful workers, disguising themselves as apostles of Christ. And no wonder! Even Satan disguises himself as an angel of light. So it is not strange if his ministers also disguise themselves as ministers of righteousness. Their end will match their deeds" (2 Corinthians 11:13-15 NRSV).

- "I am astonished that you are so quickly deserting the one who called you in the grace of Christ and are turning to a different gospel—not that there is another gospel, but there are some who are confusing you and want to pervert the gospel of Christ" (Galatians 1:6-7 NRSV).

- "Now the Spirit expressly says that in later times some will renounce the faith by paying attention to deceitful spirits and teachings of demons, through the hypocrisy of liars whose consciences are seared with a hot iron" (1 Timothy 4:1-2 NRSV).

The apostle John also warned about false teachers:

- "Many deceivers have gone out into the world, those who do not confess that Jesus Christ has come in the flesh; any such person is the deceiver and the antichrist! Be on your guard" (2 John 7-8 NRSV).

Who will secretly bring in destructive opinions. They will even deny the Master who bought them—bringing swift destruction on themselves. NRSV Apparently the false teachers were not making any claims to be prophets, but their danger was just as great. Coming from within the churches, they worked to *secretly bring in* (the Greek word also means "to smuggle") *destructive opinions.* These false teachers knowingly sought to turn people away from the truth by working subversively to bring false teaching that would only lead to destruction and judgment. They introduced it carefully, at first bringing it alongside the gospel message, as a mere aside or addition. But any deviation from the truth is no longer the truth. These false teachers were in the churches, but their heresies most likely came from outside, pagan sources.

BEWARE
All the apostles battled false teaching that infiltrated the new churches and threatened to turn the believers away from the truth. Like the false prophets of old, the false teachers were twisting God's Word. These teachers were dangerous, for their teachings could cause many to turn away from the truth or never find the truth at all. We must be careful to avoid false teachers today. Believers should evaluate any book, tape series, or TV message according to God's Word. Look for scriptural undergirding that backs up their points. Beware of special meanings or interpretations that belittle Christ or his work.

Peter explained that these heresies would *deny the Master.* The word "Master" is *despotes*; the NIV translates "Master" as "sovereign Lord"—the title refers to Christ. The word for "deny" means to contradict, reject, or disavow. Thus, these heresies could have taken the form of (1) denying Christ's second coming (discussed in 1:16-21), or (2) denying Christ's lordship by disobeying his teaching and practicing immorality (mentioned in 2:2, "shameful ways"). Some false teachers were belittling the significance of Jesus' life, death, and resurrection. Some claimed that Jesus could not be God. Others claimed that he could not have been a real human being. These teachers often allowed and even encouraged all kinds of wrong and immoral acts, especially sexual sin (see 2:10, 14).

Whatever form the false doctrines took, they amounted to these teachers' denying Christ *who bought them.* The price Christ paid was his blood—his death on the cross. The word "bought" (*agorasanta* comes from *agorazo,* also translated "redeem") indicates the relationship between Christ and his followers. The word "redeem" is used in the Bible for God redeeming his people when he delivered them out of slavery in Egypt (Exodus 6:6; see 2 Samuel 7:23). It implied that since God had brought his people out of slavery, they owed allegiance to him. In the New Testament, to "redeem" a person meant to buy that person out of slavery. The slave could be purchased and then continue to be a slave or be granted freedom. In either case, the new master paid a price. Christ paid the price with his life. Peter pointed out that the false teachers had no allegiance to Christ, their Master. The false teachers failed to understand (or chose to deny) the fact that while faith in Christ brings liberty, it also brings responsibility. In their teachings and by their lifestyles, the false teachers were denying the Lord, who had bought them. By these words, Peter revealed the seriousness of denying such a Master, for turning away from him would bring *swift destruction* on oneself. This "swift destruction" would not happen immediately—for many false teachers worked and prospered. When that certain destruction came, however, it would be swift and final.

The question arises, How could these false teachers, who had been believers and whom the Lord had "bought," end up in eternal destruction? There are five main views about this question:

1. These false teachers had been believers, but had lost their salvation. The problem with this view is that it contradicts other Scriptures that say a person cannot lose his or her salvation (see John 3:16; 5:24; 10:28-29; Romans 8:28-39).

2. These false teachers had joined the Christian community and seemed to be part of it, but they later denounced Christ and tried to convince others to do the same (see note on 2:20-21).

3. These false teachers were "bought" in the sense of "created," but not "saved." The problem here is that a different word would have been used if Peter had meant this.

4. These false teachers only said that they were saved, "bought" by Christ's blood. But they were lying. Possibly, but who can know?

5. These false teachers had been "bought" by the blood of Christ, as Christ's blood is sufficient to save everyone who ever lived if everyone chose to believe. However, the false teachers never accepted Christ as their Savior and thus were never saved in the first place. Potentially Christ died for everyone, but only those who believe and follow will be saved.

Of the five views, the second and fifth are the most plausible.

2:2 Many will follow their shameful ways and will bring the way of truth into disrepute.[NIV] Despite the certainty of their destruction, the false teachers, unfortunately, will be successful in two areas. First, they will turn *many* from the truth into following *their shameful ways,* referring to sexually immoral practices. Such practices were common in pagan societies and often were part of pagan religions. Popularity was certainly not the right criterion for the truth. Second, they will *bring the way of truth into disrepute.* They would discredit the Christian gospel taught by Jesus Christ, who is the Way, the Truth, and the Life (see John 14:6; see also Psalm 119:30). In his first letter, Peter had explained at length the importance of Christians living blamelessly before the unbelieving world (1 Peter 2:11-12; 3:13-15). They had left that former life to become Christians (1 Peter 4:3-4), and the pagans might wonder why they were returning to it. Here Peter reiterated that those who followed the false teachers into shameful living would malign the gospel before the world (see also Isaiah 52:5; Romans 2:24; 1 Timothy 6:1; Titus 2:5).

2:3 In their greed these teachers will exploit you with stories they have made up.[NIV] Peter spared no words in his condemnation of the false teachers. He exposed their prime motivation—*greed.* Only money, not truth, mattered to them (see also 1 Peter 5:2). Students ought to pay their teachers, but these false teachers were attempting to make more money by *exploiting* their followers *with stories they have made up.* In other words, they were distorting the truth and saying what people wanted to hear. Such teaching encouraged financial support because these ideas were very popular. However, greed can take other forms besides money. False teachers may be greedy for power or even for response from the crowd. Greed can lead to preoccupation with numbers of converts or speaking engagements.

IDENTIFYING FALSE TEACHERS
Peter gives three warning signs for identifying false teachers:

1. *Immorality*—Do their lives contain or condone immoral practices? Does the group listening to the false teachers have a lot of immoral sexual relationships?
2. *Greed*—Teachers have a right to financial support (1 Corinthians 9:1-14; Galatians 6:6; 1 Timothy 5:17-18), but is money the teacher's or group's prime motivation? Before you send money to any cause, evaluate it carefully. Is the teacher or preacher clearly serving God or promoting his/her own interests? Will the person or organization use the money to promote valid ministry, or will it merely finance further promotions?
3. *Lying*—Is the leader offended when you ask for the scriptural backing behind his or her statements? Does he or she fudge on the facts when asked for evidence?

The teaching that people can live as they please without fear of punishment would be very popular! Yet this was simply a made-up story! Though not as evil as these false teachers, some speakers today might use the unethical practice of making up stories to manipulate people's emotions and to get a good reaction. Others might "borrow" illustrations from others and give them as their own. In addition, the false teachers may have claimed that the gospel the apostles taught was "made up," so Peter turned their words back on themselves. Paul also condemned greedy, lying teachers (see Acts 20:33-35; 1 Thessalonians 2:5, 9; 1 Timothy 3:3; 6:3-5; Titus 1:7).

STRETCHING IT

The false teachers were not dummies. Their "made-up" stories were not so ridiculous that gullible people would dismiss them as jokes. The false teachers were probably experts at stretching the truth . . . until the final product was no longer the truth. Do office sales reports ever get stretched? Is it acceptable to bend a little when a customer calls for a quote (she won't see the invoice anyway)? With competition for funding so intense, do missionary leaders stretch the truth when they describe the overseas impact of a gift?

The word of a Christian should be straight up, not bent, stretched, or expanded. Lying is the intention to deceive, not a false report honestly delivered. Don't give in to the intention. Don't sacrifice your integrity for a boss, a client, or even a "very good cause."

Their condemnation has long been hanging over them, and their destruction has not been sleeping.[NIV] The end of the false teachers will be "swift destruction" (2:1). This destruction may not arrive immediately, but when it comes, it will be swift and certain. The teachers may seem to get away with their exploitation for a while, but all that time *condemnation* was *hanging over them* and *destruction* would be their end. In 3:9, Peter explained to the believers that God's promises were sure, no matter how long they had to wait for them. Perhaps the false teachers said that because God's promises had not come about, they were nothing more than untrue stories "made up" by the disciples. Peter took their argument and explained that no matter how long it might take and no matter how successful the false teachers might seem to be, their condemnation and destruction were sure. God is not asleep; he knows what is happening and, without a doubt, will condemn and destroy the false teachers and those who blindly follow them.

2:4 **For if God did not spare the angels when they sinned, but cast them into hell and committed them to chains of deepest darkness to be kept until the judgment.**NRSV If some people still did not believe in future judgment and punishment, Peter gave examples of how God had judged evil in the past. He pointed out that *God did not spare the angels when they sinned.* This could be a reference to the angels who rebelled along with Satan (Ezekiel 28:15) or to the sin of the angels described in Genesis 6:1-4 (see also Jude 6 and Revelation 12:7). More likely, it is the incident recorded in Genesis 6, because the following verses relate to incidents also taken from that portion of Genesis—the Flood and the judgment of Sodom and Gomorrah. If God did not even spare his angels, neither will he spare the false teachers. Judgment *will* come.

The angels who sinned were *cast . . . into hell.* That phrase in Greek is one word (used only here in the New Testament), literally meaning "to cast into Tartarus." In Greek mythology, Tartarus, located in the lowest part of the underworld, was the place of punishment of rebellious gods and the departed spirits of very evil people. These angels were imprisoned in this hell, *committed . . . to chains of deepest darkness.* Some manuscripts have the reading *seirais zophou* "chains of darkness" (see KJV); other manuscripts have the reading *seirois zophou* (pits of darkness). The words for chain *(seira)* and pit *(seiros)* are so similar in Greek that they could have been mistaken for each other. This might also be the place of punishment set aside in the heavenly realm (1 Peter 3:19-20). The place of confinement cannot be identified, but it is totally in God's control. These sinful angels will *be kept* in hell, a place of punishment, *until the judgment,* referring to their final doom (Matthew 25:41). False teachers will face the same judgment as the rebellious angels.

2:5 **If he did not spare the ancient world when he brought the flood on its ungodly people, but protected Noah, a preacher of righteousness, and seven others.**NIV Another example of God's certain judgment of evil is *when he brought the flood* on the world's *ungodly people.* Peter referred to the Flood three times in his two letters (see 1 Peter 3:20; 2 Peter 2:5; 3:6). God *did not spare the ancient world*—for the great sinfulness of all mankind led him to destroy the entire rebellious civilization.

Yet even as God was destroying all the sinful people in Noah's day, he powerfully *protected* those who followed him, eight people in all: Noah and seven of his relatives (his wife, three sons, and their wives, Genesis 8:16). Salvation had been available to everyone (Peter described Noah as a *preacher of righteousness*); however, few had chosen to believe. The use of "protected" here and "rescued" in 2:7 could also be taken as a promise that God will watch over those who remain faithful to him. God's punishment is not arbitrary. Those who deserve punishment will receive his punishment; those who trust in him will receive his grace. Peter's readers should understand the comparison—those who choose the wrong path face eternal consequences.

CHOICES
The choices sound simple—follow God or rebellious humanity—but there was nothing simple about Noah's decision.

- His faith in God gave him the reputation of an outcast, a fool. No one wants to feel that way today. We rely too readily on the approval of others.
- Noah invested all he had in God's promise. He placed his entire family fortune, everything he had, inside that ark. Today, we rely on diversified portfolios to protect against uncertain markets. We don't trust our financial security to God alone.
- Noah's witness was entirely rejected. He convinced no one. As a preacher, he would have been regarded as a total failure. Today, we smartly pick careers that provide significant incentive and reward. Who would decide to invest his or her life when there are no observable results to be gained?

If the choice between God and the world seems simple and clear, perhaps you have not counted the real cost. Very few counselors today will advise the Noah track. It's just too risky. But there really is no other choice!

2:6 If he condemned the cities of Sodom and Gomorrah by burning them to ashes, and made them an example of what is going to happen to the ungodly.[NIV] A third example of God's certain punishment of evil is *the cities of Sodom and Gomorrah.* Genesis 18–19 describes the sinfulness of these cities and Abraham's effort to keep them from being destroyed. When not even ten righteous people could be found in the cities, God destroyed the cities *by burning them to ashes:* "The Lord rained on Sodom and Gomorrah sulfur and fire from the Lord out of heaven; and he overthrew those cities, and all the Plain" (Genesis 19:24-25 NRSV). After the conflagration, "Abraham . . . looked down toward Sodom and Gomorrah and toward all the land of the Plain and saw the smoke of the land going up like the smoke of a furnace" (Genesis 19:27-28 NRSV). Some versions say that these cities were condemned to extinction. This is, in fact, true, for the cities do not even exist today. Archaeologists believe they may have been buried by the waters of the Dead Sea.

Peter explained that the horror of these cities' ending is *an example of what is going to happen to the ungodly.* Great will be the suffering of the ungodly; their ending will result in punishment, gloom, and banishment from the presence of God. In our day, God's punishment on the unrighteous seems less of a preaching and teaching priority. Do we, like the false teachers, think we have outgrown this clear doctrine of Scripture? We have a lot of emphasis on tolerance of others and the self-help benefits of the Bible, but we must not dilute God's clear words of warning. To turn away from God is to turn to ruin. From such ruin, there will be no escape. Don't neglect teaching about God's judgment.

WILL GOD JUDGE?
If God did not spare angels, or people who lived before the Flood, or the citizens of Sodom and Gomorrah, he would not spare these false teachers. These words that promised justice were a great comfort to those who were oppressed. God will punish all evildoers. These words also served as a warning to wanderers to not stray away from the truth. Some people would have us believe that God will save all people because he is so loving. But it is foolish to think that God will cancel the last judgment. Don't ever minimize the certainty of God's judgment on those who rebel against him.

2:7-8 And if he rescued Lot, a righteous man greatly distressed by the licentiousness of the lawless (for that righteous man, living among them day after day, was tormented in his righteous soul by their lawless deeds that he saw and heard).NRSV Just as Noah had been protected from the Flood that destroyed the earth, so Lot, Abraham's nephew, had been rescued from Sodom and Gomorrah's destruction. Lot had chosen to settle "among the cities of the Plain and moved his tent as far as Sodom. Now the people of Sodom were wicked, great sinners against the Lord" (Genesis 13:12-13 NRSV). When God destroyed the cities of Sodom and Gomorrah, *he rescued Lot,* because Lot was *a righteous man greatly distressed by the licentiousness of the lawless.* Lot lived in Sodom and apparently was a man of some importance there, for when the angels went to take Lot from the city, they found him sitting in the gateway of the city, where city officials met. "Licentiousness" means open and excessive indulgence in sexual sins. Licentious people have no sense of shame or restraint (an example of the licentiousness in this city can be found in Genesis 19:1-9). Peter described Lot as a *righteous man* who was horrified by the evil in the city. Angel visitors rescued Lot and his family by taking them away from the city before it was destroyed.

The Genesis account does not make Lot appear to have been very "righteous" at all. In fact, it portrays Lot as having little backbone, little concern about immorality, drunk, and so deeply involved in the city that the angels had to literally drag him away from it. Peter's description of Lot as "righteous" came from Jewish tradition, which explained Abraham's prayer for the righteous in the city as focusing on Lot in particular. Or the wording may mean that he was a good man, a decent man, especially in comparison to the evil men of Sodom. The description of his torment over the *lawless deeds* that he saw and heard could also be rendered that, despite their lawless deeds, he was upright in what *he* saw and listened to. Lot, for all his flaws, stood out as a righteous man in an extremely evil society. When God chose to bring swift and complete judgment on the evil of these cities, he also graciously saved his own.

Believers today, tormented by the sin they see around them, can take heart in the knowledge that one day God will make everything right. The wicked will be punished; the righteous (God's chosen people) will be rescued.

Just as God rescued Lot from Sodom, so he is able to rescue us from the temptations and trials we face in a wicked world. Lot was not sinless, but he put his trust in God and was spared when Sodom was destroyed. God will punish those who cause the temptations and trials, so we need never worry about justice being done.

DO WE CARE?
Lot is described here as tormented in soul over the evil around him. Who gets tormented today about sins in our society? More often, we just get tired

- of crime statistics. The market in illegal drugs is booming, and crime rates climb as addicts struggle for money to feed their habits.
- of abuse reports: women beaten up, wives treated as slaves, kids injured by parents. It's becoming viciously common.
- of politicians' dallying, of welfare recipients gambling on lotteries, of sports heroes bummed out over megasalaries when they want even more, of preachers' dallying, too.

Headlines scream of greed, cruelty, and injustice, but sadly, many Christians today don't feel much torment. Are we too apathetic or too insulated from real pain?

God's people know that change begins with a tremor in the soul. God will move you to make a real difference, but you have to be awake to see and hear how far society has removed itself from God's plan.

2:9 Then the Lord knows how to rescue the godly from trial, and to keep the unrighteous under punishment until the day of judgment.[NRSV] This "then" phrase completes the "if" phrases of 2:4, 5, 6, and 7—if the Lord has done all this in the past, then he obviously

knows how to rescue the godly from trial. These words were comforting to Peter's readers and continue to be comforting to believers
today. God knows each of us and keeps track of our suffering.
Noah and Lot had stood the "trial," staying true to God alone while
surrounded by sin and hatred. The early Christians also lived in a
hostile environment, often facing persecution. If they could stand
firm, they would be rescued "from trial." Revelation 3:10 promises,
"Because you have kept my word of patient endurance, I will keep
you from the hour of trial that is coming on the whole world to test
the inhabitants of the earth" (NRSV). The word "from" translates *ek,*
which means "out of" (not *apo,* which means "away from"). Noah
was rescued from the Flood, but only after years of building an ark
while being derided by his neighbors. Lot was rescued from
Sodom, but only after living in silent torment for years over the
extreme sinfulness of his surroundings.

Many Christians believe that true believers will not go through
trials. But Jesus clearly taught that we will face persecution (John
15:18–16:11; see also Mark 10:30). Throughout history, Christians
have already faced enough persecution to shock any comfort-seek-
ing twentieth-century follower of Christ. So we dare not conclude
that all of this will occur only in the future. Christianity does not
guarantee a trial-free life; instead, it guarantees that God will be with
us through trials and will, in his time, rescue us from them.

The examples cited above also show that God knows how *to keep
the unrighteous under punishment until the day of judgment.* Peter's
wording refers back to 2:4, which speaks of the rebellious angels
being "kept" until the "judgment." Scholars have debated the meaning of this verse. Peter may have meant that the unrighteous (his
focus was still the false teachers and their followers, 2:3) were
"under punishment"; that is, God was punishing them in this life and
will punish them after death, even as he awaits that final Day of
Judgment when they will face "destruction" (2:3; Revelation 20:11-
15). Others have taken Peter's words to mean that sinners who have
died are presently suffering as they await the final judgment. Finally,
others place the words in the future tense—that the unrighteous are
being kept now for a future judgment. The last interpretation seems
most likely because Peter points to final deliverance for the righteous at the Lord's return, so the false teachers' destiny is set for
them at the great judgment (Revelation 20:11-15).

Peter comforted his readers with God's changeless nature: God
has rescued the righteous and punished the wicked in ages past,
and he continues to do so. There will be a final reckoning, a final
"day of judgment," when God will finally separate good from
evil and give the final and eternal rewards.

**2:10 This is especially true of those who follow the corrupt desire of
the sinful nature and despise authority.**^{NIV} The certainty of the punishment described in the previous verses is for all evil people, but *is
especially true* of the false teachers. These false teachers were following *the corrupt desire of the sinful nature.* This wording refers to
sexual promiscuity, immorality, and even perverted sexual practices.
Apparently, the false teachers taught that Christian freedom placed
believers above moral rules (see 2:19). They were promoting sen-
sual indulgence. In addition, they *despise authority.* This "authority"
could refer to church leaders, angelic powers (as in the remainder of
this verse, below), or to the false teachers' denial of "the sovereign
Lord who bought them" (2:1). Most likely, the authority despised by
the false teachers referred to all three; they didn't want anyone over
them. The false teachers lived as they pleased and laughed at the
prospect of a Second Coming and judgment by God. Peter wanted
to make it clear that people would not get away with such sin.

**Bold and willful, they are not afraid to slander the glorious
ones.**^{NRSV} Peter further described these evil false teachers as *bold*
(presumptuous) *and willful* (arrogant, self-willed). Only such an
attitude could account for their defiance of authority as described
above. Furthermore, *they are not afraid to slander the glorious
ones.* (A similar passage is found in Jude 8-10.) Scholars have considered these "glorious ones" to be church leaders, angels, or fallen
angels. The most widely held opinion is that these "glorious ones"
are the fallen angels—the guilty celestial beings who deserve condemnation—thus, they are the fallen angels also mentioned in 2:4.
The false teachers "slandered" the spiritual realities they did not understand (2:12), perhaps by taking Satan's power lightly and doubting the existence of supernatural evil powers. They lived immoral
lives and, when rebuked for doing so and thus following Satan,
they would simply laugh at the idea of Satan at all.

SATAN IS REAL
Many in our world today mock the supernatural. They deny the
reality of the spiritual world and claim that only what can be
seen and felt is real. Like the false teachers of Peter's day, they
are fools who will be proven wrong in the end. Don't take Satan
and his supernatural evil powers lightly. Although Satan will
be destroyed completely, he is at work now trying to render
Christians complacent and ineffective.

**2:11 Whereas angels, though greater in might and power, do not
bring against them a slanderous judgment from the Lord.**^{NRSV}

Peter pointed out the false teachers' audacity in "slandering the glorious ones" by explaining that not even the good angels in heaven, *though greater in might and power* than evil angels, *do not bring against them a slanderous judgment from the Lord.* This could have the sense that although the false teachers slandered the evil angels, the angels of heaven never used their own insults when they pronounced God's judgment on the evil angels, but said, "The Lord rebuke you!" (Jude 9). While not even the angels would accuse Satan on their own authority, the false teachers arrogantly did so, revealing their ignorance of God *and* of Satan. Their complete irreverence in the form of immoral living (thus mocking God's laws) and slander of the evil angels (thus flaunting their self-attested authority) would result in severe punishment.

> A proud man is always looking down on things and people; and, of course, as long as you're looking down, you can't see something that's above you. *C. S. Lewis*

Though the NRSV translation is preferred, the NIV translates *para kuriou* as "in the presence of the Lord." This gives the impression that evil angels can appear before God in some heavenly court. Some scholars believe that Peter had in mind the incident recorded in the apocryphal book of 1 Enoch in which the devil contested over the body of Moses after he died. The devil claimed Moses' body because Moses had committed murder. According to that story, the angels deferred to God for judgment (refer to the discussion of this story in Jude 9). Theologically it makes more sense to take the meaning as "from the Lord" because God's good angels would have brought judgment from God to the rebellious angels, who were no longer in heaven.

OVERGROWN EGO

Perhaps the false teachers' biggest problem was having egos so overgrown that they had no respect for authority—good or evil, lawful or satanic.

- Egos that claimed: "No law condemns me. I am above every law."
- Egos that boasted: "God is my aide, angels my servants. I am the greatest."
- Egos that promised: "Only my will limits me. Only my boldness guides me. I am the master of my fate."

If you think this portrait of Peter's adversaries is too far-fetched, remember that in the 1930s even Christian people in Germany were attracted to the Nazi party, a movement full of ego that recognized no authority but its own. Beware of being so independent that you reject all authority.

2:12 But these men blaspheme in matters they do not understand.
They are like brute beasts, creatures of instinct, born only to
be caught and destroyed, and like beasts they too will per-
ish.NIV *These men* refers to the false teachers. To arrogantly rebel
against God and speak as though Satan's influence meant nothing
(see 2:11) is to *blaspheme in matters they do not understand.* All
their supposed knowledge was worthless; they really understood
nothing. Without mincing words, Peter further described these
false teachers as *brute beasts, creatures of instinct.* They were no
better than animals. They lived and spoke from mere instinct
(that is, from sinful human nature). Like "brute beasts," the false
teachers would be *caught and destroyed.*

Peter was not endorsing the wanton destruction of animals. We
must not, however, read a modern environmental agenda or
knowledge of the animal kingdom back into Peter's words. We
know we should not slaughter animals wantonly or for our own
pleasure. We know that many animals display intelligence, loyalty, and even show restraint in killing prey. It is probably more
helpful to think of "brute beasts" as animals in heat or rogue pred-
ators that just kill for the sake of killing.

Such harsh words reveal the seriousness of the false teachers'
sin. Those who teach have great responsibility. Jesus had said,
"And if anyone causes one of these little ones who believe in me
to sin, it would be better for him to be thrown into the sea with a
large millstone tied around his neck" (Mark 9:42 NIV). Teachers
who lead others astray will face great punishment. The false
teachers of Peter's day had set aside self-restraint in order to follow their passions. But following one's passions leads to self-
destruction and to eternal punishment *(they too will perish).*

2:13 They will be paid back with harm for the harm they have done.
Their idea of pleasure is to carouse in broad daylight.NIV Using a
play on words, Peter explained that these false teachers will receive
harm for the *harm* they have done, in turning people aside from the
gospel truth to their lies. These teachers, bold and willful (2:10),
had been so obvious in their sinfulness that it was shameful that
any of the believers should follow them. While the false teachers
tried to pass themselves off as superior teachers with great knowledge, they caroused *in broad daylight.* No self-respecting Roman,
no matter how immoral, would "carouse" (referring to drunkenness
or sexual misconduct) in the daylight; such acts were meant to be
done under cover of darkness (see, for example, Acts 2:15; 1 Thessalonians 5:7). These men were so arrogant, however, that they did
not even attempt to cover up their behavior; they took *pleasure* in
being degenerate in broad daylight!

PRIME-TIME SIN
Sin seems to prosper at night. Peter accepts that reality and notes how doubly wrong it is to carry one's revelry into daytime hours. What is it about darkness that tempts us to sin?

- For most people, dark hours signal time to reward oneself for hard work done. At night, they feel that their desires deserve gratification.
- Daytime means putting on one's best face to achieve success in business, education, whatever. At night, the "best face" becomes the real person.
- Children are awake during the day and early evening. Better to behave for their sakes.
- Much of carousing relates to sexual invitation and seduction.

What's to be done? First, redirect your system of after-work rewards, choosing healthy recreation over lounging and drinking. Second, work toward integrity in your person, matching the daytime "you" with the nighttime. Third, love your spouse (God's gift to you) a lot. And not least, be aware that vast advertising campaigns and entertainment industries set you up for nighttime temptation. Don't let that armada of enticements choke your life. God's best for you is full and good, not dark or lewd.

They are blots and blemishes, reveling in their pleasures while they feast with you.^{NIV} Such behavior made them no longer fit to be with the Christians. The false teachers were like *blots and blemishes*—like stains on white fabric, they ruined the Christians' gatherings by their very presence. The *feast* may refer to part of the celebration of the Lord's Supper. The "love feast" was a full meal that ended with Communion (see 1 Corinthians 11:20-22). These feasts may have been held in the daytime so as to show the purity of what occurred during these special meals. Although the false teachers were sinning openly by *reveling in their pleasures,* they took part in these meals with everyone else in the church. The word translated "pleasures" *(apatais)* can also mean "deception," giving the connotation of "deceitful pleasures." Perhaps their degenerate behavior at these daytime meals made them especially visible. In one of the greatest of hypocritical acts, they attended the sacred feasts designed to promote love and unity among believers, while at the same time they lived and spoke in opposition to Christ. As Paul told the Corinthians, "Therefore, whoever eats the bread or drinks the cup of the Lord in an unworthy manner will be guilty of sinning against the body and blood of the Lord" (1 Corinthians 11:27 NIV). These men were guilty of more than false teaching and promoting evil pleasures; they were guilty of leading others away from the truth. For this "harm," they would be "paid back."

2:14 They have eyes full of adultery, insatiable for sin. They entice unsteady souls. They have hearts trained in greed. Accursed children!NRSV Peter had no soft words for these false teachers, no excuses for their behavior. Their sinful words and actions came from deep within; their thoughts and motives were evil.

- *They have eyes full of adultery* means that they could not look on women without lusting for them. They were turning church meetings into opportunities for sexual encounters.

- They were *insatiable for sin* because they were bound in sin, acting like brute beasts that follow instinct without any rational faculties (2:12). These men were in bondage to sin and to the power of Satan (2:10).

- *They entice unsteady souls* means that, like a fisherman baiting fish, the false teachers waited out their catch. They didn't waste time with the strong believers, but sought out those who were not firmly grounded in the faith, or had doubts, or were "outside" the fellowship for one reason or another. Pretending patience and interest, they could entice these people away from the faith and into their dangerous "net."

- *They have hearts trained in greed* means that the false teachers had exercised themselves (the Greek word for "trained" is the word from which we derive "gymnasium") in being greedy and in getting what they coveted. These men were really good at being greedy because, no matter how much they got, they always wanted more.

These teachers who were duping Christians away from the faith were filled with pride, immorality, sensuality, greed, lust, blasphemy, slander, and self-will. No wonder Peter called these men *accursed children.* This was a common Hebrew phrase to describe those who would face certain destruction from the hand of God.

2:15 They have left the straight road and have gone astray, following the road of Balaam son of Bosor, who loved the wages of doing wrong.NRSV Peter once again looked to the Old Testament for an illustration to apply to these false teachers. In their greed and sinfulness, they had deliberately *left the straight road* of obedience to God and gone *astray.* They followed in the steps of another man who had led many astray. Numbers 22–24 tells the story of Balaam, son of Beor, who was hired by a pagan king to curse Israel. (The spelling of *Bosor* for Beor may reflect a Galilean pronunciation of the Hebrew name.) He did what God told him to do for a time, but eventually his evil motives and desire for money won out (Numbers 25:1-3; 31:16). Like the false teachers of Peter's day, Balaam *loved the wages of doing wrong.* The false teachers were not interested in serving God; instead, they were using religion for financial gain and personal advancement (see also Jude 11 and commentary there).

FALLEN LEADERS
Christian leaders who fall into sexual sin, particularly adultery, should cause us great concern. The Old Testament law said that it is wrong for a person to have sex with someone other than his or her spouse (Exodus 20:14). Jesus said that the *desire* to have sex with someone other than your spouse is mental adultery—if the *act* is wrong, then so is the *intention* (Matthew 5:27-28). To be faithful to your spouse with your body but not your mind is to break the trust so vital to a strong marriage.

Adultery is harmful in several ways: (1) it causes people to excuse sin rather than eliminate it; (2) it destroys marriages; (3) it is deliberate rebellion against God's Word; and (4) it always hurts others besides those immediately involved.

How do we stop this avalanche of sin? More energy needs to go into premarital counseling to ensure that marriages are good matches. Christian leaders need marriage enrichment and counseling to prevent problems from slipping in. Elders should hold a pastor accountable for his personal life, not just his pulpit ministry.

2:16 But he was rebuked for his wrongdoing by a donkey—a beast without speech—who spoke with a man's voice and restrained the prophet's madness.^NIV Balaam had been hired by King Balak of Moab to put a curse on the people of Israel, for he feared their numbers and the power of their God. Balaam liked the offer of a handsome reward for placing a curse on the people. He claimed to do only what God told him, but the money was a strong temptation. Balaam probably thought that he could figure out a way to obey God, yet get the money anyway. On his way to see King Balak, three times Balaam's donkey saw the angel of the Lord standing in their path, ready to kill Balaam. Each time, the donkey stopped and refused to go forward. Each time, Balaam beat the donkey. Finally, the donkey spoke back. Then an angel *rebuked* Balaam for his wrong attitude and wrong motives. Balaam realized that the donkey had saved his life, restraining his *madness,* for it was sheer madness to think that he could go against God. Finally, Balaam obeyed God and refused to curse the Israelites. Like Balaam, the false teachers' attitudes were akin to madness. Balaam at least listened to the donkey. The false teachers listened to no one. Thinking they could oppose God and get away with it, they were steeped in sin, took great pleasure in it, and lured others to join them. Like Balaam, the false teachers expected to get away with their sin, but they would receive their reward.

Some scholars have noted with concern the differences between Peter's explanation of the Balaam story and the Old Testament account. For example, Balaam's father is Beor, not Bosor (Numbers 22:5). Some suggest that Peter's version of the name reflected his Galilean pronunciation (Matthew 26:73). Others say that Peter was making a play on the name and the Hebrew word for "flesh" *(basar)*. Balaam's immoral character revealed itself in that he was "son of flesh."

Another concern is that Balaam was not actually rebuked by the donkey. The donkey merely spoke to ask why Balaam was beating him. The angel actually rebuked Balaam. Peter may have been referring to the story in Jewish tradition, where the donkey did rebuke Balaam. Or Peter may have been citing the story this way in an attempt to make the point that even a dumb donkey was smarter than this supposed prophet, and that even dumb animals were more knowledgeable than the false teachers.

WHO TURNED OUT THE LIGHTS?
It's hard to imagine anything living for long in total darkness. Some plants and animals do, as we have learned from oceanographers. But humans do not. We need light, and if nature cannot supply it, we find some way to generate it by fire, electricity, or chemicals.

How awful to be without light. You can't play anything or make anything. You can't go anywhere for fear of falling. You're stuck.

How frightening. Is danger close? You can't prepare. You can't react.

How lonely. Who's out there? You don't know. Friend or foe, what's it matter? You can't even see yourself.

God's Good News is salvation from darkness into light. God welcomes you into the kingdom of light. Don't wait. Apart from God, it's dark out there.

2:17 These are waterless springs and mists driven by a storm.NRSV The false teachers' messages ended only in disappointment. Like a spring that gave no water, their messages could not deliver what they promised. Like clouds that brought no rain, their messages were without substance and could be "blown away" by the slightest wind of truth. What seems unbelievable is that the false teachers could make people believe their empty promises and enticements. The followers actually believed they were getting "water." (See also Jude 12-13.) These teachers taught lies. Their fate had already been sealed because **for them the deepest darkness has been reserved.**NRSV The word *darkness* stood for the final fate of all wicked people. The false teachers would be forever cast from God's light into the "deepest darkness" of hell itself. The greatest punishment awaits them (see James 3:1).

2:18 **For they mouth empty, boastful words and, by appealing to the lustful desires of sinful human nature, they entice people who are just escaping from those who live in error.**NIV The false teachers drew attention to themselves by their *boastful words.* They spoke often and loudly, but their words were ultimately *empty.* They had no substance, no truth. Instead, they *enticed people* by offering new believers the lifestyles that they themselves followed—living in complete disregard for moral laws. *By appealing to the lustful desires of* every person's *sinful human nature,* the false teachers were able to draw new Christians away from the gospel truth. A salvation that is future only, that allows people to indulge every sinful desire and passion here on earth without punishment, can be enticing. Who would believe such a message? Not the strong followers of Christ, so the false teachers focused on those who were *just escaping from those who live in error;* that is, those new converts still "unsteady" in the faith (2:14), not yet firmly rooted, not yet completely free of pagan associations and habits. "Those who live in error" referred to the pagans. To these young believers, the empty, boastful words sounded convincing.

EMPTY WORDS
The false teachers of Peter's day were boastful. Bombastic, high-sounding words can be a cover for false religion today. We must beware of teaching that mixes culture and Christianity without drawing clear lines of moral behavior. Anyone who omits teaching self-denial and loyalty to God as more important than personal pleasure may be appealing to the sinful nature. Judge teachers by checking their substance and observing their moral behavior.

2:19 **They promise them freedom, but they themselves are slaves of corruption; for people are slaves to whatever masters them.**NRSV The *freedom* the false teachers promised was freedom to live as one pleased. However, such a *promise* of freedom was empty, for the false teachers were not free. Instead, *they themselves are slaves of corruption.* They began to taste the freedom found in Christ, but they perverted it by resisting the rules of love their new Master gave. They tossed these aside, in the name of freedom, only to find themselves enslaved once again. Why? Because *people are slaves to whatever masters them.* Many believe that freedom means doing anything they want. But no one is ever completely free in that sense. The freedom Christ brings is freedom from sin, not freedom to do whatever we want. Too often freedom from rules, structure, or obedience leads to an addiction or preoccupation with the new pleasures freedom offers. But these actions can quickly enslave a person.

If people refuse to follow God, their only option is to follow their own sinful desires and become enslaved to what their bodies want. Only Christ can promise and deliver true freedom, for only those who submit their lives to Christ are set free from slavery to sin. Jesus had talked about true freedom to the false teachers of his day: "To the Jews who had believed him, Jesus said, 'If you hold to my teaching, you are really my disciples. Then you will know the truth, and the truth will set you free.' They [the religious leaders] answered him, 'We are Abraham's descendants and have never been slaves of anyone. How can you say that we shall be set free?' Jesus replied, 'I tell you the truth, everyone who sins is a slave to sin. Now a slave has no permanent place in the family, but a son belongs to it forever. So if the Son sets you free, you will be free indeed'" (John 8:31-36 NIV). (See also Romans 6:16 and 1 Corinthians 6:12.)

2:20-21 If they have escaped the corruption of the world by knowing our Lord and Savior Jesus Christ and are again entangled in it and overcome, they are worse off at the end than they were at the beginning.^{NIV} The word *they* could refer either to the false teachers, to the unstable believers that the false teachers were enticing, or to both. Because of the context of this chapter, it seems that Peter had in mind the false teachers; also, the whole paragraph deals with condemnation of the false teachers. The Greek word *gar* (for), untranslated in the NIV, connects it with the previous verse, where it speaks of anyone becoming a slave of depravity. However, the main emphasis is on the false teachers. They had identified themselves as orthodox believers and had *escaped the corruption of the world.* Yet they then turned aside from this faith, becoming once again *entangled* in and *overcome* by the society in which they lived—an immoral and corrupt society, alienated from God. The false teachers had learned about Christ and how to be saved, but then had rejected the truth and returned to their sin. They were also endangering their followers by encouraging them to join their apostasy. These people, Peter

wrote, *are worse off at the end than they were at the beginning*
because they rejected the only way out of sin, the only way of salvation. Like a person sinking in quicksand who refuses to grab
the rope thrown to him or her, the one who turns away from
Christ casts aside his or her only means of escape.

Indeed, Peter went even further: **For it would have been better for them never to have known the way of righteousness
than, after knowing it, to turn back from the holy commandment that was passed on to them.**[NRSV] These people would have
been better off never having known the truth than knowing the
truth and deliberately violating it. Peter offered a comparison, not
an option, between the two. He said ignorance is better than apostasy because the one who persists in self-delusion in fact refuses
God's help and forgiveness. In the case of the false teachers, they
not only violated it, but taught others to do so, giving them an
even greater responsibility (see Jesus' words in Mark 9:42). A
child who disobeys his parents out of ignorance of the rules is better off than a child who deliberately and willfully disobeys. Jesus
had also spoken of the fate of those who deliberately turn from
the truth. Once again speaking to the false teachers of his day, the
religious leaders, Jesus said, "When the unclean spirit has gone
out of a person, it wanders through waterless regions looking for
a resting place, but it finds none. Then it says, 'I will return to my
house from which I came.' When it comes, it finds it empty,
swept, and put in order. Then it goes and brings along seven other
spirits more evil than itself, and they enter and live there; and the
last state of that person is worse than the first. So will it be also
with this evil generation" (Matthew 12:43-45 NRSV).

Most likely these teachers had been part of Christianity in
some way but had not been truly born again. There is teaching in
the early church that shows that they recognized some who
claimed to be believers but were not regenerated (see 2 Corinthians 13:5; 2 Timothy 2:18-19; 1 John 3:7-8). The apostle John
wrote, "They went out from us, but they did not really belong to
us. For if they had belonged to us, they would have remained
with us; but their going showed that none of them belonged to
us" (1 John 2:19 NIV).

Believers who have turned from the truth are in a more dangerous plight than those who never knew the truth. They saw the
light and returned to the darkness. They walked off the path (*the
way of righteousness,* see also Matthew 21:32), and turned away
from *the holy commandment that was passed on to them* (referring to the law of Christ, which they rejected in their quest for
"freedom"). In the early church, apostasy was considered an espe-

cially horrible sin; to be baptized and then to turn from the faith amounted to committing the unforgivable sin, for it meant turning one's back on God, never to return. Thus Peter wrote these stunning words that they would have been better off never having known God's truth than deliberately blaspheming his grace, love, and forgiveness by rejecting them. See Hebrews 6:4-6 and 10:26 for more on those who turn back from faith.

THE WRONG END ZONE
Pity the football player who runs a full sprint into the wrong end zone, scoring against his own team, like USC's "Wrong-Way" Riegels at the 1929 Rose Bowl. No one ever forgets that kind of mistake. It lives in history books.

Peter pities those who know God, then turn away. To have the truth but follow evil is as low as life gets. If you are discouraged, tempted to quit, or running with the opposition, God wants you back. Find a Christian friend who will hear you out, pray with you, and become your spiritual coach, helping clarify your goals through the confusion and doubt.

2:22 But it has happened to them according to the true proverb: "A dog returns to his own vomit," and, "a sow, having washed, to her wallowing in the mire."^{NKJV} Those who knew the truth and turned away from it (2:20-21) were among the lowest of the low. To Jews, no creatures were lower than dogs and pigs. The first proverb is taken from Proverbs 26:11; the second probably was a well-known saying in the first century. The meaning of both proverbs is the same: Those who return to evil after being cleansed are no better than dogs that throw up and then return to their vomit, or sows that are washed only to go back to rolling around in the mud. Those who make an outward profession of religion without a Spirit-controlled inner transformation will soon return to their old way of life. Dogs and pigs do what they do naturally; evil people will return to their natural inclination toward sin and thereby face judgment. We must heed the advice of Hebrews 3:12-13: "Take care, brothers and sisters, that none of you may have an evil, unbelieving heart that turns away from the living God. But exhort one another every day, as long as it is called 'today,' so that none of you may be hardened by the deceitfulness of sin" (NRSV).

2 Peter 3

The previous chapter focused on denouncing the false teachers. This chapter returns to the faithful believers, offering them love and encouragement to remember God's words to them (3:1-2), to remember God's timing is different from their expectation so that they could counter the scoffers (3:8), to be faithful (3:14), and to stay away from false teaching (3:17).

3:1 **Dear friends, this is now my second letter to you. I have written both of them as reminders to stimulate you to wholesome thinking.**NIV Addressing his readers as *dear friends* ("friends" in the faith, for he did not know all of his readers personally), Peter turned his attention from the false teachers to the believers whom he wanted to encourage. Describing this writing as *my second letter to you* supports the belief that the first letter was 1 Peter. Scholars have debated this issue extensively. Some believe that this statement refers to 1 Peter (regardless of who actually wrote 2 Peter); others think it refers to another letter now lost. They base their argument on an understanding that 1 Peter could not be described as a reminder *to stimulate* the believers *to wholesome thinking.* Whatever the case, Peter, as a concerned church leader, had written a previous letter to the believers. He described both letters as *reminders* (see 1:12-13; the same Greek words are used in 1:13, there translated "refresh your memory").

Peter's purpose was to remind the believers that their lives ought to be characterized by *eilikrine dianoian,* translated "wholesome thinking" (meaning sincerity or purity of understanding; "sincere intention" in NRSV). Plato had used this phrase to refer to pure reason uncontaminated by the senses. The Greek word *eilikrines* literally means "sun-judged." A piece of pottery was "sun-judged" when it was held up to the sunlight in order to see any flaws or cracks. The thinking and intentions of God's people must be able to stand up under scrutiny and not be led astray by immoral desires (Philippians 4:8-9).

WHOLESOME MINDS
If Peter were writing today, what concepts and ideas would
he warn us against? He would warn us against beliefs that

- the difference between right and wrong is all a matter of personal choice. You ought to feel good about your beliefs and
  not offend anyone else's choices.
- religion provides value only if it helps a person adjust to life
  and get a sense of self-worth. Religion that worries people is
  spooky and medieval.
- the worst sin is being intolerant of someone else's ideas.
  After all, who are you to judge another person's preferences?

In contrast, Christians today believe that God is real, that
God has spoken, that he is in control, and that all people
should believe in him. Let God's Word determine your thinking.
He, not the world around us, sets our standards.

**3:2 That you should remember the words spoken in the past by the
holy prophets, and the commandment of the Lord and Savior
spoken through your apostles.**^{NRSV} The way to maintain "wholesome thinking" (3:1) is to *remember the words* of Scripture. What
had been *spoken in the past by the holy prophets* and recorded in
Scripture? These were the prophecies concerning the coming judgment (the Day of the Lord) and the coming of the Messiah, who
would usher in judgment and restore the kingdom of God. They also
recalled the words of Jesus Christ, who gave his *commandment* and
then gave his *apostles* (referring to the Twelve) the authority to teach
that commandment. What was this "commandment"? Most likely it
refers to the law as upheld by Jesus in the Sermon on the Mount and
propagated by the apostles in presenting the moral requirements of
the Christian faith (see 2:21).

Paul had written that all believers are "members of the household of
God, built upon the foundation of the apostles and prophets, with Christ
Jesus himself as the cornerstone" (Ephesians 2:19-20 NRSV). The Holy
Spirit unified the prophets and apostles in an unchanging message of
hope and truth. The prophets had written of the Messiah, who would
come to bring judgment and restore the kingdom; those words had
come to pass. The apostles had spoken and written that Jesus the Messiah would return to bring judgment. Thus believers should live expectantly, knowing that those words will also come to pass.

**3:3 First of all you must understand this, that in the last days
scoffers will come, scoffing and indulging their own lusts.**^{NRSV}
We, along with the first-century believers, ought to be prepared
for anything because we have been warned what to watch for and
how to live. Peter wrote that *first of all* (meaning "above all" as

in 1:20), we must *understand* what to expect in the *last days.* The "last days" began with Christ's resurrection and will continue until his return, when he will set up his kingdom and judge all humanity. Jesus and the apostles warned that during that interim, including the time period we live in, *scoffers will come* (see 1 Timothy 4:1-2; 2 Timothy 3:1-9). Once again, Peter was referring to false teachers (whom he attacked in chapter 2) who deny Jesus Christ and thereby deny his second coming (3:4). This should be no surprise. Jesus had warned against the deception of false teachers (Mark 13:21-23), as had Paul (Acts 20:28-31; 2 Thessalonians 2:1-12) and John, who called them "antichrists" (1 John 2:18-23). See also Jude 17-19.

These false teachers will abound, *scoffing and indulging their own lusts.* Peter called the believers to remember the Scriptures and to live to please God; but the false teachers will scoff at the Scriptures and will live to please themselves and their sinful desires. They will love money and attention, all the while distorting the truth, dividing the believers and causing many to go astray. Paul called them "hypocritical liars, whose consciences have been seared as with a hot iron" (1 Timothy 4:2 NIV). They continued to act as part of the church, desiring to appear as teachers of the truth; yet they were actually serving Satan's evil purposes. Ironically, the very presence of these men who scoffed at prophecy was itself fulfillment of prophecy. The more the false teachers scoffed, the more the Christians should be settled in their faith, knowing that this was only further assurance of Christ's second coming.

The scoffers today are those who base their lives and teaching on sinful desires, those who ignore the teaching of Christ's return and coming judgment, and those who base their view of God's role in history on outward circumstances, economic trends, and international events while neglecting the teachings of Scripture.

SCOFFERS AND INQUIRERS
Peter warned against scoffers. In some churches, it's considered discourteous to question anything. If you raise a question, you're challenging authority and acting like a scoffer. Ironically, that kind of church is a scoffer's dream-come-true. Where questions are not allowed, false teachers flourish like maggots in a garbage can.

To inquire is a good thing. Inquirers raise honest, heartfelt questions; scoffers avoid real questions in favor of arguments that diminish God's stature and ignore God's Word. Inquirers want to know God better; scoffers want to hear themselves talk.

While guarding against scoffers, healthy churches encourage inquirers. A church should never be a place where your mind closes down. Are you a scoffer or an inquirer?

3:4 And saying, "Where is the promise of his coming? For ever since our ancestors died, all things continue as they were from the beginning of creation!"[NRSV] The false teachers' scoffing focused on the *promise of his coming,* referring to Christ's second coming. Jesus had promised that he would come again (Mark 13:24-27), but many years had passed and nothing had happened. Indeed, concern about the delay of Christ's second coming had caused Paul to write words of encouragement to other believers. Some believers in Corinth questioned the truth of Resurrection (1 Corinthians 15:12-58). Some in Thessalonica were concerned that their loved ones who had died had missed the Second Coming (1 Thessalonians 4:13–5:11); others in that city had stopped working in order to wait for Christ's return and had become a burden to the church (2 Thessalonians 3:6-15). James also wrote to the believers, encouraging them to have patience as they awaited the Lord's return (James 5:7-11). The scoffers based their argument on the fact that *since our ancestors died, all things continue as they were from the beginning of creation.* "Nothing has ever really changed, so why think that it ever will?" they asked. "Ancestors" most likely refers to the line of Old Testament leaders, beginning with the patriarchs, as in John 6:31; Acts 3:13; Romans 9:5. Some scholars suggest the translation "ancestors" indicates the deaths of Christian relatives, as well as prominent Christians such as Stephen (Acts 7:58) and James (Acts 12:2), either by martyrdom or natural causes. Many first-century Christians believed that Jesus would come in their lifetime. When Christians began to die without experiencing the Lord's return, some began to doubt. These were prime targets for the false teachers, who pointed out that perhaps it was all a lie and Christ was never going to return. Because there would be no judgment, these men had no problem "indulging their own lusts" (3:3).

The false teachers argued that ever since creation, the world has continued in a natural order, a system of cause-and-effect.

> Men argued then from the appearances of things, and especially from the regular routine of cause and effect. They did not realize that from time to time there had been the intrusion of the divine personal will into the course of history, introducing a higher set of laws and arresting the ordinary succession of events; as for instance, the Flood and the miracles of Old Testament history. Why, then, should not the ordinary course of Nature be broken in upon by the Second Advent, when the Lord shall gather his saints about him and reign gloriously? What God has done, he can do again! There is a Person and a will behind the slight veil of the present life. *F. B. Meyer*

They did not believe that God would intervene or allow anything out of the ordinary (such as miracles) to occur. Therefore they scoffed at teachings about a Second Coming and the end of the world.

3:5-6 They deliberately ignore this fact, that by the word of God heavens existed long ago and an earth was formed out of water and by means of water.NRSV What these scoffers were forgetting in their argument (that the world had remained unchanged since creation) was that God had created the world. The Creation disproves their "all things continue" argument because the creation of the earth was an imposed change on the formless void (Genesis 1:1-2). The very reason the world was continuing on in a stable, predictable pattern was because God, in his grace, had created it that way. *By the word of God* the heavens were created (Genesis 1:6-8). By the word of God, *an earth was formed out of water and by means of water* (referring to the waters being gathered to allow the dry land to appear, Genesis 1:9-10).

However, this stability should not be taken for granted. The false teachers *deliberately* chose to *ignore* the fact that God had been involved in the world. For the waters that had parted in order to allow the dry land to appear had returned and covered the entire world—this was God's judgment. Peter continued: **By these waters also the world of that time was deluged and destroyed.**NIV As the creation was an act of God, so was the Flood. *World* refers to God's judgment and destruction of the inhabitants of the world, not the world itself. Peter had alluded to this in 2:5, where he had stated that God "did not spare the ancient world when he brought the flood on its ungodly people, but protected Noah . . . and seven others" (NIV).

WHERE IS GOD?
Many people ignore God as Creator. Soviet cosmonaut Gherman Titov declared in 1962 that he had been to outer space, looked around for God, but no luck. His conclusion? God is fiction.

Peter reminds Titov and all other skeptics that God's work surrounds them. What an awesome wonder outer space is, or a forest ecosystem, or a spiral chain of amino acids in a DNA molecule that gave Titov two eyes to see and earthworms none.

Cosmology studies the origin of the universe and its development. Scientists have proposed intriguing theories, but no one has figured why the Big Bang happened, where the energy came from, and how intelligent life emerged.

Look around in wonder. The Creator's handiwork is so splendid we often fail to see it. Don't lose faith in his supernatural control and intervention.

3:7 But by the same word the present heavens and earth have been reserved for fire, being kept until the day of judgment and destruction of the godless.NRSV By God's word, the heavens and the earth were created (3:5); by his word, the earth's inhabitants were destroyed in judgment (3:6); *by the same word* God will bring future judgment and destruction. God had intervened before; he will intervene again. But instead of destruction by water, Peter wrote that the heavens and earth *have been reserved for fire*. In Noah's day the earth was judged by water; at the Second Coming it will be judged by fire. This fire is described in Revelation 19:20; 20:10-15. Isaiah prophesied: "See, the Lord is coming with fire, and his chariots are like a whirlwind; he will bring down his anger with fury, and his rebuke with flames of fire. For with fire and with his sword the Lord will execute judgment upon all men, and many will be those slain by the Lord" (Isaiah 66:15-16 NIV). The prophet Malachi wrote:

"'Surely the day is coming; it will burn like a furnace. All the arrogant and every evildoer will be stubble, and that day that is coming will set them on fire,' says the Lord Almighty. 'Not a root or a branch will be left to them'" (Malachi 4:1 NIV). (See also Psalm 97:3; Isaiah 34:4; Daniel 7:9-10; Micah 1:4; Matthew 3:11-12.)

Judgment has already been decided. The *day of judgment and destruction of the godless* will come. It is only a matter of God's timing. The word "reserved" means stored up or laid away. Being "kept" means being guarded or held. Scholars have debated whether Peter was referring to a literal fiery destruction of the entire universe with new heavens and earth to follow, or to "fire of judgment." Second Peter is the only New Testament book that says the world will actually be destroyed by fire (3:10-11). The passages cited above refer primarily to the fire of God's judgment. If taken that way, the fire purifies the earth, burns up the Lord's enemies and the futile works of humanity, and makes the earth new for Christ's eternal reign. Peter's point was that destruction would come and the godless (those who have not believed) will not escape.

> Not only does the Old Testament tell us to expect the Second Coming of Christ, not only is the New Testament filled with the promise of it, but if we would study the historic documents of our major denominations, we would find that our founders all believed and accepted it. The most thrilling, glorious truth in all the world is the Second Coming of Jesus Christ. It is the sure promise of the future. *Billy Graham*

3:8 But, beloved, do not forget this one thing, that with the Lord one day is as a thousand years, and a thousand years as one day.NKJV Peter had made his point that Christ would certainly return and bring judgment, but the question still remained, "Why was the Lord delaying so long?" Peter offered two reasons in 3:8-9. First of all, the Lord does not count time as people do. He is above and outside of the sphere of time. God sees all of eternity past and eternity future. Indeed, to him *one day is as a thousand years, and a thousand years as one day.* Peter urged the believers to once again remember the Scriptures (3:2). Psalm 90:4 says, "For a thousand years in your sight are like a day that has just gone by, or like a watch in the night" (NIV). The believers must *not forget this one thing.* God may have seemed slow to these believers as they faced persecution every day and longed to be delivered. But God is not slow; he simply doesn't operate according to our timetable. (Also see 3:9, 15 for more on the second reason for God's gracious delay and his patience.)

ANY DAY NOW
To Christians wondering about God's delayed return, Peter offers a three-part challenge.

1. When has God ever failed to keep a promise? Never, and God will not fail now.
2. When has God ever fulfilled a promise in quite the exact way all of us smart people think he should? Never. So don't get too smart now.
3. What could God possibly be waiting for? Well, look around at needy souls, lost without a Savior, ignorant of God's promise. If you don't have a tear in your eye, you've missed the point of God's patience. Stop wondering; start spreading the word. Don't let any human reasoning deter you from your hope and your duty.

3:9 The Lord is not slack concerning His promise, as some count slackness, but is longsuffering toward us, not willing that any should perish but that all should come to repentance.^{NKJV} The
second reason for the Lord's delay *concerning His promise* (the promise of his return) was not *slackness*. God was not tardy or late. Unlike people, God does not forget his promises, nor is he late in following through on them. Instead, the Lord is delaying his return because he is *longsuffering* and compassionate. He wants as many people as will to come to faith in him. God, in his great love, is *not willing that any should perish but that all should come to repentance.* Jesus is delaying his second coming so that sinners will repent and turn to him. God is not "late" at all; rather, according to his timetable, he is being exceedingly patient, giving people time to turn to him. Love is the reason that he delays the destruction of the world. See John 1:4, 7, 9 and 3:16 for more on God's love for all humanity.

GOD'S PATIENCE

(All verses are quoted from the NIV.)

Exodus 34:6	"And he passed in front of Moses, proclaiming, 'The LORD, the LORD, the compassionate and gracious God, slow to anger, abounding in love and faithfulness.'"
Numbers 14:18	"The LORD is slow to anger, abounding in love and forgiving sin and rebellion. Yet he does not leave the guilty unpunished; he punishes the children for the sin of the fathers to the third and fourth generation."
Psalm 86:15	"But you, O LORD, are a compassionate and gracious God, slow to anger, abounding in love and faithfulness."
Jeremiah 15:15	"You understand, O LORD; remember me and care for me . . . You are long-suffering. . . ."
Ezekiel 18:23	"Do I take any pleasure in the death of the wicked? declares the Sovereign LORD. Rather, am I not pleased when they turn from their ways and live?"
Jonah 4:2	"I knew that you are a gracious and compassionate God, slow to anger and abounding in love, a God who relents from sending calamity."
Romans 2:4	"Or do you show contempt for the riches of his kindness, tolerance and patience, not realizing that God's kindness leads you toward repentance?"
Romans 9:22	"What if God, choosing to show his wrath and make his power known, bore with great patience the objects of his wrath—prepared for destruction?"
Romans 11:32	"For God has bound all men over to disobedience so that he may have mercy on them all."
1 Timothy 2:4	"[God] wants all men to be saved and to come to a knowledge of the truth."

God desires all people to be saved. He is not indifferent. God gave people free will. Some will exercise their free will and reject God, but this is not God's desire.

Some have attempted to make this verse mean that ultimately everyone will be saved. But nowhere does Scripture teach universal salvation. This verse means that God, in his great compassion, does not desire that anyone should "perish" (referring to eternal destruction). He wants every person to "come to repentance," to turn to him and trust him. In this verse, God's "will" refers to God's desire and plan. The unsaved world greatly concerns God. The prophet Ezekiel wrote God's words, "Have I any pleasure in the death of the wicked, says the Lord God, and not rather that they should turn from their ways and live?" (Ezekiel 18:23 NRSV). God is loving, but he also executes perfect justice. His perfect love causes him to be merciful to those who recognize their sin and turn back to him, but he cannot ignore those who willfully sin. Wicked people die both physically and spiritually. God takes no joy in their deaths; he would prefer that they turn to him and have eternal life. However, the promise of judgment and destruction show that God knows that many will not choose to follow him.

We must not sit and merely wait for Christ to return; we should live with the realization that time is short and that we have important work to do. We must participate with God in his deepest desire for the world—repentance and faith. Be ready to meet Christ any time, even today; yet plan your course of service as though he may not return for many years.

3:10 But the day of the Lord will come as a thief in the night.^{NKJV} *The day of the Lord* is the day of Christ's return and of God's judgment on the earth. Peter repeated a warning used by Jesus Christ, that this day *will come as a thief in the night.* Jesus had said, "Keep awake therefore, for you do not know on what day your Lord is coming. But understand this: if the owner of the house had known in what part of the night the thief was coming, he would have stayed awake and would not have let his house be broken into. Therefore you also must be ready, for the Son of Man is coming at an unexpected hour" (Matthew 24:42-44 NRSV; see also Revelation 3:3; 16:15). Christ's second coming will be swift, sudden, unexpected, and terrible for those who do not believe in him. But for those who follow Christ, it will be a time of great joy. Paul had written to the Thessalonian believers, "For you yourselves know very well that the day of the Lord will come like a thief in the night. . . . But you, beloved, are not in darkness, for that day to surprise you like a thief; for you are all children of light and children of the day; we are not of the night or of darkness" (1 Thessalonians 5:2, 4-5 NRSV).

Peter explained that no matter how long it might take, the Day of the Lord *will* come, and it will come unexpectedly. We should live each day as though Christ could return at any moment. Christians must be morally clean and spiritually alert. The Day of the Lord will be a time of judgment and destruction, for **the heavens will disappear with a roar; the elements will be destroyed by fire, and the earth and everything in it will be laid bare.**^{NIV} Again quoting words that he had heard Jesus say, Peter described the coming end. Jesus had said,

- "There will be signs in the sun, the moon, and the stars, and on the earth distress among nations confused by the roaring of the sea and the waves" (Luke 21:25 NRSV).

- "Immediately after the distress of those days 'the sun will be darkened, and the moon will not give its light; the stars will fall from the sky, and the heavenly bodies will be shaken'" (Matthew 24:29 NIV).

The prophets also had spoken of a future cosmic destruction:

- "The stars of heaven and their constellations will not show their light. The rising sun will be darkened and the moon will not give its light. I will punish the world for its evil, the wicked for their sins. I will put an end to the arrogance of the haughty and will humble the pride of the ruthless. I will make man scarcer than pure gold, more rare than the gold of Ophir. Therefore I will make the heavens tremble; and the earth will shake from its place at the wrath of the Lord Almighty, in the day of his burning anger" (Isaiah 13:10-13 NIV).

- "The earth is broken up, the earth is split asunder, the earth is thoroughly shaken" (Isaiah 24:19 NIV).

- "All the stars of the heavens will be dissolved and the sky rolled up like a scroll; all the starry host will fall like withered leaves from the vine, like shriveled figs from the fig tree" (Isaiah 34:4 NIV).

- "The sun and moon will be darkened, and the stars no longer shine" (Joel 3:15 NIV).

- "The mountains melt beneath him and the valleys split apart, like wax before the fire, like water rushing down a slope" (Micah 1:4 NIV).

DAY OF THE LORD
Every nation celebrates its heroes with holidays and festivals. Many people celebrate the day of their birth. The largest international celebration centers on the birth of Jesus. But the biggest holiday of all is yet to come. On the Day of the Lord:

- Grief, suffering, and injustice are finally and forever vindicated. God makes things right.
- The world we know passes away, and everything starts new. It's God's way of clearing a dusty closet and setting everything on course again.
- God's family is introduced to an eternal home, the likes of which are hard to imagine, but we know it will be bright, clean, and joyous.

Take a moment to ask, if today is *the day,* is my heart right with God?

Peter described three aspects of the conflagration:

1. That *the heavens will disappear with a roar* describes the end
   of the earth's atmosphere and the sky above. The word "roar"
   in Greek was often used for its sound; *rhoizedon* means a
   whizzing or crackling sound, and the word sounds that way.
   Thus it was a picturesque word for Peter to choose as he
   described the coming destruction of the heavens and earth by
   fire (3:7). The roar could also refer to the thunderous voice of
   God (see Psalm 18:13-15).

2. *The elements will be destroyed by fire* could mean that the
   celestial bodies will also be destroyed (the sun, moon, stars,
   and planets). This interpretation is favored by most scholars.
   However, other views state that this refers to the four main
   elements (earth, air, fire, and water) that the Stoics believed
   made up the universe, or that this refers to hostile spiritual
   powers in the heavens.

3. *The earth and everything in it will be laid bare* is also translated
   "the earth and everything that is done on it will be disclosed"
   (NRSV) or "will be found." This extremely difficult phrase has
   given rise to numerous readings and possibilities. The Greek
   words have been variously interpreted as the earth disappear-
   ing, being burned up, or being "laid bare" so that all the works
   that people counted on in this earth in place of God will be
   revealed for their futility, and then they will all be annihilated.
   (See also Hebrews 1:10-12.)

When will these events occur? Some have placed them between
the events of Revelation 20 (the thousand-year reign of Christ,
Satan's doom, the final judgment) and Revelation 21 (new heaven
and new earth, the descent of the new Jerusalem). Revelation 20:11
says, "Then I saw a great white throne and him who was seated on
it. Earth and sky fled from his presence, and there was no place for
them" (NIV).

Peter explained that this earth will not last forever. As God intervened
in the past to judge the earth by water, so one day he will intervene
again. But in that day, the judgment will be by fire, and everything will
be destroyed. Those who presume to take God's delay of this judgment to mean that they can do as they please will find themselves surprised upon his return. And when the destruction occurs, there will be
no second chances and no escape for those who have chosen to disobey the Creator. However, in the following verses, Peter turned his
attention to the believers, writing to them about how they should live
in light of the coming judgment.

FIRE SALE
Realizing that the earth is going to be burned up, we should put
our confidence in what is lasting and eternal and not be bound
to earth and its treasures or pursuits. We need God's presence
and power. We should not be overly dependent on this material
world or use it as our standard for thought and behavior. Do
you spend more of your time piling up possessions, or striving
to develop Christlike character?

**3:11-12 Since everything will be destroyed in this way, what kind of
people ought you to be? You ought to live holy and godly lives
as you look forward to the day of God and speed its coming.**NIV Peter's description of the coming destruction of the earth
ought to cause Christians to carefully examine their lives. His
question, *What kind of people ought you to be?* is rhetorical.
They already knew the answer, but he told them anyway: *You
ought to live holy and godly lives.* Such lives would be in direct
contrast to the unholy living and godlessness found in the world.
Peter had described this kind of living in 1 Peter 1:13-16, 22-25;
2:1-3, 11-21; 3:1-12; 4:1-11. Such lives, lived through faith in
Jesus Christ, will continue on after the coming destruction.
Because of that knowledge, the Christians need not fear *the day
of God;* they could instead actually *look forward* to it because
God will create "new heavens and a new earth" (3:13).

Peter wrote that the believers can also
actually *speed its coming* by continuing
to live holy (dedicated to God and separated from evil) and godly (characterized by personal piety and worship)
lives, praying (Matthew 6:10), and telling people about the gospel (Matthew
24:14). Christians are not called to sit
and wait for the inevitable end; instead,

> Without the truth,
> embodied in the second
> coming doctrine, that life
> is going somewhere,
> there is nothing left to
> live for. *Michael Green*

our mission during our time on earth is to live for God and to tell
the world the gospel message. Jesus had explained that, before
his return, "the gospel must first be preached to all nations"
(Mark 13:10 NIV). In his speech at Pentecost, Peter had told the
people, "Repent, then, and turn to God, so that your sins may be
wiped out, that times of refreshing may come from the Lord, and
that he may send the Christ, who has been appointed for you—
even Jesus. He must remain in heaven until the time comes for
God to restore everything, as he promised long ago through his
holy prophets" (Acts 3:19-21 NIV).

That day will bring about the destruction of the heavens by fire, and the elements will melt in the heat.^{NIV} In case anyone had missed it, Peter repeated his point about the final end of the world. Christians will be safe through it. They can look forward to it and speed its coming; however, they must not forget the awesome power that God will display on *that day*. As noted above, the end will bring *destruction of the heavens by fire* (3:10) and the melting of the elements *in the heat*. These will happen as a direct result of the coming of the Day of God. The earth's destruction will not be the result of any natural winding down of the universe, but the result of God's sovereign will, occurring according to his plan.

SPEEDING THE DAY
At Fermilab in Batavia, Illinois, atomic particles are accelerated to near light speed in the hope that a few will collide and allow scientists to observe and identify particles that make up an atom. Months of scientific preparation precede each experiment.

God calls us to prepare for his Day in a similar way. By concerted effort, prayer, and missionary zeal, the message of God takes hold around the world, charging the cosmos with energy until God unleashes all his power in history's climactic event.

We work together toward God's great Day. God alone knows when it will be. Today, cut out nonessentials. Do a little extra for God. Care a little more about neighbors who have no faith. Pray a little longer for a missionary. Take that job at church you were asked to consider. Give that donation. The particles are speeding up; the universe is crackling.

3:13 But, in accordance with his promise, we wait for new heavens and a new earth, where righteousness is at home.^{NRSV} Believers look forward to the end of the earth only because it means the fulfillment of another of God's promises—his creation of *new heavens and a new earth*. God's purpose for people is not destruction but re-creation; not annihilation, but renewal. The prophet Isaiah recorded God's *promise* to the people: "'As the new heavens and the new earth that I make will endure before me,' declares the Lord, 'so will your name and descendants endure'" (Isaiah 66:22 NIV; see also 65:17). God will purify the heavens and earth with fire; then he will create them anew. All believers can joyously look forward to the restoration of God's good world (Romans 8:21). In a beautiful description of the new heavens and earth, believers are assured that *righteousness is at home* there because God himself will live among his people. Revelation 21 offers a description of what this new home will be like:

■ *Then I saw a new heaven and a new earth, for the first heaven and the first earth had passed away, and there was no longer any sea. I saw the Holy City, the new Jerusalem, coming down out of heaven from God, prepared as a bride beautifully dressed for her husband. And I heard a loud voice from the throne saying, "Now the dwelling of God is with men, and he will live with them. They will be his people, and God himself will be with them and be their God. He will wipe every tear from their eyes. There will be no more death or mourning or crying or pain, for the old order of things has passed away."* *. . . I did not see a temple in the city, because the Lord God Almighty and the Lamb are its temple. The city does not need the sun or the moon to shine on it, for the glory of God gives it light, and the Lamb is its lamp. The nations will walk by its light, and the kings of the earth will bring their splendor into it. On no day will its gates ever be shut, for there will be no night there. The glory and honor of the nations will be brought into it. Nothing impure will ever enter it, nor will anyone who does what is shameful or deceitful, but only those whose names are written in the Lamb's book of life. (Revelation 21:1-4, 22-27 NIV)*

HEADING HOME
Settlers heading west along the Oregon Trail knew that one day, down the road, they would find a place to call home. The promise kept them going.
    Christians today need a reminder of what's ahead: a home where righteousness fills the air like the soothing aroma of cinnamon rolls fresh from the oven. God has prepared that home for us, just a few more bumps ahead along that dusty trail.
    Today, when your wagon wheel falls off and shade is hard to find, when your lead horse steps in a prairie dog hole and your son breaks your only shovel, pause to thank God for the promise: a place where righteousness settles down, just ahead, around the bend.

3:14 So then, dear friends, since you are looking forward to this, make every effort to be found spotless, blameless and at peace with him.^NIV Because believers can trust God's promise to bring them into a new earth, and because they *are looking forward to this* (that is, anticipating it), they ought to live to please God. To say it another way, only this powerful hope could entice us to live righteously. God's kingdom will be characterized by righteousness (3:13); therefore, believers ought to practice righteousness now, in preparation for living in the kingdom. Peter encouraged the believers to *make every effort* in this, a term he had used previously to encourage the believers to moral purity (see 1:5-7, 10, 15). We should not become lazy and complacent just because Christ has not yet returned. Instead, we should live in eager expectation of his coming. What would you like to be doing when Christ returns? That is how you should be living each day.

In 2:13, Peter had described the false teachers as "blots" *(spiloi)* and "blemishes" *(momoi)*. The believers, however, were to be completely opposite: *spotless (aspiloi)* and *blameless (amometoi)*, as Christ was "a lamb without blemish and without spot" (1 Peter 1:19 NKJV). "Spotless" and "blameless" were terms used for the selection of suitable animals used in the sacrifices. The words connote moral purity. Christ's character stands as the Christians' pattern and goal.

Furthermore, the believers were to remain *at peace with him* (referring to Christ). Because Christ himself will return, believers ought to live always to please him and get rid of any sin that breaks peace with him. Then they will be ready to go with him when he returns. This overwhelming "peace" would help Christians keep an eternal perspective against the problems they faced in this world.

3:15 Bear in mind that our Lord's patience means salvation.[NIV] As the believers waited, perhaps impatiently, for the Lord's return, Peter reminded them to *bear in mind* that the delay in the Lord's return was an indication of his *patience*. The false teachers were attributing the delay to slackness, seeking to negate God's promise. However, as Peter noted above, God "is longsuffering toward us, not willing that any should perish but that all should come to repentance" (3:9). God's patience *means salvation* for many more who will have the chance to respond to the gospel message.

Just as our dear brother Paul also wrote you with the wisdom that God gave him.[NIV] When reading the various letters of the New Testament, it is interesting to study the interrelationships among the writers. Peter was one of Jesus' twelve disciples. He later became the undisputed leader of the church in Jerusalem. Paul came along later, converted on the Damascus road by a vision of Jesus Christ (Acts 9). Paul was also considered an apostle, but he spent much time in his letters explaining his calling (see, for example, 2 Corinthians 10–12; Galatians 1:11–2:10). Paul explained,

■ *When they saw that I had been entrusted with the gospel for the uncircumcised, just as Peter had been entrusted with the gospel for the circumcised (for he who worked through Peter making him an apostle to the circumcised also worked through me in sending me to the Gentiles), and when James and Cephas [Peter] and John, who were acknowledged pillars, recognized the grace that had been given to me, they gave to Barnabas and me the right hand of fellowship, agreeing that we should go to the Gentiles and they to the circumcised. (Galatians 2:7-9 NRSV)*

Galatians 2:11-14 describes a time when Paul publicly rebuked Peter for being inconsistent in his dealings with Jews and Gentiles. While that has left some to believe that friction remained between Peter and Paul, they had great respect for each other as they worked in the ministries to which God had called them. Peter and Paul had very different backgrounds and personalities, and they preached from different viewpoints. Paul emphasized salvation by grace, not law, while Peter wrote about Christian life and service. Peter could speak sincerely of Paul as *our dear brother* (denoting him not only as a fellow Christian, but more important, as a fellow apostle).

By the time of Peter's writing, Paul's letters already had a widespread reputation. Peter backed up his words with the believers' apparent knowledge that Paul had also written to them about this very topic. It remains unclear to which of Paul's letters Peter was referring. Scholars have attempted to discover this by looking at Paul's letters in light of the subject matter. Exactly what was Peter referring to that Paul also wrote about? Most likely, this refers directly back to 3:14, where Peter encouraged the believers to live holy lives in view of the sudden and certain return of Christ. Paul wrote about this topic in most of his letters at various lengths (in 3:16, Peter says that Paul wrote about these matters in all his letters). It is possible that Paul's letters were beginning to be assembled and read together, becoming well known across the world. Scholars also have interpreted what Peter meant when he referred to Paul's letters by referring to the letter's destination (because of Peter's words that Paul *also wrote you,* referring to the same audience). Peter's words may be more generic. Peter realized that any community that read this letter would most likely have read some of Paul's correspondence in which this teaching was included.

Peter recognized the value of Paul's letters in the growth of the church, for he described Paul as writing them *with the wisdom*

that God gave him. In other words, these were inspired works. In
3:16, Peter referred to them along with "the other Scriptures,"
indicating that the letters were on a par with the Holy Scriptures.
(See Paul's words about this in 1 Corinthians 2:6-16.)

**3:16 He writes the same way in all his letters, speaking in them of
these matters. His letters contain some things that are hard to
understand, which ignorant and unstable people distort, as
they do the other Scriptures, to their own destruction.**[NIV] The
teachings of the apostles were never distorted by the person or
area of ministry. Whether the letter came from Paul or Peter, the
message could be depended on to be the same, for it had come
from God himself. Peter had certainly read Paul's letters, so he
appealed to Paul's authoritative writings, explaining that Paul had
written about the same matters *in all his letters* (referring back,
once again, to 3:14). Notice that Peter wrote of Paul's letters as if
they were on a level with *the other Scriptures.* Already the early
church was considering Paul's letters to be inspired by God. Both
Peter and Paul were aware that they were speaking God's word
along with the Old Testament prophets (see 1 Thessalonians
2:13). In the early days of the church, the letters from the apostles
were read to the believers and often passed along to other
churches. Sometimes the letters were copied and then passed on.
The believers regarded these writings to be as authoritative as the
Old Testament Scriptures.

Some readers may have been put off by some of the *things that
are hard to understand* in Paul's letters. Once again, it remains
unknown which passages Peter meant. Some scholars suggest
that this refers to Paul's teaching about justification by faith. This
teaching had caused the false teachers (like those Peter railed
against in this letter) to claim that once they were saved they
could do whatever they liked. In Romans 3:3-26, Paul had argued
at length about such a conclusion from his teachings. The false
teachers had intentionally misused Paul's writings by distorting
them to condone lawlessness. No doubt this had made the teachers popular because people always like to have their favorite sins
justified, but the net effect was to totally destroy Paul's message.
Paul may have been thinking of teachers like these when he
wrote in Romans 6:15: "What then? Shall we sin because we are
not under law but under grace? By no means!" (NIV).

Peter warned his readers to avoid the mistakes of those wicked
teachers by growing in the grace and knowledge of Jesus. The
better we know Jesus, the less attractive false teaching will be.
Sincere Christians ought to continue seeking to understand, not
being like those who are *ignorant and unstable* (once again jab-

bing at the false teachers), who took the difficult passages and
twisted (or "distorted") them to mean whatever they wanted.
Peter explained that this should not come as a surprise, for the
false teachers twisted all of Scripture to mean whatever they
wanted. However, this would result in *their own destruction,*
described in chapter 2.

**3:17 You therefore, beloved, since you are forewarned, beware
that you are not carried away with the error of the lawless
and lose your own stability.**NRSV Once again, Peter addressed his
readers as *beloved* (or "dear friends"), implying his love and concern for them. Indeed, that was the very basis of this letter. He
wanted them to be *forewarned* about the danger of false teachers,
explaining the false teachers' tactics and future destruction.
Being forewarned, the believers would not be *carried away with
the error of the lawless,* losing their own *stability.* To "be carried
away" means to be led astray into error. The term pictures a person following along behind a crowd. The implication is that keeping company with false teachers or those who follow them will
inevitably cause the believer to also be led astray. People not
grounded in the truth can find themselves led away by arguments
that seem logical or beliefs that seem easier to understand. But
these amount to no more than "the error of the lawless" and will
cause believers to become "unstable" like the false teachers
(3:16). "Therefore, beloved Christians," appealed Peter, "be forewarned so that you can stand firm and faithful until the end."

**3:18 But grow in the grace and knowledge of our Lord and Savior
Jesus Christ. To him be the glory both now and to the day of
eternity. Amen.**NRSV Peter concluded this brief letter as he had
begun, by urging his readers to *grow* (the verb is a present imperative, meaning "continue growing") *in the grace and knowledge*
of the Lord and Savior Jesus Christ—to get to know Christ better
and better. No matter where we are in our spiritual journey, no
matter how mature we are, the sinful world always will challenge
our faith. We still have much room for growth. If every day we
find some way to draw closer to Christ, we will be prepared to
stand for truth in any and all circumstances.

Believers "grow in grace" as they understand that they are living by God's grace alone—so everything they do is a result of
that grace. Believers "grow in knowledge" as they search and
study the Scriptures, pray, listen to sound teachers, and apply that
knowledge to their daily lives. If they do these, they will not need
to fear being influenced by false teachers. This knowledge is not
just any knowledge; it is knowledge *of our Lord and Savior Jesus*

Christ. Christ is Lord, divine and omnipotent; he is Savior, the one who accomplished humanity's salvation. To him alone belongs *glory* in this age and in the new eternal age to come. *Amen,* so be it.

NOW WHAT?
Peter's case rests. The false teachers have been exposed. Believers have been forewarned. Now what?

Our daily task is to grow in the knowledge of Jesus Christ. That's best done by Bible study, prayer, and meeting with other Christians for discussion and worship. It's also done by living God's way on the job and at school, by choosing God's way in policies that govern our nation, by discovering all we can about the world God created, by standing strong for justice and mercy, forgiveness and truth.

Peter closes his letter with a special phrase, "the day of eternity"—that great day when Christ returns and God establishes justice forever in a heaven of love. To that day we look, giving God all our effort and devotion in full trust and confidence.

JUDE

INTRODUCTION TO JUDE

Half-truths, statements taken out of context, misleading descriptions, words changed in meaning, and outright fabrications are designed to deceive, to hide the truth. Liars have many motives: to make a sale, to win an election, to hide wrongdoing, to enhance an image, to beat a rival, to cheat someone, to gain the favor of a coach, teacher, friend, parent, employer, or spouse. Whatever the reason, the real character of the liar is exposed when the truth is revealed.

In the early years of the church, liars arose—truth-twisters who deliberately rejected God's Word and the lordship of Christ and designed, instead, their own theology. The motive for these men was to gain power and money. Responding to this threat to the church, the apostles and other church leaders published warnings, urging Christians to be alert, to know the truth, and to reject the liars and their lies. That's what motivated Jude to pen his short letter.

As you read Jude, think about the possible false teachers in your world and determine to "contend for the faith" (v. 3).

AUTHOR

Jude: son of Joseph, brother of James, and half brother of Jesus.

Immediately the writer of this short letter identifies himself as "Jude, a servant of Jesus Christ and a brother of James" (v. 1), so the question is which James and which Jude (a form of the Hebrew name Judah—Greek "Judas"—a common Jewish name). Some believe that the author is Judas the apostle—not Judas Iscariot, but the other Jude (Luke 6:16; Acts 1:13). But that Judas is listed as the "son" of James, not the "brother." Also, it would seem that if the writer of this book were "Jude, the apostle" that he would identify himself as such. There are other possibilities, of course: an unknown brother of James the apostle, the brother of an unknown James, an unknown author writing under the

name of Jude, and so forth. All of these speculations have little
or no evidence to support them.

The most widely accepted answer is that Jude and James are
the sons of Joseph mentioned in Matthew 13:55 and Mark 6:3
and, thus, the half brothers of Jesus. Eventually, James had
become the head of the church in Jerusalem (see Acts 12:17;
15:13-21; Galatians 1:18-19; 2:11-13). He also wrote the Bible
book bearing his name (in about A.D. 47–49). The renown of
James would explain why Jude described himself as "a brother
of James" (v. 1). This is an unusual description since at this time
a person usually would describe himself as someone's son rather
than as someone's brother.

Like James, Jude did not believe in Jesus at first. In fact, they
had rejected him (Mark 3:21) and had ridiculed him (John 7:1-5).
After the Resurrection, however, Jesus "appeared to James"
(1 Corinthians 15:7). Evidently this is what convinced James that
Jesus was, in fact, the Messiah, the Savior, God in the flesh. Perhaps Jude was with James at the time, or perhaps James led his
brother to the Lord. Whatever the case, both men became vocal
witnesses for Christ and leaders in the young church. Note also
that both men begin their books by describing themselves not as
equals or family but as *"a servant* of Jesus Christ" (James 1:1;
Jude 1).

Little else is known of Jude. He, along with Mary and his other
brothers, were in the upper room just before Pentecost (Acts
1:14), and he traveled with his wife as he performed missionary
work (1 Corinthians 9:5).

Quotations and possible references to this letter appear in writings of Clement of Rome (A.D. 96). Other church fathers, including Clement of Alexandria (155–215), Tertullian (150–222), and
Origen (185–253) accepted it as canonical. Jude was also
included in the Muratorian Canon (170) and was accepted by
Athanasius (298–373) and the Council of Carthage (397).

SETTING

Perhaps written from Palestine in about A.D. 65.

Jude's location and the date of his writing are unknown. As
James' brother and active in the Jerusalem church, the most
likely place would seem to be Palestine. But Paul implies that
Jude and his wife may have served as traveling missionaries
("Don't we have the right to take a believing wife along with us,
as do the other apostles and the Lord's brothers and Cephas?"—
1 Corinthians 9:5). If this is true, Jude could have been almost

anywhere in the Roman Empire when he wrote this letter. Also, because neither 2 Peter nor Jude refers to the destruction of the Jerusalem temple, both letters probably were written before A.D. 70.

Both the location and date of this letter are affected by the fact that it is similar to 2 Peter. Consider these common phrases and similar passages (all from the NIV):

- "There will be false teachers among you" (2 Peter 2:1)

  "For certain men whose condemnation was written about long ago have secretly slipped in among you" (Jude 4).

- "For if God did not spare angels when they sinned, but sent them to hell, putting them into gloomy dungeons to be held for judgment; if he did not spare the ancient world when he brought the flood on its ungodly people . . ." (2 Peter 2:4-5).

  "The Lord delivered his people out of Egypt, but later destroyed those who did not believe. And the angels who did not keep their positions of authority but abandoned their own home—these he has kept in darkness, bound with everlasting chains for judgment on the great Day" (Jude 5-6).

- "This is especially true of those who follow the corrupt desire of the sinful nature and despise authority. Bold and arrogant, these men are not afraid to slander celestial beings" (2 Peter 2:10).

  "In the very same way, these dreamers pollute their own bodies, reject authority and slander celestial beings" (Jude 8).

- "But these men blaspheme in matters they do not understand. They are like brute beasts, creatures of instinct, born only to be caught and destroyed, and like beasts they too will perish" (2 Peter 2:12).

  "Yet these men speak abusively against whatever they do not understand; and what things they do understand by instinct, like unreasoning animals—these are the very things that destroy them" (Jude 10).

- "They are blots and blemishes, reveling in their pleasures while they feast with you" (2 Peter 2:13).

  "These men are blemishes at your love feasts, eating with you without the slightest qualm—shepherds who feed only themselves" (Jude 12).

- "These men are springs without water and mists driven by a storm. Blackest darkness is reserved for them" (2 Peter 2:17).

  "They are clouds without rain, blown along by the wind. . . . They are wild waves of the sea, foaming up their shame; wandering stars, for whom blackest darkness has been reserved forever" (Jude 12-13).

- "In the last days scoffers will come, scoffing and following their own evil desires" (2 Peter 3:3).

  "In the last times there will be scoffers who will follow their own ungodly desires" (Jude 18).

The coincidence of similarity between Jude and 2 Peter can be explained in three ways:

1. *Peter used Jude as a resource.* If this is true, then Jude would have to have been written before Peter wrote 2 Peter (A.D. 67). Also, he would have had to be close to Peter, or, if Jude wrote from Jerusalem, there would have to have been time for the letter to get to Peter in Rome. A date of A.D. 65 would fit this possibility.

2. *Jude used 2 Peter as a resource.* In this case, 2 Peter would have to have been written before Jude (and the location is also a factor). A date of about A.D. 69 would fit this possibility.

3. *Both Jude and Peter used a common resource.* This possibility would allow many possible dates and locations.

The similarity between the two letters indicates that they probably were written at about the same time, since they both addressed the same issue faced by the church, a pre-Gnostic heresy.

AUDIENCE

Jewish Christians scattered throughout the world.

Little is known for sure about the intended readers of this letter except that it is addressed, "To those who have been called, who are loved by God the Father and kept by Jesus Christ" (v. 1). This description sounds as though Jude was writing to all believers and not a specific church or segment of the church. His expressions "among you" (v. 4) and "your love feasts" (v. 12) seem to indicate that he has churches in mind. And Jude's appeal to Old Testament personalities and stories (for example, the Exodus, the destruction of Sodom and Gomorrah, Moses, Cain, Balaam,

Korah's rebellion, and Enoch) seems to indicate that his intended audience had a strong Jewish heritage. As a Jewish believer himself, Jude's tendency would have been to minister among Hebrew Christians, like his brother James, who specifically addressed his letter "to the twelve tribes" (James 1:1).

Some think that Jude was writing to the same audience for whom 2 Peter was intended, because of the heresy addressed by both letters. But there is no evidence for this. Evidently these false teachers were becoming a problem for most of the churches. Paul addressed a similar problem in his letter to the Colossians.

It is likely, therefore, that Jude wrote this letter to Jewish Christians to whom he had ministered, in Palestine and elsewhere.

OCCASION AND PURPOSE FOR WRITING

To warn believers about false teachers and their heresy.

Jude wrote that at first he had intended to "write . . . about the salvation we share" (v. 3); however, the Holy Spirit compelled him to warn his friends and fellow believers about the false teachers who had infiltrated their churches (v. 4). These men were ignoring the teachings of the apostles (v. 17), ridiculing theology (vv. 10, 18), and twisting the message of God's grace in order to excuse their sexual immorality. Jude urged his readers to "contend for the faith" (v. 3), build themselves up in their understanding of God and his Word (v. 20), pray (v. 20), reject all false teaching (v. 23), and focus on Christ (vv. 24-25).

Beyond the description in the text, little is known about these false teachers. However, the teachers' arrogance, immorality, and claim to superior knowledge sound as though they were forerunners of what became Gnosticism in the second century. For more on Gnosticism, see the introduction to 2 Peter.

MESSAGE

False Teachers, Apostasy.

False Teachers (vv. 4, 8, 10-19). Jude warned against false teachers and leaders who reject the lordship of Christ, undermine the faith of others, and lead people astray. He pointed out that these men had already infiltrated the church, making them even more dangerous. He also explained that these leaders and any who follow them will be severely punished by God.

Importance for Today. We must stoutly defend Christian truth, avoiding all compromise of the basics of the faith and rejecting all who would twist Scripture to fit their own immoral agenda.

Make sure that you avoid leaders and teachers (even in the church) who change the Bible to suit their own purposes. Genuine servants of God will faithfully portray Christ in their words and conduct. Watch out for anyone who tries to make Jesus anything less than the King of kings and Lord of lords and who tries to make the Bible anything less than the inspired, inerrant Word of God.

Apostasy (vv. 4-9, 10-11, 14-19, 22-25). Jude also warned against apostasy—turning away from Christ—presenting examples from the Old Testament of those who turned away and were punished. We must remember that God punishes all who rebel against him. We must be careful not to drift away from a firm commitment to Christ.

Importance for Today. People who do not seek to know the truth in God's Word are susceptible to apostasy. Become a student of the Scriptures and keep your focus on Christ. Guard against any false teachings that would distract you or pull you away from God's truth.

VITAL STATISTICS

Purpose: To remind the church to be vigilant against heresy and to remain strong in the faith

Author: Jude, brother of Jesus and James

To whom written: Jewish Christians, and all believers everywhere

Date written: About A.D. 65

Setting: The church was being threatened by heresy and false teaching.

Key verse: "Dear friends, although I was very eager to write to you about the salvation we share, I felt I had to write and urge you to contend for the faith that was once for all entrusted to the saints" (v. 3 NIV).

OUTLINE

1. The danger of false teachers (1-16)
2. The duty to fight for God's truth (17-25)

Jude

Jude's letter focuses on "apostasy"—when people turn away from God's truth and embrace false teachings. Jude reminded his readers of God's judgment on those who had left the faith in the past. This letter warns against false teachers—in this case, probably those who were promoting an early form of Gnosticism. Gnostics opposed two of the basic tenets of Christianity—the incarnation of Christ and the call to Christian ethics. Jude wrote to combat these false teachings and to encourage true doctrine and right conduct.

Some people avoid studying the Bible because they think doctrine is dry and boring. Yet this should be exciting and important work. Theological opinions and options have led to revolutions, battles, and ongoing disputes in the world, even today. Those who refuse to learn correct doctrine are susceptible to false teaching because they are not grounded in God's truth. It is imperative to understand the basic doctrines of the Christian faith in order to recognize false doctrines and prevent wrong teaching from undermining our faith and hurting others.

Jude is a short letter with only one chapter. Verses are referred to by verse number only. For example, (v. 2) refers you to verse 2.

1 Jude, a servant of Jesus Christ and brother of James.NRSV
Jude was a common Jewish name. Scholars have various opinions about Jude's identity. Some identify him with the apostle Judas (John 14:22; Acts 1:13); however, verse 17 of this letter seems to reveal that the author was not an apostle. Others say he was a companion of Paul known as "Judas called Barsabbas" (Acts 15:22). However, the overwhelming majority consider him to be Jude (or Judas), a half brother of Jesus (Matthew 13:55; Mark 6:3). In his introduction, Jude identified himself as *brother of James.* This James was not one of the apostles named James, but another of Jesus' half brothers (he is referred to in Galatians 1:19). Mary was their mother, and Joseph was their father. (Although Mary was Jesus' true mother, God was Jesus' true Father.) In the days of Jesus' ministry on earth, his brothers did

not believe in him (John 7:3-10). However, Paul recorded that Jesus, after his resurrection, made a personal appearance to James (1 Corinthians 15:7). Jesus' time with James must have affected James profoundly, for he became a believer. At some point, Jude also was converted (Acts 1:14). (For more information on Jude and James, see the introduction to Jude.)

James, the Lord's brother, was martyred in A.D. 62, a few years before this letter was written. James was well known among the believers and his name still was highly regarded; thus Jude could simply identify himself as James' brother, knowing that there would be no mistaking his identity. Jude and James were not apostles, but James had been one of the leaders in the church in Jerusalem; later he became head of the church (Acts 12:17; 15:13; 21:18) and author of the New Testament book of James. Apparently Jude held some authority (as revealed in this letter). He most likely traveled as a missionary (see 1 Corinthians 9:5) and naturally would have wanted to write a letter to his converts whose faith was being threatened by false teaching.

> It is not the possession of extraordinary gifts that makes extraordinary usefulness, but the dedication of what we have to the service of God. *F. W. Robertson*

Oddly enough, Jude did not refer to himself as a brother of Jesus Christ. It would seem that this would have carried even more authority. Like James (see James 1:1), Jude simply identified himself as *a servant of Jesus Christ,* not as Jesus' brother. This may have been because the use of the terms "brother" and "sister" had come to refer to the spiritual relationship all believers had to Jesus Christ and to one another. Thus, Jesus' half brothers refrained from referring to themselves by their family relationship with Jesus. As believers, they focused on their spiritual relationship with their Lord and considered themselves privileged to be called his servants. They had been bought (or redeemed) from slavery to sin with the price of Christ's blood (1 Corinthians 7:23). Paul also referred to himself as Christ's servant (Romans 1:1; Galatians 1:10; Philippians 1:1).

The word translated "servant" means "slave," one who is subject to the will and wholly at the disposal of a master. To describe themselves thus, the believers were expressing their absolute devotion and subjection to Christ Jesus. The New Testament teaches that true leaders must serve others. Jesus exemplified this throughout his life (see Mark 10:35-45; Philippians 2:5-8).

Imagine what childhood memories Jude and James must have

recalled as they considered their new spiritual relationship with Jesus. Surely Jesus must have been an exceptional older brother. Perhaps they flinched at some of their words of mockery (as recorded in John 7:3-5). But they became believers, contenders for the faith, and true servants of their Lord and Savior.

To those who have been called, who are loved by God the Father and kept by Jesus Christ.^{NIV} Jude did not specify any destination for his letter. Instead, he addressed it to believers, whom he described in a beautiful triad:

1. *Those who have been called.* This phrase pictured what happened in the past—believers have been called to be saved. Being "called" also is referred to as "elected," "chosen," or "predestined." God's Spirit calls people out of darkness into the light of Christ, convinces them of their sinfulness, shows them what Christ can do for them, and then helps them to accept Christ. This occurs by God's grace and love alone. (See also Romans 1:6-7; 8:28-30; 11:29; 1 Corinthians 1:24; Ephesians 4:4; 1 Peter 1:2; 2 Peter 1:3, 10-11.)

2. *Loved by God the Father.* The verb form of "loved" refers to a past action that continues into the present. God's love prompted his call; his love will continue now and forever. God's love never changes. The believers across the ancient world, often facing persecution, could count on the fact that they were and always would be enfolded by God's love. God had become their "Father" by adopting them as his children. (See also Galatians 3:26–4:7.)

3. *Kept by Jesus Christ.* Believers are "kept" (or guarded) by Jesus Christ for the certain rewards of Christ's promised blessing. Peter explained that believers could be assured of "an inheritance that can never perish, spoil or fade—kept in heaven" (1 Peter 1:4 NIV). Also, believers have security in their salvation: "through faith [believers] are shielded by God's power until the coming of the salvation that is ready to be revealed in the last time" (1 Peter 1:5 NIV). Believers are kept safe for Christ, guarded as his property, to be claimed upon his return. At Christ's second coming, believers will be ready to receive their full salvation and to live eternally with him. (See also Romans 8:18-39; 2 Timothy 1:12.)

2 May mercy, peace, and love be yours in abundance.^{NRSV} In another triad, Jude described his prayer for the believers. He wanted them to have *in abundance* (that is, in overflowing measure) mercy, peace, and love.

1. *Mercy* carries with it the Old Testament picture of God's loving-kindness or compassion. God's mercy helps believers day by day. Jude knew that the believers were facing difficult situations in the world—a society focused on selfish pleasure, ready to persecute believers at any provocation, with false teachers looking to tear the churches apart. Mercy helps believers in their times of need (Hebrews 4:16). That believers would have mercy in abundance meant that they were secure in God's merciful call and protection.

2. *Peace* refers to the peace that Christ made between us and God through his death on the cross. Only God can give true and lasting peace. Jews wish each other "peace" (*shalom* in Hebrew). Peter referred to the peace of Christ (see 2 Peter 3:14). Jesus said, "Peace I leave with you; my peace I give you. I do not give to you as the world gives. Do not let your hearts be troubled and do not be afraid" (John 14:27 NIV). The believers needed an abundance of inner peace and quiet confidence as they faced the turmoil in their world and as they stood up to the false teachers.

> Peace *with* God brings the peace *of* God. It is a peace that settles our nerves, fills our mind, floods our spirit, and in the midst of the uproar around us, gives us the assurance that everything is all right.
> *Bob Mumford*

3. *Love* comes from God, for God himself is love (1 John 4:7-8). Believers who are grounded in God's love can resist the lies of the false teachers and remain solid in their stand against persecution and temptation. God will generously grant their requests and meet their needs.

LOVE
"All you need is love" announces the Beatles' classic tune. It's totally right, yet gives the wrong solution. The love of another person, even intimate and personal, may be satisfying for a time; in the long run, however, it will turn out to be insufficient for a person's deepest needs. The love of God, which fills the heart with peace and assures the soul of mercy, provides the framework for all other loves. Without it, human love fails.

When Jude wanted to share abundant love for his readers, he urged them toward fullness, happiness, contentment, and generosity. God's love forgives, strengthens, and leads us. It gives all other loves a purpose and a hope. In what ways have you experienced God's abundant love? How will you love him in return?

---

3 Beloved, while eagerly preparing to write to you about the salvation we share, I find it necessary to write and appeal to you to contend for the faith that was once for all entrusted to the saints.^{NRSV} Although Jude's brief letter does not mention his intended readers, it addresses specific concerns about false teaching that was threatening the churches. Yet that may not have been Jude's original intention. He probably decided to write to encourage believers. However, an urgent concern about false teaching caused him instead to write *this* letter denouncing the false teachers and appealing to the Christians to *contend for the faith.* Jude probably wanted this letter to be circulated because false teaching was a serious problem for all the churches. Thus, he specified no particular church or area.

The believers were addressed as *beloved* (also translated, "dear friends"), a term often used by those who wrote with authority to the Christians. (For example, Paul used the term in 1 Corinthians 10:14; Peter, in 1 Peter 2:11 and 2 Peter 3:1; John, in 1 John 2:7 and 3:2.) Jude had wanted to write a joyous letter to believers *about the salvation we share,* that is, a letter about the Christian faith that he and all believers had in common. Instead, Jude had to set that idea aside because a much more urgent and unhappy topic needed to be addressed. False teachers were threatening the churches, endangering the believers' faith.

The word "contend," *epagonizesthai,* occurs only here in the New Testament. Often it is used in secular literature to describe the intense struggle in an athletic contest. Jude called the believers to action, to contend for the faith. "Contending" would not be easy; it called for hard work, diligent study, willingness to stand against society's desire to water down the gospel, speaking up for the truth and bearing the burden of interpreting the timeless truth to a changing society. The believers could not (and would never be able to) sit back and idly enjoy the mercy, peace, and love of their faith (v. 2). Rather, their Christian faith must be defended against the onslaught of false teaching. "The faith" refers to the entire body of beliefs taught by the apostles and held by the Christians (see Acts 2:42). The teachings of Christ and his apostles had been *once for all* (without change to the content) *entrusted to the saints* (to all believers). All Christians had been entrusted with the faith—to keep it pure and to teach it to others. Therefore, all Christians should stand ready to defend the faith as they would defend any prized possession.

Jude emphasized the important relationship between correct doctrine and true faith. The truth of the Bible must not be compromised because it gives us the real facts about Jesus and salvation. The Bible is inspired by God and should never be twisted or manipulated.

NO COMPROMISE
How do ordinary Christians contend for the truth today? Think about these ideas:

- It is every Christian's job to study the Bible. Don't ever imagine that pastors and seminary professors hold a monopoly on this task. Without study, you cannot know what to contend for.
- Knowledge in the brain is only part of contending for truth. Prayer is vital. God gives the Holy Spirit as a teacher. Unattached to God, you may know everything, but understand nothing.
- Many private interpretations fracture the truth of the gospel; Christians must remain unified on the essentials. Associate with a church that loves God and encourages learning. Then use your common resources for the hard work of contending. Lone crusaders invariably create hostile splinter groups.

There are certain doctrines that we should contend for, those that are central to our faith and salvation (such as the Trinity, the deity of Christ, atonement). On others we can agree to disagree (such as Calvinism/Arminianism, charismatic issues, methods for spiritual growth, spiritual disciplines).

- Truth must be served as well as studied. Demonstrate the truth by working for it. Build a house, organize a fun night, start a food pantry, help with youth—all in the name of Christ, the Truth.

4 For certain intruders have stolen in among you.NRSV Jude explained the reason for his compulsion to write this letter of appeal: *certain intruders* (that is, false teachers) had entered the church, "stealing in" among the believers. How could this happen? These may have been traveling teachers who had come and had established themselves in communities and churches with the sole aim of perverting the Christian gospel. (For example, in Galatians 2:4, Paul talked about the Judaizers who had infiltrated Christian groups.) Their teaching didn't sound so "false" at first; it was subtle and easy to follow, so it had lulled some believers away from the truth. The false teachers knowingly sought to destroy the church from within, working in an underhanded manner to bring in their ideas. But their false teaching would only lead to judgment. Although these teachers introduced their perverted teaching carefully, any deviation from the truth is no longer the truth. For example, many taught that Christians can do whatever they like without fear of God's punishment. This reflects a weak view of God's holiness and his justice. Peter explained it this way: "They will secretly introduce destructive heresies, even denying the sovereign Lord who bought them" (2 Peter 2:1 NIV). Both Peter and Jude used the same Greek word, meaning "to smuggle" or "to worm their way in." Thus these false teachers did not belong in the church and were no better than intruders among the believers.

People who long ago were designated for this condemnation as ungodly, who pervert the grace of our God into licentiousness and deny our only Master and Lord, Jesus Christ.^{NRSV} Some have seen in these words the doctrine of double predestination (that some are chosen for salvation and others chosen for damnation according to the foreknowledge of God). The phrase "were designated for" comes from the verb *prographo* meaning "to write down beforehand" (hence, the NIV translation "whose condemnation was written about long ago.") It is not necessary to go that far in the interpretation. More likely, it refers to previously written condemnation of anyone who is a false teacher or false prophet (see Paul's words in Galatians 1:8-9).

God's true prophets had warned against false prophets (see, for example, Isaiah 44:25; Jeremiah 50:36). Jesus had warned his disciples that false teachers would come (Matthew 7:15; 24:11, 24; Luke 6:26). The apostles often denounced false teachers in their letters (see 2 Corinthians 11:5; Galatians 1:6-9; Philippians 3:2; Colossians 2:8, 16-19; 1 Timothy 1:3; 6:3; 2 Timothy 3:6; 2 Peter 2; 1 John 4:1). These false teachers would eventually receive their just reward: They *long ago were designated for this condemnation as ungodly.* "Ungodly" means unrighteous, lawless, those people whose sinful conduct stems from the total lack of respect for God. Jude explained that no matter how long it might take, and no matter how successful these teachers might appear to be, eventually they would be condemned by God himself, as explained in the remainder of this letter.

Jude cited two reasons for this certain condemnation:

1. They *pervert the grace of our God into licentiousness.* This refers to the moral side of their heresy. The true gospel teaches that people are freed from sin by believing in Jesus Christ as Savior and Lord. This happens by God's grace alone. "Grace" gives Christians freedom from sin and from the law. However, the purpose of this freedom is to move people to holy living and service to God. "Licentiousness" means debauchery, an open and excessive indulgence in sexual sins. Licentious people have no sense of shame or restraint. The false teachers "perverted" or twisted God's grace, saying that freedom from sin means that people can live any way they please, fulfilling their sinful pleasures without inhibition. In their arrogance, these false teachers

claimed that their privileged status within God's grace put them above moral law.

Paul refuted this same kind of false teaching in Romans 6:1-23. Even today, some Christians minimize sin, believing that how they live has little to do with their faith. But what a person truly believes will be revealed by how he or she acts. Those who truly have faith will show it by their deep respect for God and their sincere desire to live according to the principles in his Word. Twisting God's grace to allow for flagrant sexual sin is a horrible perversion of the gospel. For doing this, the false teachers and their followers would pay dearly.

2. They *deny our only Master and Lord, Jesus Christ.* This refers to the doctrinal side of their heresy. With their flagrant sexual sinning in the name of God's grace, these false teachers were denying Christ as their Master and Lord, replacing him with themselves and their appetites. While claiming to know God, their actions denied him (see Titus 1:16). They taught lies, and in so doing they denied the basics of the Christian faith (1 John 2:22). Such a denial also ends in judgment and destruction. Jesus had told his disciples, "Whoever denies Me before men, him I will also deny before My Father who is in heaven" (Matthew 10:33 NKJV).

So how are believers today to discern false teaching? Heresies can be discovered through asking probing questions. We can guard against heresies by asking these questions about any religious group:

- Does it stress man-made rules and taboos rather than God's grace?

- Does it foster a critical spirit toward others, or does it exercise discipline discreetly and lovingly?

- Does it stress formulas, secret knowledge, or special visions more than the Word of God?

- Does it elevate self-righteousness, honoring those who keep the rules, rather than elevating Christ?

- Does it neglect Christ's universal church, claiming to be an elite group?

- Does it teach humiliation of the body as a means to spiritual growth rather than focusing on the growth of the whole person?

- Does it disregard the family rather than holding it in high regard as the Bible does?

THE TWIST
Even some of our churches today have false ("ungodly")
teachers who "have stolen in" and are twisting the Bible's
teachings to justify their own opinions, lifestyles, or wrong
behaviors. In doing this, they may gain temporary freedom
to do as they wish, but they will discover that in distorting
Scripture they are playing with fire. God will judge them for
excusing, tolerating, and promoting sin. We must hold our
teachers to the highest standards for the content that they
teach.

**5 Though you already know all this, I want to remind you
that the Lord delivered his people out of Egypt, but later
destroyed those who did not believe.**[NIV] To prove that the "designated condemnation" (v. 4) was certain to come upon the
false teachers and all unbelievers, Jude cited three examples of
God's punishment in the past (vv. 5-7). The believers *already*
knew these examples. Jude wanted *to remind* them about how
God had judged sin and rebellion in the past. Such judgment
also awaited the sin and rebellion of the false teachers. In verse
5, Jude reminded his readers about God's people, Israel, who,
although they were delivered from Egypt, refused to trust God
and enter the Promised Land (Numbers 14). God's people had
been recipients of God's deliverance, seeing his incredible
miracles in accomplishing their exodus *out of Egypt.* But when
they arrived at the entrance to the Promised Land, many
rebelled against God, refusing to believe that he could or would
protect them. Their unbelief resulted in destruction. From the
original group, only Caleb and Joshua (and their families) were
allowed to enter Canaan. The writer to the Hebrews explained
it this way: "Who were they who heard and rebelled? Were
they not all those Moses led out of Egypt? And with whom was
[God] angry for forty years? Was it not with those who sinned,
whose bodies fell in the desert? And to whom did God swear
that they would never enter his rest if not to those who disobeyed? So we see that they were not able to enter, because of
their unbelief" (Hebrews 3:16-19 NIV).

Jude used Israel's experience on the threshold of the Promised Land to explain that even some among God's people can
turn away. The false teachers had come from the ranks of the
believers. While not truly followers of Christ, they were saying and doing many of the right things, even as they were
teaching their wrong doctrines. They understood that they
could find deliverance from bondage to sin (like bondage to

Egypt), yet they were choosing sin over salvation. The obvious result, Jude wrote, would be that they, like the disobedient Israelites, would be *destroyed.*

6 And the angels who did not keep their own position, but left their proper dwelling, he has kept in eternal chains in deepest darkness for the judgment of the great Day.^{NRSV} This second example of God's punishment of disobedience describes certain *angels,* not those who live in heaven and glorify God, but those *who did not keep their own position, but left their proper dwelling.* Once pure, holy, and living in God's presence, they gave in to pride and joined Satan to rebel against God. They left their positions of authority and their dwelling with God, resulting in eventual doom. Peter explained that God "did not spare the angels when they sinned" (2 Peter 2:4 NRSV). Scholars differ regarding to which rebellion Jude referred. This could refer either to the angels who rebelled with Satan (Ezekiel 28:15), or more likely to the sin of the "sons of God" described in Genesis 6:1-4 (an interpretation given in the book of Enoch in the Apocrypha, when angels came to earth and took women as sexual partners; see also Revelation 12:7). Though not in the Bible, Jewish theology at this time held that some fallen angels (demons) were held in chains and some were free to roam this world to oppress people. For more on the book of Enoch, see verse 14. Jude's readers apparently understood his meaning, as well as the implication that if God did not spare his angels, neither would he spare the false teachers. Pride and lust had led to civil war and to the angels' fall. The false teachers' pride and lust would lead to judgment and destruction. God did not spare his angels; neither would he spare them.

As for these disobedient angels, God *has kept* them *in eternal chains in deepest darkness for the judgment of the great Day.* (See 2 Peter 2:4 and 17 for more on "chains in deepest darkness.") These angels were imprisoned in Tartarus (see comments on 1 Peter 3:19-20; 2 Peter 2:4). Some scholars describe the "eternal chains" as metaphors for the confinement of "deepest darkness"; others take them to be literal chains in a dark pit somewhere in this earthly sphere. Most likely this place of punishment is in a heavenly realm that is set aside for punishment (see comments on 1 Peter 3:19). These sinful angels will be "kept" in a place of punishment until the great Day of Judgment, when they will face their final doom (Matthew 25:41).

DEEPEST DARKNESS
What could such a prison be like? Take your worst nightmare
and worsen it. Scarier than the grossest horror film, spookier
than walking through a cellar full of spiders without a
flashlight—this place is no place you want to be.
   Take the hint. Avoid catastrophe by staying loyal to God.
Don't join the unbelieving rebels. Avoid their destination. Don't
risk such despair as these verses describe. Put your hope in
God alone, who saves us for heavenly light through faith in
Jesus Christ.

**7 Likewise, Sodom and Gomorrah and the surrounding cities,
which, in the same manner as they, indulged in sexual immorality and pursued unnatural lust, serve as an example by
undergoing a punishment of eternal fire.**NRSV. Finally, as a third
example of God's judgment of disobedience, Jude pointed out
that *Sodom and Gomorrah and the surrounding cities* had been
destroyed by God. The inhabitants were so full of sin that God
wiped the cities off the face of the earth. The people were following their own sinful natures, indulging in *sexual immorality* and
pursuing *unnatural lust.* Genesis 18–19 describes the sinfulness
of these cities. Genesis 19 tells about when angels, in the form of
men, visited Sodom. Some homosexual men in the city wanted to
rape these "men" who were visiting Lot; thus they "pursued
unnatural lust" by desiring sexual relations with the visiting
"men." Homosexuality and perversion brought *a punishment of
eternal fire* when God "rained down burning sulfur on Sodom
and Gomorrah" (Genesis 19:24 NIV). After the conflagration,
"Abraham . . . looked down toward Sodom and Gomorrah and
toward all the land of the Plain and saw the smoke of the land
going up like the smoke of a furnace" (Genesis 19:27-28 NRSV).
So complete was God's judgment and destruction that the cities
no longer exist today. Archaeologists believe they may be under
the waters of the Dead Sea.
   The Bible describes homosexual sex as "immoral" and "unnatural." Any attempt to label it merely as an "alternative lifestyle"
contradicts the Bible. Several other passages talk about homosexuality (Leviticus 18:22; Romans 1:26-27; 1 Corinthians 6:9-11;
and 1 Timothy 1:9-11). From these passages, we learn

- *The Bible clearly condemns homosexual sex.* God's plan for
  natural sexual relations is his ideal for his creation.

- *Alongside God's condemnation of sin is his offer of forgiveness.*
  Homosexuality may be considered acceptable in our society

(and even in some churches), but society does not set the standard for God's law. Many homosexuals believe that their desires are normal and that they have a right to express them. But God does not obligate nor encourage us to fulfill all our desires (even normal ones). Desires that violate his law must be controlled. God can forgive sexual sin just as he forgives other sins.

- *Temptation can be overcome by God's grace.* People who have homosexual desires can and must resist acting upon them. God offers his grace and mercy and will show the way out of sin into the light of his freedom and love.

- *Like all sinners, homosexuals are called to repent.* Because the Bible calls homosexual sex a sin, it must be repented. However, repentant homosexuals need to find a place of refuge and support within the church. God can transform their lives. The church should be a haven of forgiveness and healing for repentant homosexuals without compromising its stance against homosexual behavior.

The destruction of these cities served *as an example* of what will happen to people who refuse to obey God. The fire that rained on the evil cities pictures the fire that awaits unrepentant sinners. Many people don't want to believe that God will punish people with "eternal fire" for rejecting him. But this is clearly taught in Scripture. Sinners who don't seek forgiveness from God will face eternal darkness. Jude warned all who rebel against, ignore, or reject God.

8 In the very same way, these dreamers pollute their own bodies, reject authority and slander celestial beings.NIV Jude called the false teachers *dreamers,* referring to their use of dreams and visions for sources of their prophecy. Drawing from his three analogies above, Jude indicted the false teachers in three areas:

1. They *pollute their own bodies.* Like the citizens of Sodom and Gomorrah, they follow wherever their sinful desires lead them, even into homosexuality. Peter wrote that they followed "the corrupt desire of the sinful nature" (2 Peter 2:10 NIV), referring to sexual promiscuity, looseness, and licentiousness (v. 4). These people taught that Christian freedom placed believers above moral rules. No one living in such a way should attempt to speak for God. By doing so, these false teachers brought great judgment on themselves.

2. They *reject authority.* This "authority" could refer to church leaders, angelic powers (as below), or the Lord himself.

Most likely, the false teachers rejected the authority of all of these. They lived to please themselves and dismissed the prospect of a Second Coming and judgment by God.

3. They *slander celestial beings.* These "celestial beings" (also translated "glorious ones") may refer to church leaders, angels, or fallen angels. Many scholars say that Jude was referring to the good angels. While angels are not to be worshiped, they ought to receive respect and awe because of their position and authority. Jude may have been describing the false teachers' flouting of belief in the power and authority of Jesus Christ *and* of God's messengers, the angels. Just as the men of Sodom insulted angels (Genesis 19), these false teachers were insulting God's angels. These scholars take verse 9 to mean that the archangel Michael did not dare to slander even Satan; how arrogant that the false teachers would dare to slander God's holy angels!

In light of the comparable verse in 2 Peter 2:11, the celestial beings mentioned here most likely are the fallen angels—the guilty celestial beings who deserve condemnation. The false teachers "slandered" the spiritual realities they did not understand, perhaps by taking Satan's power too lightly. Thus, the statement in verse 9 that the archangel Michael did not dare to slander Satan himself shows the arrogance of these false teachers.

Jude was emphasizing that the false teachers were immoral, insubordinate, and irreverent. Jude hardly needed to say more. The believers had no reason for listening to or following such people.

9 But even the archangel Michael, when he was disputing with the devil about the body of Moses, did not dare to bring a slanderous accusation against him, but said, "The Lord rebuke you!"[NIV] Michael's title, *archangel,* a term found only here and in 1 Thessalonians 4:16, reflects the ranking of angels that was part of Jewish tradition. The Bible regards an archangel as a high or holy angel appointed to a special task. In Daniel 10:13, 21 and 12:1, Michael is a mighty angel. This incident mentioned by Jude is not recorded in Scripture, but it can be found in an ancient book titled, "The Assumption of Moses." The story, obviously known to the early believers, explains that the archangel Michael had been sent to bury Moses' body. Deuteronomy states that "Moses the servant of the Lord died there in Moab, as the Lord had said. He buried him in Moab, in the valley opposite Beth Peor, but to this day no one knows where his grave is"

(Deuteronomy 34:5-6 NIV); however, there is no mention of this struggle for Moses' body.

According to "The Assumption of Moses," when Michael prepared to do his task, he began *disputing with the devil* over Moses' body. Satan is a fallen angel. He is real, not symbolic, and is constantly fighting against those who follow and obey God. The story explains that Satan said Moses' body rightfully belonged to him because Moses had committed murder (see Exodus 2:12). He said that he had rights over all the earth and that Moses' body fell under that category as well. While Michael had every reason to expose Satan's lies, he *did not dare to bring a slanderous accusation against him.* Michael, instead of using his own authority, left the matter in his Master's hands, saying simply, *"The Lord rebuke you!"* He did not rely on his own power and authority.

Jude wanted the believers to understand that if even archangels are careful about how they address other powers, even evil ones, how much more should mere people watch their words when speaking of celestial powers, good or evil. If even a powerful angel of God did not dare to speak a judgment on God's behalf, then neither should the false teachers claim to speak for God when they knew nothing about him.

FIGHTING THE DEVIL

SRA is the acronym given to a wide range of heinous activities called Satanic Ritual Abuse. Specifically, these activities include animal and human sacrifice, immoral acts, and harm to children done by alleged satanists.

SRA is the topic of several recent best-selling religious books, beginning with author Mike Warnke and continuing through Lauren Stratford and others, who outlined their SRA experiences in riveting, graphic prose. In many cases, however, including the two just cited, these books are filled with exaggerated events and imaginary encounters. Investigators who uncovered the lies were themselves accused of deceit and duplicity, but their findings were never challenged. SRA enjoyed a wave of hysteric popularity, and authors sold fantastic stories, but as a result publishers blushed and a somewhat skeptical public audience grew to wonder, "Who can you trust?"

Jude teaches two lessons, which the SRA fad underscores: (1) Don't get fascinated with the details of the devil. Avoid conversation with Satan. Nothing good comes from it. Let the Lord God handle the devil. (2) In your avoidance, realize that deceit is at the very heart of Satan's character, and be guardedly skeptical about what you hear. Count on God's Word for truth, and on Satan's words for nothing at all.

10 Yet these men speak abusively against whatever they do not understand; and what things they do understand by instinct, like unreasoning animals—these are the very things that destroy them.^{NIV} In contrast to the archangel Michael's refusal to slander even Satan himself (v. 9), the false teachers slandered celestial beings (v. 8) and spoke abusively *against whatever they do not understand.* Many of these false teachers claimed to possess a superior, secret knowledge that gave them authority. They considered themselves to be the only ones to truly "understand" God. Yet by their slander, they revealed not superior knowledge, but profound ignorance. In fact, for all their pride, they were no better than *unreasoning animals.* Their only understanding was *by instinct*—how to fulfill their sexual desires. While claiming superior knowledge and status, these false teachers had only the most basic knowledge—how to fulfill their lust. They had no understanding beyond that of the animals; their status was not above the rest of humanity, but was, in reality, below it.

Their refusal to heed God's voice left them enslaved to sin and their sinful passions. The only things these men truly understood were the passions and lusts that enslaved them. Even though they claimed to be able to indulge themselves without retribution, eventually they would be destroyed by those sins.

11 Woe to them! They have taken the way of Cain; they have rushed for profit into Balaam's error; they have been destroyed in Korah's rebellion.^{NIV} Jude reminded his readers of three classic examples of men who had lived as they pleased and had been punished for doing so. These stories illustrate attitudes that are typical of false teachers—pride, selfishness, jealousy, greed, lust for power, and disregard of God's will. No wonder Jude exclaimed *Woe to them!* Their grave errors would result in complete destruction.

1. *Cain* murdered his brother out of vengeful jealousy (Genesis 4:1-16). There are various interpretations of *the way of Cain.* Jude may have been referring to Cain's desire to devise another way of worship rather than the way God intended (Hebrews 11:4), to Cain's intense envy of his brother, or to Cain's selfish, evil heart that led him to murder. The apostle John wrote, "Do not be like Cain, who belonged to the evil one and murdered his brother. And why did he murder him? Because his own actions were evil and his brother's were righteous" (1 John 3:12 NIV). Just as Cain murdered his brother, so the false teachers "murder" people's souls. Just as Cain did not care about his brother, murdering him out of

envy, so the false teachers did not care about their followers, willingly leading them along the pathway to destruction. Like Cain, the false teachers were defying God's authority and acting out of sinful passion.

2. *Balaam* prophesied out of greed, not out of obedience to God's command (Numbers 22–24; see also 2 Peter 2:15-16). The false teachers were following in the steps of Balaam, a man who had led many astray. A pagan king had hired Balaam, a prophet, to curse Israel. At first, Balaam obeyed God; eventually, however, his evil motives and desire for money won out. Like Balaam, the false teachers were not interested in serving God; they *rushed for profit into Balaam's error,* using religion only for financial gain and personal advancement. What was this "error"? Scripture explains that Balaam led the Israelites into immorality and idolatry (Numbers 25:1-3; 31:16). Balaam had tried three times to curse Israel, but had been unable to do so. He may have told the Israelites that God's favor rested upon them so they could live as they pleased without fear of retribution. Such a teaching was popular, but wrong. The false teachers, like Balaam, cared nothing about the God for whom they presumed to speak. They were completely consumed by the love of money. Like Balaam, they would perish (see Numbers 31:8).

3. *Korah* rebelled against God's divinely appointed leaders, wanting the power for himself (Numbers 16:1-35). Korah, Dathan, Abiram, and 250 leaders of Israel "came as a group to oppose Moses and Aaron and said to them, 'You have gone too far! The whole community is holy, every one of them, and the Lord is with them. Why then do you set yourselves above the Lord's assembly?'" (Numbers 16:3 NIV). By leading this revolt against God's divinely appointed leaders, Korah was actually revolting against God. The punishment was literally earthshaking: "The ground under them split apart and the earth opened its mouth and swallowed them, with their households and all Korah's men and all their possessions. They went down alive into the grave, with everything they owned; the earth closed over them, and they perished and were gone from the community" (Numbers 16:31-33 NIV). Like Korah, the false teachers had revolted against the divinely appointed leadership of the apostles and church leaders, setting themselves up in opposition.

Through these three Old Testament pictures, Jude painted these false teachers. They were without love (like Cain), greedy for money (like Balaam), and insubordinate to God-appointed authorities (like Korah). So certain was the end of these false teachers that Jude wrote about it in the past tense: *they have been destroyed.*

FALSE HEROES
Jude's antiheroes were dealers in murder, money, and power. They ignored God and defied common human virtues. People who followed them were going to get hurt.

Follow leaders who know and love God, not Pied Pipers leading the crowd toward pain and ruin. Jude used three archvillains from the Bible to describe the kind of people we should avoid and never look up to as examples.

Around your dinner table tonight, ask

- Who in the world would be a bad example to follow?
- Who at school or at work would be a bad example to follow?
- Why do people follow bad leaders?
- Who are some good people to admire and follow (at school, in church, at work, in the nation)?

12-13 These men are blemishes at your love feasts, eating with you without the slightest qualm—shepherds who feed only themselves.^{NIV} When the Lord's Supper was celebrated in the early church, believers would eat a full meal before sharing the bread and wine of Communion. The meal was called a *love feast* and was designed to be a sacred time of fellowship to prepare one's heart for the Lord's Supper. However, the false teachers were joining these "love feasts," becoming *blemishes* in what should have been a time of rejoicing in the Lord. They were ruining the Christians' gatherings by their very presence. The word translated "blemishes" could also be translated "hidden rocks or reefs." This ancient use of the word pictures the false teachers as dangerous, unseen rocks along a shoreline, ready to sink even the most seaworthy ship. Jude spared no words in describing the danger of these false teachers' involvement with the believers. In the worst sort of hypocrisy, these intruders who had stolen in among the believers (v. 4) were participating in the love feast while at the same time living and speaking in opposition to Christ. Not only this, but they may have been acting immorally as well, for Peter wrote that the false teachers were "reveling in their pleasures while they feast with you" (2 Peter 2:13 NIV).

They did this *without the slightest qualm* (also translated, "without fear"). They thought nothing of their hypocrisy; it never crossed their minds that they would be punished for such actions. These false teachers' involvement in the love feasts was only to get them into the church and gain them a hearing among the believers. They cared nothing for the believers, their celebration, or the God the believers worshiped. The false teachers were like shepherds who refused to feed the sheep, but who went on *feeding themselves* (see Ezekiel 34:8; John 10:12-13). Instead of looking after others' needs, the false teachers' only concern was their own needs. Instead of leading others to safety, the false teachers were leading them astray.

> I find this a solemn warning to those who, like myself, are professional theologians. We must constantly ask ourselves if our studies and knowledge are benefiting anybody at all.
> *Michael Green*

In four vivid word pictures taken from nature, Jude further described the false teachers. First, **they are waterless clouds carried along by the winds.**NRSV The false teachers were all show but no substance. Like waterless clouds, they promised rain but floated on by without a drop for thirsty soil. While they might claim superior knowledge, the false teachers had nothing of substance to assuage anyone's spiritual thirst.

Second, the false teachers are **autumn trees without fruit, twice dead, uprooted.**NRSV A fruitless tree in autumn may refer to a sterile tree, which was as good as dead because it produced no fruit. An *uprooted* tree was completely dead. Jude compared the false teachers to trees promising fruit but giving none. They were "once dead" because they had never taken root (they were never believers), and they had never borne spiritual fruit in their lives. They were *twice dead* because just as fruitless trees are uprooted and burned, so the false teachers would face eternal punishment.

Third, the false teachers were **wild waves of the sea, casting up the foam of their own shame.**NRSV Like the wild waves that make lots of noise as they restlessly thrash about, the false teachers restlessly and loudly were spewing their teaching. Jude used the image recorded in Isaiah, "But the wicked are like the tossing sea that cannot keep still; its waters toss up mire and mud" (Isaiah 57:20 NRSV). As debris and filth caught in the foam are cast up on the shore, so the false teachers' *shame* (referring to their shameful actions) would be "cast up" for all to see.

Fourth, the false teachers were **wandering stars, for whom the deepest darkness has been reserved forever.**NRSV For centuries, the fixed stars in the heavens have guided seafarers and navigators in travels around the earth. But *wandering* (or shooting) *stars* offer no guidance and no light. They appear bright for a few moments but shoot across the sky and disappear into darkness. The false teachers were as useless as wandering stars because they offered no direction and no light. Their teachings might seem "bright" for a while, but these teachers would find that for them *the deepest darkness has been reserved forever.* Their eternal judgment and punishment are certain; they have reservations that cannot be changed or canceled.

EMPTY WORDS
The false teachers talked a lot but had no substance; their words were lies. Life is filled with promises. We build families on promises, spend careers on promises, and trust God himself for the great promise of a joyous future. If promises fail, life collapses.

Do your best to make good on your word. So many people depend on your integrity. So much happiness rides on your honesty. Don't promise what you can't or won't deliver, as did the false teachers. Their lives were wasted because their promises were empty.

14-15 **It was also about these that Enoch, in the seventh generation from Adam, prophesied, saying, "See, the Lord is coming with ten thousands of his holy ones."**[NRSV] We know a little about Enoch from the Old Testament: "When Enoch had lived 65 years, he became the father of Methuselah. And after he became the father of Methuselah, Enoch walked with God 300 years and had other sons and daughters. Altogether, Enoch lived 365 years. Enoch walked with God; then he was no more, because God took him away" (Genesis 5:21-24 NIV). Enoch was in the lineage of Jesus Christ (Luke 3:37). The apocryphal book called Enoch describes Enoch as *in the seventh generation from Adam.* He was the seventh in order because Adam was counted as the "first" in the Jewish way of recording generations. During the period between the writing of the Old and New Testaments, Enoch had become a popular figure in Jewish writing. He was thought to be a figure of the Messiah and was considered to have had expert knowledge about the heavens. The writer of Hebrews said, "By faith Enoch was taken from this life, so that he did not experience death; he could not be found, because God had taken him away. For before he was taken, he was commended as one who pleased God" (Hebrews 11:5 NIV).

Jude was quoting from a prophecy in the book of Enoch

(1 Enoch 1:9), written in the time between the Testaments
(second century B.C.) and familiar to the early Christians.
While this book did not become a part of the canon of Scripture, Jude considered this prophecy to be correct and authoritative, and he quoted words that were familiar to his readers and
affirmed by other Scriptures. This prophecy clinched Jude's
argument of future judgment. Enoch had prophesied that the
Lord would return in great glory, bringing with him *ten thousands of his holy ones.* Scripture also describes Jesus returning
to earth with many angels ("holy ones")—see Deuteronomy
33:2; Daniel 7:10; Zechariah 14:5; Matthew 16:27; 24:30-31;
25:31; Hebrews 12:22.

Jude continued to quote from Enoch's prophecy, saying that the
Lord would return to earth **"to judge everyone, and to convict
all the ungodly of all the ungodly acts they have done in the
ungodly way, and of all the harsh words ungodly sinners have
spoken against him."**NIV The word *ungodly* appears four times in
this sentence, underlining the true character of the false teachers.
"Ungodly" means unrighteous, lawless, the sinful conduct of people
who have no respect for God (see v. 4). Their character, actions, and
words will result in a guilty conviction on the day when the Lord
returns *to judge everyone.* Those who believe will be saved and live
forever. However those "ungodly" people who disobeyed God and
have refused to believe will be convicted of their "ungodly" actions
that were committed in the "ungodly" way, especially speaking
harsh words against Jesus Christ.

Some have wondered why Jude would have quoted from a book
that is now considered noncanonical ("canon" refers to the authoritative list of accepted books). The word "apocrypha" means "hidden"
and refers generally to two types of writing, the Apocrypha and the
pseudepigrapha. The Apocrypha refers to certain books that relate to
material in some of the Old Testament books. They were approved
by Jewish councils for private study but not for public reading as the
Word of God. They were included in the Greek version of the Old
Testament (the Septuagint), but were rejected from the Hebrew
canon at the council at Jamnia. Roman Catholics approved twelve
books to be part of their canon at the Council of Trent in the six-
teenth century, but Luther and the Anglican church (thus all Protestants) did not accept them as the Word of God. The pseudepigrapha
refers to Jewish writings that don't relate directly to the Old Testament books. These also were excluded from the Old Testament
canon—the book of Enoch is one of these. These books played a
key role between the writing of the Old and New Testaments and
give valuable Jewish background to the New Testament. Indeed,

Jude's use of the book of Enoch caused many to wonder if it should be included in the Bible. The fact that Jude quoted from Enoch does not imply that Enoch's teachings are inspired and should have been included in Scripture. For example, Paul quoted some noncanonical statements that he considered to be true. In Acts 17:28, he quoted Aratus and Cleanthes; in 1 Corinthians 15:33 he quoted Menander; and in Titus 1:12 he quoted from a Cretan poet and philosopher, Epimenides—in no case was Paul implying that all of these men's words should be considered as inspired Scripture! Jude believed the quotations to be true, but not the entire book. The words quoted by Jude are reinforced by many Scripture passages that refer to Christ's return. Jude wanted to show the certainty of the false teachers' doom.

16 These are grumblers and malcontents; they indulge their own lusts; they are bombastic in speech, flattering people to their own advantage.^{NRSV} After denouncing the false teachers by calling them "ungodly" four times in the previous verse, Jude next explained four areas of ungodliness. First, as *grumblers and malcontents* they constantly found fault in everyone and everything, except in themselves, of course. They probably also grumbled against God, discontent with life and the restrictions of God's law. Such people can never be made happy or content. When people stray from God, they may become habitual complainers, unable to see God or good in anything (see Exodus 16–17; Numbers 14–17; 1 Corinthians 10:10).

Second, *they indulge their own lusts.* This has already been made clear by Jude's words in verses 4, 8, 10-13, and 15. Without regard for God's laws or even for basic morality, these men shamelessly indulged their lusts, acting on their passions and desires. Their only god was self, and they worshiped that god wholeheartedly.

Third, *they are bombastic in speech.* This means they were boastful men, swollen with pride. They had denied Christ and spoken against him (v. 15); these bombastic words might have been their erroneous doctrines spoken loudly with the hopes of impressing others and making a name for themselves.

Fourth, these false teachers were *flattering people to their own advantage.* Flattery is phony, and the false teachers used it as a cover-up for their real intentions. Instead of loving people, they used them, using flattery if necessary to get what they wanted.

Jude could hardly have said worse about anyone. Sparing no words for these false teachers, he laid their attitudes, words, and actions out for all to see. He meant for the Christians to take this irrefutable evidence and decide for themselves about these men.

FLATTERY

Compliments affirm; flattery manipulates. A good speech, successful recital, or B+ in geometry are all occasions for affirming the one whose effort has won esteem. Flattery, on the other hand, offers false praise with the purpose of getting something big in return.

Fund-raisers flatter the wealthy as prelude to "the financial challenge we face." Getting a big donation is their only goal. Men flatter women as a prelude to sexual advances. Office seekers flatter politicians, and salespeople may flatter buyers, even when the "goods" for sale are religious. That kind of misleading flattery ruins souls.

Affirm often; flatter only in obvious jest. Then your words will have "face value" honesty, and people will not wonder what you really mean and want.

THE DUTY TO FIGHT FOR GOD'S TRUTH / 17-25

The audience to whom Jude wrote was vulnerable to heresies and to temptations toward immoral living. Jude encouraged the believers to remain firm in their faith and trust in God's promises for their future. This was vital because they were living during a time of increased disloyalty to the faith. We too are living in the last days, much closer to the end than were the original readers of this letter. We too are vulnerable to doctrinal error. We too are tempted to give in to sin. Although there is much false teaching around us, we need not be afraid or give up in despair—God can keep us from falling, and he guarantees that if we remain faithful, he will bring us into his presence and give us everlasting joy.

17-18 But, dear friends, remember what the apostles of our Lord Jesus Christ foretold. They said to you, "In the last times there will be scoffers who will follow their own ungodly desires."[NIV] In addition to examples from the Old Testament of God's punishment of sin (vv. 5-7) and citations from prophecy about the Second Coming (vv. 14-15), Jude appealed to the believers to *remember what the apostles* had said. The words of the apostles were already being considered authoritative and on the level with Scripture. Jude's wording indicates that he was not himself one of the apostles, for he referred to the apostles as *they*. That the apostles had spoken these words *to you* indicates that at least some of Jude's readers had been contemporaries of the apostles.

Jude encouraged the Christians to remember the apostles' warnings against false teachers—and there were many. The words quoted here, *"In the last times there will be scoffers who will follow their own ungodly desires,"* parallel 2 Peter 3:3. Peter wrote, "First of all you must understand this, that in the last days scoffers will come, scoffing and indulging their own lusts" (NRSV). The "last days" began with Christ's resurrection and will continue until his return, when he will set up his kingdom and judge all humanity. Jesus and the apostles forewarned all believers that during that interim, including the time period in which we live, "scoffers will come." To "scoff" means to show contempt for something by one's actions and language, to mock. These false teachers scoffed at the truth and taught their own lies. They despised all morality and religion. Jesus had warned against the deception of false teachers (Mark 13:21-23), as had Paul (Acts 20:28-31; 2 Thessalonians 2:1-12; 1 Timothy 4:1; 2 Timothy 3:1-5), Peter (2 Peter 2:1–3:7), and John (1 John 2:22; 4:1-3; 2 John). Because Jesus and the apostles had warned against false teachers, the church must also be prepared.

TWO-SIDED BIBLE STUDY
When Jude urged us to remember what the apostles foretold, he was encouraging vigilance. We need to be vigilant because false teachers can jeopardize our Bible study. The first side of Bible study—discovering God's great love for us—takes most of our time. But the second side—warnings about God's judgment—sounds worrisome and heavy and so may not get its fair share of attention.

We should study the Scriptures to stay on course as we grow in God's strength. The Bible warns against persons and movements that divert believers from God and spoil faith. Don't get sidetracked by

- movements in which God and his love are neither evident nor welcome
- persons who distort the Bible's message by requiring moral and ethical conduct that is not specified in Scripture
- teachers and leaders who scoff at God
- teachings that ignore or minimize the Lord's return

Regular, balanced Bible study keeps God at the center and false teaching in the distance.

---

19 It is these worldly people, devoid of the Spirit, who are causing divisions.NRSV These false teachers should have been easy to spot. They were not godly ministers; rather, they were *worldly people,* living to please themselves and their sinful desires. They lived merely on the natural level. They loved money and attention.

They were *devoid of the Spirit.* They never believed in Christ, and they never received the Holy Spirit. Paul had written, "Therefore I tell you that no one who is speaking by the Spirit of God says, 'Jesus be cursed,' and no one can say, 'Jesus is Lord,' except by the Holy Spirit" (1 Corinthians 12:3 NIV; see also John 14:17; 16:13). The false teachers claimed to speak for God, but they would be unable to confess Jesus as Lord because they did not have the Holy Spirit. Thus they mocked Scripture and lived shamelessly without godly fear (v. 12). See James 3:13-18 for a good test to apply to teachers to see if their teaching manifests the presence of the Holy Spirit.

They set themselves above all other Christians because of their assumed superior knowledge and understanding of their "freedom" in Christ. Those allegedly enlightened enough to join them regarded themselves as distinct and superior from others in the church. Thus, Jude condemned these false teachers for *causing divisions.*

Ironically, the very presence of these false teachers who scoffed at the apostles' teachings and at the prophecies of the Second Coming was a fulfillment of prophecy. The apostles had indicated that these false teachers would be abundant in "the last days" (see 1 Timothy 4:1-2; 1 John 2:18-26). Their presence only further assured the believers that Christ would soon return.

20 But you, dear friends, build yourselves up in your most holy faith and pray in the Holy Spirit.NIV Even as the false teachers attempted to cause divisions (v. 19), the believers (once again addressed as *dear friends,* as in v. 17) could stand against the false teachers if they followed Jude's advice in four areas. First, they must build on the firm foundation of their faith, standing strong and unified (see also 1 Corinthians 3:9-17; Ephesians 2:20-22). They could do this by staying close to other believers and by continuing in worship, including taking the Lord's Supper. As in verse 3 above, their *most holy faith* refers to the entire body of beliefs taught by the apostles and held by Christians. The believers could "build themselves up" in their faith by studying and learning the Scriptures (Acts 2:42; 2 Timothy 2:15; Hebrews 5:13–6:3; see also Ephesians 4:12-16). We should note that believers are to work together as they build themselves up as a community, as Christ's temple. It was "your faith" as opposed to the false teachers' heretical teaching; it was "most holy" because it came from the most holy God. This faith alone transforms lives and gives eternal life.

Second, Jude encouraged the believers to *pray in the Holy Spirit,* meaning to pray in the power and strength of the Holy Spirit. The Holy Spirit prays on behalf of believers (Romans 8:26-27; Galatians 4:6; Ephesians 6:18), opens their minds to

Jesus (John 14:26), and teaches believers more about their
Lord (John 15:26). This most likely includes, but is not limited
to, prayer in tongues. Because the false teachers were "devoid
of the Spirit" (v. 19), they could not truly pray and their
prayers would not be heard. Indeed, they may have put aside
prayer altogether, to their own detriment. Prayer is the lifeline
that connects all Christians to their Savior. Believers must
never stop praying.

IN THE SPIRIT
Jude urged the believers to "pray in the Holy Spirit." Real
prayer takes many forms, but fake prayer lacks one essential:
the Holy Spirit. Praying in the Spirit means

- you pray to know God's mind before you insist on telling God
  about your opinions
- your happiness rests more in God's assurance of love and
  forgiveness than whether your prayers for X, Y, and Z get
  answered today
- your heart and mind rejoice in God, confirming that you
  belong to him, no matter how many struggles you face

Today, be quiet before God, ask the Holy Spirit to fill your
heart, then pray. God will take your stress away and give you
peace and strength for the day.

**21 Keep yourselves in God's love as you wait for the mercy of
our Lord Jesus Christ to bring you to eternal life.**[NIV] Jude
described a third way for the believers to stand strong against
false teachers: *Keep yourselves in God's love.* This means that the
believers must stay close to God and his people, not listening to
false teachers who would try to pull them away (John 15:9-10).
To stay in God's love is to remember that God *first* loved us—he
took the initiative to accomplish salvation. Jesus said, "As the
Father has loved me, so have I loved you. Now remain in my
love. If you obey my commands, you will remain in my love"
(John 15:9-10 NIV). Obedience is the key. The false teachers had
flouted obedience and thus had stepped out of God's love.

Fourth, the believers should *wait for the mercy of our Lord Jesus
Christ to bring you to eternal life.* The promises will come true.
Christ will return and bring his people into eternal glory with him.
While believers have already received his "mercy," they must wait
for the consummation of that mercy when their salvation will be
made complete. Peter wrote, "You ought to live holy and godly lives
as you look forward to the day of God and speed its coming. . . .
Since you are looking forward to this, make every effort to be found

spotless, blameless and at peace with him" (2 Peter 3:11-12, 14 NIV). Believers wait in confident expectation. God's promises are not "ifs" but "whens." They must know, beyond any doubt, that their Savior will soon return for them.

22-23 Be merciful to those who doubt; snatch others from the fire and save them; to others show mercy, mixed with fear—hating even the clothing stained by corrupted flesh.NIV Although the false teachers were hopelessly entrenched in their sin and Satan's grip, the believers had a responsibility to those who had fallen prey to false teaching. Scholars differ in their interpretations of these verses because the various ancient manuscripts have different readings. According to some manuscripts there are only two groups (as in the NKJV, which says "And on some have compassion, making a distinction; but others save with fear, pulling them out of the fire, hating even the garment defiled by the flesh"), while other manuscripts have three groups (as is presented in the NIV above and NRSV).

The first group consists of those believers who have listened to the false teachers and have begun to doubt God's truth. They still have reservations, so they have not yet joined the false teachers. These people are not to be ridiculed; rather, they are to be shown mercy and carefully drawn back into the church by providing them with the true teaching of the gospel. Believers who are well taught in the faith can *be merciful to those who doubt* by quietly and calmly talking with them, explaining the false teachers' error, and reminding them of the truth they had originally received. (Scholars who divide this verse into two groups say that the "snatching from the fire" phrase applies to these doubters.)

The second group has gone beyond doubting. Agreeing with the false teachers, they are on the road to destruction. They need someone to literally step in their path and *snatch* them *from the fire.* The "fire" refers to the eternal punishment awaiting the false teachers (v. 4). If we saw someone about to be burned by fire, we would quickly grab that person and pull him or her out of harm's way. That's the attitude the true believers are to have toward those sliding toward false teaching. We need to grab them and pull them away before it is too late. We need ministers and teachers who know how to refute false teaching and defend Christianity so that they can rescue the misinformed.

The third group refers to those already in the false teachers' camps—those who have already joined them. These people also need *mercy,* but believers are to mix their mercy *with fear,* that is, extreme caution. To hate *even the clothing stained by corrupted flesh* means that believers are to hate the sin, but love the sinner.

Believers must never compromise on the truth or on God's commands about right and wrong. While believers might try to rescue those deceived people, they must do so without allowing themselves to become contaminated by the false teaching. This will be a difficult task, one to be undertaken with healthy fear and respect for the spiritual warfare when God's power meets head-on with Satan's power. Believers have God on their side, but they must remember not to attempt anything in their own power lest they too fall prey to the false teachers' lies.

SAFE FOOTING
Effective witnessing saves people from God's judgment. We witness to some through our compassion and kindness; to others we witness as if we were snatching them from the eternal fire. Many times we must treat different people with different methods: We may encourage doubters with truth and more evidence; we may warn others with discipline. Always we must remember God's mercy. Yet, as Jude warned, our mercy must be mixed with fear. In trying to find common ground with those to whom we witness, we must be careful not to fall into the quicksand of compromise. When reaching out to others, we must be sure that our own footing is safe and secure. Be careful not to become so much like non-Christians that no one can tell who you are or what you believe. Influence them for Christ—don't allow them to influence you to sin!

---

24 To him who is able to keep you from falling and to present you before his glorious presence without fault and with great joy.NIV As the letter began, so it ended—with assurance. In this great doxology, Jude stressed the mighty power of God to keep us securely in him. God *is able to keep* believers from falling prey to false teachers. Although false teachers were widespread and dangerous, although it would be dangerous to attempt to rescue slipping fellow Christians, the believers should not retreat or be afraid. Instead, they should trust God and remain rooted and grounded in him. The psalmist wrote, "For you have delivered me from death and my feet from stumbling, that I may walk before God in the light of life" (Psalm 56:13 NIV).

God can be trusted to *present* all believers *before his glorious presence.* We should praise him for this great promise. The believers could trust that God would do as he promised and one day bring them to himself. But that will not be a day of punishment (as it will be for the false teachers). Rather, it will be a day of joy, for God will present his people *without fault and with great joy.* To be sinless and perfect ("without fault") will be the ultimate condition of the believer when he or she finally sees Christ face-to-face. When Christ appears, and we are given our new bodies, we will be like him (1 John 3:2). Coming into Christ's presence will be a time of "great joy" for God and for all believers.

FEAR OF FALLING
Why do trapeze artists bring gasps from a circus crowd? or parachute instructors give mind-controlling advice to first-time jumpers? Why do rock climbers use rope, and kids fix training wheels to a bike?

It's the gravity problem: our fear of falling. Jude wrote that God can keep us from "falling."

In spiritual life, the jagged cliffs are all around us. Slipping seems so easy, so convenient. What's so terrible about a little lie, one night away, some quick fun?

When you worry about falling (or being pulled over the side!), remember God. He keeps us well connected on a rope the devil cannot cut through. When temptation surrounds you, pray. When evil thoughts invade your mind, rehearse Bible promises. When doubts dampen your faith, call a Christian friend for a talk. In all this, trust God to hold you steady, keep you balanced, and bring you home.

---

25 To the only God our Savior be glory, majesty, power and authority, through Jesus Christ our Lord, before all ages, now and forevermore! Amen.[NIV] Contemplating the great joy awaiting all believers and the fulfillment of God's promises of eternal glory, Jude praised God with a beautiful doxology. Jude had originally intended to write about the salvation all believers shared (v. 3); he got his chance here. This one final verse captures the focus and goal of believers' salvation and faith. Christianity is not a series of made-up ideas or free-floating thoughts; it is faith in a person—not just any person, but *the only God* who also became *our Savior . . . through Jesus Christ.* To this God alone the believers should ascribe

- *glory*—God's powerful radiance, his greatness, his complete moral superiority and splendor

- *majesty*—God's transcendent greatness

- *power*—God's self-contained might, his control over the world

- *authority*—God is sovereign over all physical and moral laws in the entire universe

These qualities reside in God alone. Jesus Christ is *our Lord,* meaning that he too has all glory, majesty, power, and authority as God himself. This was true before the ages began; it is true in the present day. And it will continue to be true *forevermore.*

The prophet Isaiah wrote, "Remember the former things, those of long ago; I am God, and there is no other; I am God, and there is none like me. I make known the end from the beginning, from ancient times, what is still to come. I say: My purpose will stand, and I will do all that I please" (Isaiah 46:9-10 NIV).

BIBLIOGRAPHY

Bauckham, Richard J. *Jude, 2 Peter.* Word Biblical Commentary Series. Waco, Texas: Word, Inc., 1983.

Blum Edwin A. *1 and 2 Peter, Jude.* The Expositor's Bible Commentary, vol. 12. Grand Rapids: Zondervan Publishing House, 1981.

Clowney, Edmund P. *The Message of 1 Peter: The Way of the Cross.* Downers Grove, Ill.: InterVarsity Press, 1988.

Douglas, J. D., and Philip W. Comfort, eds. *New Commentary on the Whole Bible: New Testament Volume.* Wheaton, Ill.: Tyndale House Publishers, 1990.

Green, Michael. *The Second General Epistle of Peter and the General Epistle of Jude.* Tyndale New Testament Commentaries. Grand Rapids: Wm. B. Eerdmans Pub. Co., 1988.

Grudem, Wayne. *First Peter.* Tyndale New Testament Commentaries. Grand Rapids: Wm. B. Eerdmans Pub. Co., 1988.

Hawthorne, Gerald F., and Ralph P. Martin, eds. *Dictionary of Paul and His Letters.* Downers Grove, Ill.: InterVarsity Press, 1992.

Kelly, J. N. D. *A Commentary on The Epistles of Peter and of Jude.* Black's New Testament Commentaries. London: Adam and Charles Black, 1977.

Marshall, I. Howard. *1 Peter.* Downers Grove, Ill.: InterVarsity Press, 1991.

Michaels, J. Ramsey. *1 Peter.* Word Biblical Commentary Series. Dallas: Word Books, 1988.

Walvoord, John F., and Roy B. Zuck. *Bible Knowledge Commentary: New Testament Edition.* Wheaton, Ill.: Victor Books, 1983.

INDEX